D0706096

DATE DUE

APR 2 8 2014	
MAR 0 4 2016	

BRODART, CO.   Cat. No. 23-221

TEENAGE WITCHES

Teenage Witches

Magical Youth and the Search for the Self

Helen A. Berger
Douglas Ezzy

RUTGERS UNIVERSITY PRESS
NEW BRUNSWICK, NEW JERSEY, AND LONDON

Copyright © 2007 by Helen A. Berger and Douglas Ezzy

All rights reserved

No part of this book may be reproduced or utilized in any form or by any means, electronic

or mechanical, or by any information storage and retrieval system, without written permission from the

publisher. Please contact Rutgers University Press, 100 Joyce Kilmer Avenue, Piscataway, NJ 08854–8099.

The only exception to this prohibition is "fair use" as defined by U.S. copyright law.

Library of Congress Cataloging-in-Publication Data

Berger, Helen A., 1949–

Teenage witches : magical youth and the search for the self / Helen A. Berger and Douglas Ezzy.

p.   cm.

Includes bibliographical references and index.

ISBN-13: 978-0-8135-4020-7 (hardcover : alk. paper)

ISBN-13: 978-0-8135-4021-4 (pbk. : alk. paper)

1. Witchcraft.   2. Teenagers—Miscellanea.   I. Ezzy, Douglas.   II. Title.

BF1571.5.T44B47 2007

133.4'30835—dc22   2006021864

Manufactured in the United States of America

ACC LIBRARY SERVICES AUSTIN, TX

To Helen's nieces and nephew,
Nora, Alex, and Marcelle,
&
Douglas's children, Tim and Emily,

&
with deep gratitude and respect
to all the young Witches
who invited us
into their
lives

CONTENTS

ILLUSTRATIONS

ACKNOWLEDGMENTS

We have many people to thank for making this book possible. Helen's research in England was funded by a grant from the College of Arts and Science at West Chester University. Douglas received funding for his research in England from a University of Tasmania Institutional Research Grant (Ref. No. E0013757). In England many people helped us with our research. Eileen Barker, who was instrumental in the creation of Inform, put us in touch with that organization. The people at Inform and Vivianne Crowley made introductions for us with the Pagan Federation in the United Kingdom. The Federation kindly endorsed our study and put an advertisement on their youth Web site, Children of Artemis, asking teenagers who were willing to participate in our study to contact us. Michael York and Richard Swizler generously gave Helen their London flat to use as her base as she traveled around England to interview young Witches. Michael also provided us with feedback on our second chapter. Carol Wolkowitz helped by placing advertisements around her university and in a local occult bookstore. She and her husband, Martyn Partridge, also hosted Helen during her travels by British Rail around England. James Beckford, in the midst of a busy schedule, picked Helen up at the train station and drove her to the university. Adrian Harris, Melissa Harrington, Jenny Blain, Robert Wallis, and Graham Harvey all generously provided Douglas with accommodation, companionship, and thought-provoking discussion.

In the United States many colleagues assisted by placing advertisements about the project around their university or asking their students if they or someone they knew were interested in participating. Harriet Hartman, Wendy Griffin, Tanice Foltz, and Mary Olsen deserve particular thanks. In Australia the Pagan Alliance endorsed the project and advertised it. Douglas would particularly like to thank Lesley-Caron Veater, who provided him with accommodation and a cozy lounge room in which to interview people.

We are indebted to the faculty at Center for the Dynamics of Ritual at Heidelberg University in Germany, and Oliver Krüeger in particular, who invited us to present our early research on teenage Witches in the United States and Australia. Their comments have helped us think about the process of teenagers becoming and being Witches. Felicia Wallace helped with the works cited, and Joanne Simpson in the United States and Eve Hicks in Australia did wonderful jobs of transcribing the interviews. Brad Kinne, high priest of the Temple of the Seekers, provided some of the photographs, and Joanne Simpson printed most of the photographs that appear in this book. Our universities, West Chester University of Pennsylvania and the University of Tasmania, made this book possible by respectively providing Helen and Douglas sabbaticals to write. Adi Hovav, our editor at Rutgers University Press, was a source of support and feedback, as were two external reviewers, James R. Lewis and Lynn Schofield Clark. They helped make the book better. We are also each indebted to our partners. Helen's husband, John H. Wolff, as always, was supportive throughout the project and in the end did more than his share of housework to enable the book to be completed. Douglas's partner, Kira White, was also supportive in many ways and tolerant of his strange working hours. Our greatest debt is to the young people who shared their stories with us and welcomed us into their lives.

introduction

Who are teenage Witches, and what are they really doing? Drawing on ninety interviews with young people who call themselves Witches, have been practicing Witchcraft for at least one year, and began practicing when they were teenagers, this book answers these questions. Teenage Witches are not that different from most of their generation, except that they are seekers attempting to find a spiritual path. They come from both religious and nonreligious homes, although in the United States most come from families that are at least somewhat religious. They tend to see themselves as different and to enjoy that status. Many have already faced major life crises, such as depression and the deaths of loved ones. Before finding Witchcraft, most were interested in the occult. But they tend to be more interested in the spiritual aspects of Witchcraft, only occasionally practicing magic. They participate in rituals to celebrate the seasons and to venerate the Goddess and God. The Goddess in particular is important to most teenage Witches, who identify with the female divine and see her as a symbol of Mother Earth.

There are two mistaken images of young Witches: either kids with pointy hats and broomsticks who fight demons, or misguided delinquent teenagers, perhaps seduced by cult leaders. Counter to such images, the vignettes of Beverly, Charles, and Ruth that follow this introduction are typical of what we were told by the ninety young people we interviewed. Beverly's mother, a Presbyterian minister, died when Beverly was nine years old. Beverly is a young U.S. woman struggling to make sense of this death and of her emerging bisexuality. She finds some answers in the rituals and practices learnt first from books and then at a local Goddess spirituality group. Charles, an Englishman, first heard about Witchcraft on the Internet and then on television shows such as *Buffy the Vampire Slayer*. Books and the Internet are his primary teachers, and he has met a Pagan girlfriend through the Internet. He takes his religion seriously, and it clearly has had a significant positive influence on his life. However, he has only physically met two other Witches, one of whom is his girlfriend, and he is not a member of any organized group. Ruth's story in the third vignette illustrates a common theme, young people's struggle with depression. For this Australian, Witchcraft provides a path of self-acceptance and confidence that was part of the process of overcoming her depression. Beyond these stories, each chapter of the book other than the last is preceded by a vignette that illustrates its theme.

Participants and scholars of Witchcraft have for more than a decade noted the increase in the number of teenagers who explore Witchcraft, but this book is the first to systematically investigate teenage Witches. Because these teens are often believed to be drawn in by the spells and to be superficial in their involvement, we began our study with that image in mind. But one of the delights of research is to find that one's first impressions are not always borne out. As we show in *Teenage Witches*, most young Witches are serious about their religion. This does not mean that they are not at times naïve or lacking in knowledge about either Witchcraft or the religions some of them have left. But it does mean that they take their religious practice seriously and on the whole are attempting to learn more. Our expectation that there would be significant national differences proved unfounded. There are some small national differences, which we discuss, but we found many more similarities than differences among the young people in the three countries—in part, because they read many of the same books, watch the same television shows and movies, listen to the same music, and interact on the Internet.

Contemporary Witchcraft, perhaps more than any other religion, is deeply entwined with the media of late modernity. The Internet, mass-marketed books, television shows, and glossy magazines play a central role in disseminating information about Witchcraft. Furthermore, in many senses the individualism and reflexivity of Witchcraft is consistent with the broader trends of late modern, or postmodern, society. These are some of the reasons that teenage Witchcraft, as opposed to any other teenage religion, fascinates us as sociologists. Witchcraft, and particularly teenage Witchcraft, is an illustration par excellence of the postmodern condition.

The interviews on which this book is based each lasted between forty-five minutes and two hours. We tape-recorded them and had them transcribed word for word. Each vignette that follows this introduction and that precedes each chapter is drawn from the words of a young Witch in a single interview. The words in italics are ours, added to clarify meanings and to provide detail. We have edited the interviews, sometimes removing short phrases such as "you know," "sort of," and "like," as well as repeated phrases and words, and deleting interviewer comments such as okay or yes. Ellipses (...) indicate the deletion of more than a few words. We have put square brackets [like this] around words we added to clarify the speaker's meaning. We have changed people's names and other identifying details to ensure the anonymity of the young people and of anyone else they mention, other than public Witches.

This book is the result of a collaboration that has taken place mostly over the Internet. As Helen is an American and Douglas is an Australian, we fittingly met in England at a conference on new religious movements organized by Inform at the London School of Economics. Helen, who has been researching Witches and Neopagans since 1986, was contemplating a new project on the growing phenomenon of teenage Witches. Douglas, whom she met for the first time at the conference, had more recently turned from the study of work and illness to look at Paganism in Australia. After he read a paper on the growing commercialization of Paganism and discussed Web sites oriented to teenage girls (Ezzy 2001), Helen and he had a ten-minute conversation and Helen invited him to collaborate with her on this research. The invitation and acceptance were impetuous on both our parts, but we found that we work well together and each brought skills, knowledge, and residence in a different English-speaking nation to the project.

Both of us are sociologists, which has given us a common methodological, intellectual, and theoretical background. We both aim to represent the stories and experiences of the Witches as objectively as we can. We found that collaborating on the research improved the rigor of our analysis, as we challenged and refined each other's conclusions.

Being at opposite ends of the globe was useful for the research, as it made it easier for us to begin a truly international study. Initially we thought we would compare only the United States and Australia, but we came quickly to realize it was important to include England, first because the religion began there, and second because we believed the study would be incomplete without including a European country in our analysis. Ours is the first study that systematically looks at Witchcraft in three countries on different continents. Most research has been confined to one continent, and usually to one country. We hope others will look at non-English-speaking nations and compare our findings with theirs.

Having a male and a female do the research was helpful in trying, to the degree that it is possible, to control for what might be a gender bias in the interviews. In recent academic study of contemporary Paganisms, researchers have openly positioned themselves with respect to the beliefs and practices of the groups under study (Blain et al 2004), seeking to transcend the insider/outsider debate. And although neither of us is a Witch or a teenager, in some senses we span the insider and outsider positions, as Douglas shares a Pagan respect of the earth as sacred and Helen is not a Pagan.[1]

Our decision to study teenage Witchcraft was multifaceted. As mentioned earlier, Witchcraft, and particularly teenage Witchcraft, is an exemplar of the postmodern condition. As discussed in Chapter 1, the hallmarks of late or postmodernity include the globalization of knowledge and of cultural and symbolic systems. The media in the form of movies, books, television shows, and the Internet is key in this process. There is today a questioning of all truth claims, including those of science. As we discuss throughout *Teenage Witches*, Witchcraft incorporates all these trends. Furthermore, the international nature of our research provides a rare opportunity to examine parallels in religious experience on three continents. Most international studies tend to be statistical, based on surveys. Ours is a qualitative study based on long interviews and demonstrates similarities across continents in processes of identify formation and magical practice encouraged by a globalized media and community. Finally, there has been public concern about teenagers becoming Witches. They are often viewed as being seduced into the religion. *Teenage Witches* interrogates and challenges the stereotypes that surround teenage Witchcraft. The teenage Witches who talked to us live in a fascinating world, where they are exploring a spirituality that they feel speaks to them and their needs. In the process they are transforming the religion and in many ways also transforming themselves.

TEENAGE WiTCHES

Vignette

Beverly—A Minister's Daughter (United States)

I would say that I was always one [a Witch]. I just discovered what I was. . . .
When I was seven, I realized that I didn't believe in God the way my parents did and I started to formulate my own ideas about God and religion and all that. And when I was twelve, I think by that point I had pretty much solidified things the way that I currently believe. And when I was thirteen, I officially declared myself a Witch and was initiated. . . . I was initiated by a small group of friends who I had met through a women's spirituality group, some of which counted themselves as Witches and others as Pagans and others just as feminists who were practicing a trend of spirituality that was not the norm.

The group that Beverly initially joined at the age of twelve was at a local Unitarian Universalist church. My dad knew one of the women who had founded the group, and he hooked me up with her and she started bringing me to the group and I met a lot of my initial Pagan friends there. . . .
Well, I went to that women's group, but it was weird because most of them were my dad's age or older. . . . My dad is very supportive. He is actually a [Presbyterian] minister, so I didn't think he was going to be very supportive at first. But, yeah, once I told him, he was a little confused at first, but he is pretty cool with it.

Beverly's mother had also been a Presbyterian minister. Although Beverly traces her dissatisfaction with Christianity to an earlier date, her mother's death has influenced her spirituality. My mom passed away when I was nine. I actually feel like that was a big turning point in my life. Obviously because I had lost my mother—but also because it made me think a lot more about

3

death and I don't think that's what nine-year-olds really do. And I think that is a large piece of why I have the spirituality that I have now. . . . Basically my mother I considered to be my best friend when she passed away, and between the feeling of great loss, like many other people I turned to spirituality and I turned to religion as a comfort, and I also didn't really have an idea of what happened after people died. Most of my family [said to me], "She is in a better place," or very nonspecific comforting phrases to make me feel better and I began to think, "No, really, what happens after people die?" . . .

It is hard to remember exactly at what point I came to what conclusion, when I came to what belief, but right now, looking back on it, my basic idea [was] that all energy and all life is interconnected and that "going to a better place" is really staying right here. I think that there is no point at which life is nonlife. It is just transitioning into another point. I think of life as a cycle but also as a spiral, and by dying her individual consciousness debatably was lost, but my understanding [is] she could have—I'm trying to think how to put it. My idea of death is very much in tune with the physics principle of the law of conservation of energy. Energy doesn't die or disappear, it is just reformatted, it is reworked, and her energy could be part of the ocean, it could be part of the sky, it could be part of a bug or some grass, or it could be part of a baby that was born after she died, or it could be part of pretty much anything.

I don't specifically talk to her. I do sometimes say things to her, but I don't really feel like I am getting answers back so much. But the night before the tenth anniversary that she died, I dreamt about her and it was the first time I have dreamed about her in years, possibly since she had died. And we spoke and it was the first time that I felt like I got answers from her and when I woke up I was crying. It was very touching. It was really intense.

It is in part what occurred between Beverly and her mother before her death that makes Beverly feel that she was always a Witch. Part of what I think has made me always a Witch, before I really called the spells, I did things [to] shape events. My mother and I actually used to talk—for lack of a better word—telepathically. I haven't really realized that kind of interaction with another person, but, yes, it seemed normal to me. I often had difficulty understanding when we were speaking and when we were just thinking. . . . I think that there are a lot of mental abilities that people just haven't discovered or let themselves fully experience and I think most of my mother's family is pretty talented.

Although Beverly feels she was always a Witch, she first learned about the religion when she was twelve. The summer that I turned twelve, and I had a friend, who is my best friend now, visiting at our summer camp, and I had just read *The Mists of Avalon.* I was in this space where—I really wish that I could have been born in a place where I could have lived on an island with a bunch of priestesses and grew up that way. That would have been awesome. I was talking to a friend of mine and we got talking about religion and what we believed and she had read a couple of books on Witchcraft, including Scott Cunningham, *Wicca for the Solitary Practitioner,* and I think she had also read *Spiral Dance* by Starhawk. I know she had at least read Cunningham and a couple of others, and she said: "I have been checking this out. It is similar to what I believe, but it is not really clicking for me, but it sounds like this is what you are talking about. You would really want to check it out." And I am like: "I'm not a Witch. Bug off. Don't tease me." I kept thinking, "Well, it is cultist stuff, so it has to be evil." And she loaned me a couple of her books and I started reading it and basically I started reading to try and disprove her, to say I am not part of this, she doesn't know what she is talking about. And I did that for years, and I still haven't been able to do it [prove her friend was wrong]. So I kept reading and saying, "Yeah, this is what I am thinking." And especially Starhawk, I think she is very poetic and it is really touching to read some of her stuff. It's like, wow! I never would have thought to phrase it that way, but yes, that is what I think.

Beverly is twenty-three years old and completing her undergraduate degree in religious studies with a gender studies minor. Since high school she has been open about her religious affiliation. In high school I got harassed a lot. I had kids tell me I was going to burn in hell. I had kids threaten to kill me. I had kids tell me that I was the child of Satan, and things like that. Sometimes it would really hurt, and other times it would just seem so ridiculous. I would just be like: "How can I go to hell if I don't believe in it? I don't think that hell exists. I don't think that Satan exists, you know, and you can tell me all you want that I am going to go there, but in my idea of the world, it just can't happen." . . . Most of my friends outside of high school were either in their forties or fifties or in their early twenties. It was also strange for me because I also came out in high school as being bi [sexual], so I didn't really have a lot of friends in high school. Between the Witch thing and being queer they didn't like me so much.

Beverly considers herself a solitary practitioner, although she is currently working in a group. I did a spell to get the coven together. . . . I did it on a number of different levels. I think that spells work better when you [also do work on the] mundane level as well. So I talked to all my friends who I already knew were interested in Witchcraft or Pagan spirituality and asked if they had any interest. I put a post up on Witchvox . . . and said, "I am forming a women's Wiccan group, would you send me an email if you are interested."[1] And then I did a spell for about three nights.

The women who joined Beverly's coven range in age from twenty to thirty-five years old. It is a group of about seven women—two of them don't really come because they live out of state, but they come when they can, when they are in the area. Their parents live in the area, and they have moved away, they are friends from high school, so we stay in touch, and they come and visit, join in, but basically we meet at the high holidays [the eight yearly sabbats]. We try to meet at both the new and the full moons. Sometimes we don't meet at both, depending upon scheduling. Like, the full moon was yesterday and we actually didn't meet because of the Washington protest for peace. A number of the members went down there and were pretty exhausted today, so we weren't able to get together, but, yeah, it is very informal. I don't think we all come from the same tradition, but we are all solitary who have practiced at some time or another with other people and are looking for a little bit more community at this point.

Most of the time I am solitary and when I do work with other people, it is one or two other people at a time and it is mostly men. I have worked with male friends. . . . I have done a lot of teaching of men, or boys, depending upon when it was, and actually my current boyfriend has an interest, but I am trying not to push it on him or anything. So I am not exactly teaching him, but we talk about it sometimes and we have practiced once or twice.

Even though Beverly tells us that she more commonly works with men than with women, she defines herself as a Dianic Witch. Dianics typically worship only the Goddess to the exclusion of the God and work in all-women's groups. Beverly says she is a feminist and sees a link between her notion of gender equality and her participation in Witchcraft. I wish there was more of a connection between all Witches and feminism. I think maybe partially because I read Starhawk and thought that that was the pinnacle of Witchcraft reading, I always thought that feminism and Witchcraft were closely associated. But I think the more people I meet, the more I realize that I am more and more of a minority. I would classify myself as a Dianic in the sense that I see my feminism as being an innate part of my spirituality and that I can't practice without a feminine background. But I don't think that is the way it is for everyone, and I am beginning to slowly realize that.

Beverly is a thoughtful woman. Raised in a religious home, she remains religious, even though she has changed her religious affiliation from Protestantism to Witchcraft. A major aspect of her religion is the Goddess, the female divine who in her aspect as Mother Earth is connected to the environment. Both feminism and environmentalism are important to Beverly and part of her religious identity. I think the Goddess is that unity of energy. So I guess life is always an experience with the divine. Sometimes I feel it more intensely than others. I have had moments in the woods, or at the ocean, or just being by myself in which I felt an intense bliss, an intense knowledge. And I just felt like I knew, or I could know anything I wanted to, and that I could do anything I wanted to, and that I really was loved by the universe. . . . I think that that feeling [meant] that the Goddess was with me. And it has brought me to tears before. It is beautiful. I have also experienced that in church. It has been a long time since I experienced that in church, but I went to see a friend of my father's speak on Easter, when I was probably fourteen or fifteen and I had already decided that I was a Witch and wasn't really into it, but I was listening to him. He was talking about Jesus and he was talking about God and I felt his love for God in the same way that I feel [love for the Goddess], and it overwhelmed me, and I very much felt God right then.

The natural world is an important element of Beverly's spirituality. She sees the Goddess in nature. The ocean is an amazing place. I don't really know how to describe that, other than whenever I feel the need to be with the Goddess I go to the ocean. *For Beverly the essence of Witchcraft is* discovering a balance with life and nature, and trying not to harm anything, including yourself, which I will admit I'm not completely 100 percent good at, but it's a goal. *Part of this balance between life and nature is becoming comfortable with the cycles of the year and the cycle of life and death.* I think that death and life are essentially one. . . . Death isn't the end of life; it's the end and the beginning. Just like you prune a bush to make it grow better, or you burn a blueberry field so that the crop comes back stronger, you can't really have life without death.

Religion for Beverly is important. She enters conservative Christian chat rooms to discuss religious tolerance. She tells us she also has a really big pentagram fleece on my door that I made for Yule, and I have had it up since late December, and I always wear a pentagram. Sometimes I wear other symbols in lieu of it, like I will wear a star, or a triple moon, or something like that, but pretty much religiously I wear a pentagram. The one I have recently is really big; it is really hard to miss. I just started working in a place that is fairly conservative, so I dug out my fist-sized pentagram, which is a little much for me, but it certainly got the point across.

At the heart of Beverly's experience of Witchcraft is her struggle to make sense of some difficult life experiences, such as the death of her mother and her bisexuality. These experiences make her feel "different." In Witchcraft Beverly finds rituals, friendships, and beliefs that help her come to terms with these experiences and this sense of difference. (On this recurring theme in our interviews with Witches, see Chapter 3.)

The Goddess is a central image for most young Witches. Beverly is more clearly a feminist and an environmentalist than many of the other Witches we interviewed, but to varying degrees Witchcraft encourages environmental awareness and a sensitivity to, and confidence in, the feminine (see Chapter 5).

Beverly's father, a Christian minister, is surprisingly supportive of his daughter's religious journey. Other parents, such as Charles's in the following vignette, were more concerned. The harassment Beverly reports from school friends is not uncommon, although not all Witches are as open as Beverly about their practice. The encouragement to explore Witchcraft she received from another school friend is also common. In contrast to Charles's isolation, Beverly has met a wide variety of Pagans in her local community.

Beverly draws a fascinating comparison between her experience of the love of God in a church and her experience of the bliss of being in the presence of the Goddess as part of her Witchcraft practice. Both experiences are clearly profound and moving, and Beverly does not suggest that one is wrong and the other right. In a similar way, Beverly describes her spiritual connection with her mother, who was a Christian minister, focusing on the experience rather than on the correctness of the beliefs. While Beverly is a member of a number of Pagan groups, she considers herself a solitary, finding her own path through the challenges presented by her life.

Vignette

Charles—From *Big Brother* to Witchcraft (England)

I was really into *Big Brother* [a reality show] when it was first on—the television program—and I was talking to this person on the Internet that was really into it and she mentioned in passing that she was Wiccan and I thought, "What the hell is Wiccan?" So I asked and then she gave a rough explanation and then a couple of days later I was watching *Buffy*. . . . So they [the characters in *Buffy*] sat down and said, "Yeah, I'm Wiccan." I'm like, "Well, what is this word I keep hearing about?" So I go [to] www.google.com, Wicca, and it hits all of this information and I just started reading at one end and when I got to somewhere near the middle I thought, "Yeah, this is quite appealing." It's a loose religion. It's not really conforming to anything and it's just something that interested me. . . . And I just started in a researcher kind of way picking up sources—just generally anything—[Web] sites, people's statements, press reports, books, films, TV. Just basically anything that had anything relevant to the word "Wicca."

Charles is eighteen years old and in the midst of taking his A-levels, exams taken at the end of the English equivalent of high school that determine which university, if any, and which program one is accepted into. He is doing his exams in English, drama, and biology. I was tempted to do theology, but the teacher's a bit weird, so I thought I'd steer clear of it. *Charles confides that his parents, who belong to the Church of England, are not particularly religious. They attended church when he was younger because he sang in the choir. Charles claims his interest in attending church was to sing, but he is a seeker who is interested in exploring and learning about religions.*

10

After learning the rudiments of Witchcraft from information he found on the Internet, Charles entered a Wiccan chat room. People [were] telling me how they had mystical/magical powers and could float, and I thought "Fair enough, okay." They were going around saying, "Yeah, I can fly . . ." and I thought, "Well, obviously, probably not—[there are the laws of] physics." But the more I heard people talking about it, the more I got interested in what it actually really was. When it comes down to the basics and you strip away drunken teenagers and you get something—just Wicca as it is . . . and before I realized it, a year ago I thought, "Well, why not?" So I just decided, "Yeah, that's it, I'm going to become Pagan," . . . because I really felt—I think the expression is "coming home." I just felt at home. It filled a void—something that was missing.

Asked where he found the expression "coming home," which is a common one among Neopagans, he reveals: I believe it was from a woman who calls herself Bride from one of the Internet things [chat rooms]. Basically the only [way] I could really communicate with anybody else who was the same way was over the Internet 'cause I haven't grown up in a Pagan family. I don't know any Pagans in the area. So it was my lifeline and she said, "Yeah, an expression of coming home." . . . When I thought, "Yeah, I'd like to become Pagan, I mean, what do I do? Do I have to sign a form? Do I have to, you know, go to a church or something?" They said, "No, just change your outlook on life." And I went to the bookshop, dug out some money I thought I didn't have, and picked up a book . . . [by] Scott Cunningham. I read that and thought it was quite—it gave an impression of what he thinks it is. Then I picked up a Kate West [book], read that, and thought, "Oh, well, that's what she thinks it is." And I just ended up . . . finding out what other people thought it was and forging my own way.

The first thing I ever tried to do was an invocation. You know, sit there, relax, meditate with the thought of help coming from somewhere. . . . I had a list of Celtic Gods and Goddesses and I invoked Cernunnos [the horned god associated with the hunt and thought to serve as a source for the image for the devil in Christianity]. "Well, okay, if you're there and you're listening and you're this great hunter, could [you] lend me a bit of strength so I can get through the day a bit easier?" And I sat there thinking about how there was a person up there or an entity up there that has this immense skill and strength. When I stopped, I felt a little bit better. It was like a ladder that I started climbing that helped me feel happier and helped me see things differently.

And it progressed from there—I saved up a bit of pocket money and went out and bought myself some tarot cards and started working with them; . . . the cards are actually just a way of focusing your mind—so you don't need a book which says, "Well, this card means this and this card means this." It's what the card means to you, and from that you draw on what they all mean and you come up with an idea. That's what divination is. And I started with that—progressed really rapidly. The other night my girlfriend said, "Are we going to be able to take the holiday?" and I said, "Well, hang on." Got out the tarot cards and the runes I bought the other day and just sat down and looked at it and I said, "Yeah, there's not going to be a problem." 'Cause it just felt that they're saying, "Yeah, don't worry about it." Went from there to thinking, "My God, I hope I do so well in my exams. Let's do something that might help." So I found something that says "A Fortune Spell" and I thought, "Well, that's not really what I want." . . . So I thought, "Well, what can I do?" . . . I sat there with a candle and some nice music playing in the background and I said, "I would like so much to do really well in my exams." And I guess it just put me in a better frame of mind.

Charles describes the Internet as his lifeline prior to his involvement in Wicca. I was at school. I was moderately depressed. I thought, "God, this is so boring. There must be something else other than twenty-four hour schoolwork." And I just used what I could as a method of communicating 'cause, you know, I'm an only child, my parents live downstairs, I live upstairs. I'm not really connected anywhere. I haven't got a close circle of friends. . . . I do now, but I didn't then, and so I ended up trying to find friends and . . . I found quite possibly the best way was through the anonymity of the Internet.

Charles met his girlfriend in a Pagan discussion room; . . . I think the room was discussing the finer points of drawing down the moon,[1] . . . and I sat there and I thought, "Well, I'm a little lost here," and I just said, "I'm lost," and someone said, "Yes, so am I," and I just started talking to her and we just got talking like that. . . . We just got talking, really, and I guess a couple of weeks after we'd been talking I went down to meet her. *Charles's girlfriend lives two and a half hours by bus from him:* We [first] met halfway, in London, and then went back to hers [her parental home] for a couple of days and then came back up to mine [Charles's parental home] and we just hit it off really well. We started off as friends—it wasn't like a lust thing like, "Oh, God, girl, quick—into bed." It was just someone I could share and talk to in the flesh about how I felt and it was the same for her, 'cause I mean her dad's a vicar. So, you know, problems there coming through and we just hit it off really well to start off with and we just carried on.

Asked about his spell work, Charles reports: The only thing that I really did that was a spell, . . . my girlfriend asked me to do. We sat at an altar and prayed together and did some magic over it—candle magic as a protection ring to keep me safe. Up until that point I'd had stuff stolen all the time and we did it and nothing's ever been stolen. It's been quite nice. . . . And then at Christmas after we'd been together for a year . . . she suggested that we formalize things a little more. We're not going to get married, but we thought, . . ."Well, what the Celts used to do was they'd, say, have trial marriages, so that's what that is." We got handfasted on Christmas Eve, which was something special.[2] We rigged up small tables and candles and we had cloths and chanting and nice music in the background. It was really romantic; . . . we did it as a path working.[3] We sat there and we had a tape that we'd made and it talked us through a guided meditation of us standing in a forest, walking through it in a nice romantic Hollywoodesque moment that we had for the handfasting. It was nice. I think we came down from it about an hour later and we just sat there. We looked at each other and thought, "Wow!" I guess that was when it finally hit me that Paganism is not about sitting there fighting demons with snakes, as it appears in the TV shows. It's all about in the mind, I think.

The Internet remains an important part of Charles's spiritual learning. I don't actively participate in e-groups. I like listening in 'cause a lot of the time they're discussing something I haven't got a clue about. I try to follow it and use it as a teaching thing where I learn from what other people are saying. [I am on] Britwitch, which is, I think, the largest one in the country. . . . Then I'm part of a [Pagan] Web site where all my friends that are—well, I won't say friends, but people I know that are Pagan are—and that's like if I have a problem or there's something I don't understand, I go there and just write a message on the forum and then within a couple of days someone will come back and say, "Yeah, I had the same problem. What I did was this."

Other than his girlfriend, Charles knows only one other Witch in the flesh, one that lives nearby. *Charles remains connected to the larger Witchcraft community through the Internet and through reading. Although the Internet was important in his finding Witchcraft, he currently uses it only sporadically,* about ten minutes, maybe, a day because it's very much like popping on checking to see if anyone's wanting to talk to me or anything like that. I guess it's kinda taking a back seat at the moment with study [for exams].

Charles's parents were a little worried at first, I think. I think the first impression my dad got I finally managed to get out of him was that he was deathly afraid I was going to join some American suicide cult—and I just sat them down and said, "No, it's nothing like that. You will hear things about Voodoo, Witchcraft, and stuff, but that's not what I'm into. I'm heavily into peace, love, and nature and almost hippyism." And he went, "Ah, hippies. I remember hippies"—because he was one a long time ago when he was younger. Once I'd actually sat them down and explained to them that what I was into wasn't going to harm me in any way, shape, or form—they were more worried about my self rather than my soul, I guess. I mean, you hear horror stories of people whose parents are convinced that their child is going to suffer in eternal damnation because they worship a different God.

My parents—they understand now, I guess. It took a while, but they understand and they let me keep a small altar in my room without [them] touching it. Well, I say small, it's actually grown rather large recently. I guess I'm quite ceremonial. When I do a ritual, . . . all I need is my mind. . . . But I like the feeling of clutter, I guess. So I'm a very cluttered person. . . . I have candles, I have candle snuffers, I have incense sticks, oil burners, I have small bowls, big bowls, cloths, tarot cards, runes, crystals, basically small things that I've picked up from places and they hang around there.

Charles normally does rituals alone in his room. When it's the full moon, a simple saying, "Hello, yes, I can see you're up there. Thank you for watching over me." I haven't really stuck to the main festivals, I guess because I usually forget about them. I'm not great with dates. But when it comes to Samhain, it's like, "Right. It's an important day." I'll meditate on it, think about what it really means, then I might light a candle or things like that.

I guess it's [Witchcraft] just made me feel better about myself. Knowing that if I need to use magic to get myself out of a situation that I've got myself helplessly stuck in then it's a backup, I guess. . . . It's like a safety net, thinking if things get bad and I don't know what to do, I can always turn for help—upstairs. [If] it's a case of I'm really stuck, I don't know what to do next, let's see if I can't do something to open up my mind to think about another route I could take. Something like that, I guess.

The Internet is central to Charles's experience of Witchcraft. It is not uncommon for Witches to have rarely, or never, met another Witch face-to-face. When they do meet other Witches it is often a product of first meeting on the Internet, as is the case with Beverly's coven. The Internet is more central to the Witchcraft community than it is to most other religions, in part because of the stigma still attached to identifying as a Witch—there is safety in the anonymity of the Internet. However, it also reflects a generational change in how young people gain information.

Television programs, Google searches, Internet communities, and books are central to Charles's story of becoming a Witch. It is a common story, as is the sense that finding Witchcraft is like "coming home." Beverly and Ruth in the other opening vignettes both say that they had always been Witches, although they had not always known the words to describe it.

Charles's handfasting ritual with his girlfriend illustrates that Witchcraft is used by young people to build relationships, respect, and self-esteem. The ritual Charles describes to help his self-confidence illustrates this theme (see Chapter 3). While a few teens were very depressed, such as Ruth in the next vignette, Charles reports being only bored and lonely, leading to his search for something more to life.

Some parents were less understanding than were Charles's (see Chapter 4). Charles calms his parents' fears by comparing himself to a hippy and respectfully discussing and explaining his beliefs to them. Witchcraft is an individualistic religion, and Charles underlines this aspect of his practice. Charles is a reflexive, networked, late modern Witch.

Vignette

Ruth—Coming out of Depression (Australia)

Witchcraft changed nearly everything. It just has made me who I am. It's helped me to see the positives in life—focus on the positive rather than the negatives; . . . [I am] more confident in myself as to who I am and my beliefs. *Ruth is nineteen years old and studying for an advanced diploma of naturopathy at a vocational college. She lives at home and supports herself working as a waitress on weekends and at night. She lives in a small country town in southeast Australia about one hour's drive from the nearest city. Her father is a builder and her mother is a teacher.*

I've been interested in Witchcraft for as long as I can remember. My earliest memories would be in primary school of getting together with my friends to do some spells. [At first, it was] an excuse to go outside and have a bonfire. [Laughs.] It was always at my house. My parents were always more willing than everyone else's parents to explore that area. The people that I've associated with have changed over the years, but my sister's always been there with me, although she doesn't seem as interested as myself.

Early on, it was more for the interest's sake and the fun of it. . . . You could be different. Because it would be like, "What did you do on the weekend?" "Oh, I played sport. What did you do?" "Oh, I cast a spell," or "I [laughs] did this or that." It was more to be different at that stage, sort of start being an individual. But later on it progressed into praying every day for different things, happiness for everybody and just basic things, [such as] help to make sure I remember all this stuff that I'd studied, so I [laughs] can recall it tomorrow. It's becoming more of a way of life rather than an interest. I think that the natural medicine is a huge part of what I believe is Pagan. So I'm right into the herbs.

With the support of her mother, Ruth invited friends to her place to experiment with Witchcraft rituals. We had about eight people at one stage and they weren't all Pagan by any means; some of them were sort of interested, one girl came because her sister was coming, and bits and pieces like that. But we ended up doing Mabon.[1] And we ended up raising power. And I think the chant was [the one that] lists all the Goddesses. And we were all holding hands, dancing around the circle. And when we raised enough power and we stopped, the fire actually spiraled upwards and went out, and it was [laughs] pretty cool, and then we were all standing there, and we all could have sworn that someone actually walked past us. And when we opened our eyes and we looked at each other and we all looked behind us to see, Who was that? But no one had left and we touched, and they sort of weaved in between us and went through the circle. I could have sworn it was like physical touch. [I felt] like we'd achieved something. Warm, fuzzy [laughs].

The enchantment that Ruth feels is facilitated by the altar in her bedroom that she has decorated herself. My special place is my room. I've been allowed to paint it how I like and put things on the walls. Like in old castles they've got the torches that can come off the wall—I've got two of those on one wall, with a sun and moon face in the middle, and that's painted like a brick wall and it breaks down into the forest, which is the other two walls. . . . I've got a ritual dress. Very lovely. It's medieval styled, and it's got big long sleeves, and it's got a little cape on the back of it, and it's got all the flowing lace, and it's really gorgeous, and the laceup and what not. . . . I designed my Book of Shadows because I couldn't find anything good enough to hold my book, so I designed one and had it made, which is—I think it's gorgeous—it takes pride [of] possession in my room.

I hate reading. But my mom actually bought me Silver RavenWolf's *Teen Witch* book when I was [thirteen years old]. That was my first actual book. My mom was always interested in Paganism. . . . She just came home and said, "Look, I bought you this." I read it. Very American, almost [laughs]. 'Cause she [RavenWolf] was always saying, "Us American Witches" and "over here in America," as if there was no place else, which was a bit disappointing. I liked the way she casts circle, it's actually her daughter's, I really like that. And for some reason it stuck in my memory so I know it off by heart. I've done a few of them [the spells in Raven-Wolf's book], but not all of them, by any stretch. After reading that book I bought a few books myself; . . . [recently] I've been reading more herbal books. And I read *Incenses, Oils, and Brews,* and that goes through how to make them and all that sort of thing, which was quite interesting. And I went through a stage where I just digested book after book after book, and then I just eventually stopped, for some reason. When I started getting into reading more books, my parents thought it was fantastic because I was actually reading books [laughs].

Ruth emphasizes both the egalitarian nature of Witchcraft and its individualism. Probably the main reason why I like being Pagan is it's equal. It's got Gods and Goddesses—it's equal. It's not male dominated or anything. *Although Ruth says she is not a feminist, gender equality is clearly a central concern.* Being overly feminist is I don't think a good thing. I like equalism. I like being able to view males and females as being equal, not one higher than the other. And you can be yourself and make up your own beliefs as to what you want to believe in. And Pagans are all happy with that [laughs]. You don't have to believe in this, this, and this, and you don't have to go to church on this day, or you don't have to do this ritual in this way. I like being an individual [laughs]. . . . The essence of Witchcraft? For me, . . . it's just being myself.

For Ruth, "being myself" is primarily about self-acceptance, particularly the acceptance of individual difference. For some young Witches this relates to a minority status, such as being a homosexual or a Goth. However, for Ruth, this sense of "difference" was simply a product of being an outsider at a new school. In primary school I was trying to be an individual, but I went to high school and was the only person from my primary school who went there. I just didn't fit in, couldn't make friends, got really, really [stressed and] depressed. Grade seven [about thirteen years old], I'm surprised I had any friends in high school—I was horrible [laughs]. Yeah, really nasty. Not very nice at all. But I got through year seven, and going into grade eight I just got more and more depressed, so, hmmm.

It is easy to underestimate the importance of self-esteem and social relationships for young people. For Ruth, her outsider status had profound consequences. I went through a really bad depression in grade eight—[a] suicidal depression.

And one morning I just snapped out of it. Right, you're meant to be over there, you're walking the wrong path, get over there. *Ruth linked coming out of her depression with deciding she was a Witch.* Just being more definite in "This is it—this is who I am," rather than being "Ooh, well I could be this or I could be that"—it was more, "Right, worked it out." . . . I guess I felt relaxed, weight gone, because you're just searching, searching, searching, and all of a sudden you've found it, and you're like, "Oh, thank God" [laughs]. You feel a lot better.

The Witchcraft is what got me out of the depression. . . . How did it work? I think self-empowerment would be the main thing. And what to live for in life [laughs]. I think it's that you can believe in what you want to believe in. It's not a rigid structure, you don't have to fall in with the norm, you don't have to do what everybody else is doing. Which is what I think I was trying to do, which made me depressed. So, realizing that I'm not meant to fit in with the norm [laughs]. It's not what I'm meant to do, . . . do your hair the same way as all the rest of the girls and watch the same programs. But I wasn't allowed to at home. My father would refuse to have the television on, . . . which in itself I think is pretty depressing [laughs].

A number of the young Witches describe how Witchcraft led them to be more generous or compassionate in their relationships with others. Ruth ascribes this change in her own attitude to the improvement in her self-understanding. Before I realized that I was meant to be Pagan and I was meant to have my own beliefs, I wasn't a very nice person [laughs]. It's changed me in even down to how I act to people. Before, [I was] really quick to judge people, whereas now I'm more open. "Ok, everyone's got their own ideas—what's your idea?" . . . Before, [I labeled people] without actually getting to know them first and to see whether they are that sort of person or not. . . . [Witchcraft] made me more open-minded. I just try and accept people for who they are and what they want to believe in, rather than actually put, "Oh, you're meant to be doing this, and you're meant to be doing that."

I guess I'm a bit more willing to do things for people just for the fun of [it] rather than trying to gain something from it. One of my classmates went through a hard time and she really needed some help with anatomy, and her exam's coming up this week, and I just said, "Look, I'll help ya." . . . I think it's just being more open-minded. You do unto others as you would have done to yourself. What you send out comes back times three.

Part of the reason for Ruth's self-confidence and openness about Witchcraft is the supportive attitude of her parents. But one of the good experiences [I had] was because my parents were open with it with all of their friends—well, depending on whether they're highly religious or not. My parents actually came to me and said, "Well, our friends' daughter is interested in Paganism and I was wondering whether you could go over there and show her your Book of Shadows and talk her through what you do." And people actually coming to me to ask me whether I can share knowledge with them about what I believe in. It was a nice feeling that people would come to me for that.

In the past year Ruth has made contact with the Pagan community in the nearby city. Ruth estimates she has probably met about forty people who are Witches, mainly through her local Pagans in the Pub meetings. I seem to run into people who are Pagan now that I'm open with it, rather than before when you're a bit closed with it. *She attended a Pagan Alliance–organized ritual last year.* It was winter going into summer. So we did the little role play and summer triumphed this time. It was good. It was really enjoyable.

Ruth feels that she is guided in her choices by a spiritual being. I'm not sure if it's a Goddess or the God, or whatever you want to call it, but . . . when I've been off track quite badly, I will have moments where I'll just go, "Oh, hang on, that's what I'm meant to be doing." Whether it's my spirit, whether it's someone else's spirit, I don't know.

When asked to describe how she thinks magic works, Ruth offers two explanations. One suggests that it is all in the mind; the other points to a supernatural reality. [Magic works through] the power of the mind more than anything. If you want something, if you really want something to happen badly enough and you believe that it will happen, I believe it will happen. I guess I could sort of explain it as the—well, it doesn't quite fit but—the placebo effect. If you take a sugar pill and you believe that it's an aspirin and it will cure your headache, the headache goes. I mean, the pill hasn't actually got anything to do with it—it's a mental mind over matter; . . . I [also] believe that it's energy, but it's not a physical energy.

Ruth has never been to an environmental or political protest. Myself, I'm not too much into looking at the humongous global picture. I will go up and clean up the rubbish in my local area because that's my area. I like to start small and conquer the little things, to build up to the bigger things. . . . I've never voted for anyone. I have no idea what the parties are all about. *Even if Ruth has not become an environmentalist, she has developed a stronger sense of the natural world around her.* Sometimes now I just [like] to walk my dog down [by] the river and just sit there, and not do anything. And just sit there and listen to the wind and just see what's happening in that small space around me. Rather than just going, "Oh, that's just that part of the world," to actually sit there and take it in and say, "This is an amazing place we live in."

Ruth is a hopeful young woman, struggling to make sense of her place in the world. She is not particularly "different," although she describes feeling very different and not fitting in with her peers at school. She is white, heterosexual, lower middle class, and attractively dressed. Her story illustrates the individualism of Witchcraft (see Chapter 6). Ruth's individualism has not made her more selfish. Rather, it has led to greater self-acceptance. She credits Witchcraft with helping her become more generous with her time and more tolerant toward others. Echoing a common pattern, Ruth does not describe herself as either a feminist or an environmentalist (see Chapter 5). However, her Witchcraft practice has sensitized her to both gender issues and nature.

Although she began exploring Witchcraft in a playful way, it has clearly become a serious religious practice for Ruth. Books played a central role in her becoming a Witch (see Chapter 2). Her initial social interactions were with peers who typically knew less about Witchcraft than she did. Only subsequently has she developed contacts with the local Pagan community and participated in organized rituals.

At the heart of Ruth's story is a struggle to make sense of her place in life, to find a sense of purpose and direction. Witchcraft played a key role in enabling her to overcome a "suicidal depression." The complexity of late modern life presents young people with many challenges. The positive benefits of Witchcraft practice are similar to the positive benefits of participating in other religious traditions. The rituals and enchanted world of Witchcraft provide people like Ruth with a sense of direction, purpose, and hope (see Chapter 3).

CHAPTER ONE

The World
of Teenage Witchcraft

Teenage Witches in the contemporary United States, England, and Australia are first and foremost teenagers. They are concerned about schoolwork, family, and physical and mental health issues for themselves and those they care about. They think about love, their future, and the daily issues of friendships, relationships with their parents, and adequate pocket money. These are not trivial concerns; they are the basis of young people's current lives and will also impact their futures. On the whole, in our interviews with ninety young people—thirty in each country—we find individuals struggling to make sense of and live responsibly in their world. They are deeply involved in the spiritual and self-growth aspects of Witchcraft and only secondarily interested in instrumental magic. Few young Witches were raised in the religion; most have found it primarily through books and secondarily on the Internet. Like most converts, they believe that their religion provides them with many benefits, in this case self-empowerment, a sense of connection with nature, and answers to existential questions.

Teen Witches tend to be more likely to practice alone than in a group, but they maintain contact with others through books, the Internet, gatherings, and friendships. Many have already faced serious life challenges, such as Beverly, whose mother died in her childhood; Karen, whose father is physically abusive; and others whose parents are disabled or who have themselves suffered from ill health. The stories of young Witches are typically of finding meaning and hope through spiritual practices during day-to-day living and in the face of life crises (see Chapter 3).

The thought of teenagers practicing Witchcraft may conjure up an array of images, from the relatively culturally acceptable characters of *Charmed* or *Buffy the Vampire Slayer* to mental pictures of young people being seduced by a Satanic cult. Our research indicates that none of these images are accurate. When we began our study, we expected to discover "McWitchcraft"—a group of primarily young women superficially involved in spell casting, particularly love spells, having been drawn to Witchcraft by the mass media. To the contrary, on the whole we found highly spiritual self-reflective young women and men. Some commentators, particularly from the Religious Right, have linked Witchcraft with Satanism (see Ellis 2000). None of the Witches we interviewed worship the devil or are involved in Satanism—that is a different religion. Three Witches have explored it but rejected it as selfish and not sufficiently spiritual for them.

Fears have also been raised that in choosing Witchcraft, teens are joining a cult in which they will lose their free will. Sociologists of religion normally eschew the term "cult," as it has lost any real meaning, most commonly signifying a new religion that one doesn't like. As most teenagers practice Witchcraft alone and therefore have not joined a group, there is little chance of the direct influence of a charismatic leader that many parents and pundits fear.[1] Furthermore, for legal reasons many covens will not permit anyone under the age of eighteen to join without parental permission.

Witchcraft, Wicca, and Neopaganism: A Recap

"Paganism" includes a group of earth-based religions in a similar way that "Christianity" refers to a variety of churches and traditions. Some people prefer to use the term "Neopaganism" to distinguish contemporary Pagan religions from those of ancient cultures such as the Roman Empire. Wicca is one form of Witchcraft, and both are part of the larger Pagan movement. Participants of all see the divine in the natural world and celebrate

1.1 Young male Witch at pond, USA. Photo by Helen A. Berger.

the cycle of the seasons. As there is no central bureaucracy or required dogma to determine authenticity, an individual's self-definition as a Witch, Wiccan, Pagan, or Neopagan is normally taken at face value. There are several other forms of Paganism such as Druids and Ásatrú that are quite distinct from Witchcraft.[2] However, the distinctions often become blurred as people move among groups and incorporate a variety of traditions in their practice. "Wicca" is often used to refer to people who have been initiated into one of the older traditions of Witchcraft. However, as people can self-initiate, the distinction between Witches and Wiccans is further blurred. In this book we use the terms "Wicca" and "Witchcraft" interchangeably, as those we interviewed do.

Although much of the media about Witchcraft is produced in the United States, the religion has its origins in England. Gerald Gardner, an English civil servant, is credited with creating Wicca, the most influential subset of Neopaganism, in the 1940s. No solid historical evidence has been found to substantiate his claim that he was trained by a coven that had been in existence since before the advent of Christianity (Hutton 1999; Kelly 1991; Bonewits 1989), but as Ronald Hutton notes, Gardner did successfully launch a new religion. Some Witches today continue to claim that theirs is an old religion or the old religion, or that they carry on a family tradition that can be traced to pre-Christian European society. None of these claims have been substantiated by historical research, nor could most of them be substantiated in this way. The notion that Witchcraft is an old religion was absorbed into Wicca through the work of Margaret Murray (1971 [1921]), an Egyptologist who wrote a popular book and subsequently the *Encyclopedia Britannica* entry on the witch trials of the early modern period; she argued that the trials were a successful attempt by first the Catholic Church and ultimately by both Catholic and Protestant Churches to eliminate the practitioners of the older pagan earth-based religions that lingered in rural areas. Murray's work relied heavily on that of Jules Michelet (2003), who believed the trials were an attempt by the Church to eliminate the pan-European fertility cult that had preceded Christianity. Murray knew Gardner, as they both belonged to the same folklore society, and she wrote the preface to Gardner's first book (Hutton 1999).

Many new religions and sects claim origins in antiquity to legitimize themselves and to suggest they are not just made up. It is also possible that some Witches are the descendents of English "cunning people." The historian Ronald Hutton claims that through the nineteenth century cunning people in English villages were Christians but also found lost objects and healed neighbors with a combination of magic and herbs. Because of the growing evidence that Wicca is a new religion, fewer Witches today claim that it is not, although some contend that their religion has ancient roots not because there is an unbroken line to pre-Christian Europe, but because they are looking to the past for spiritual inspiration.

Hutton's (1999) history of contemporary Witchcraft is the most comprehensive to date. He notes that Gardner had been influenced by five trends that were prevalent in English society and in which he was involved before founding Wicca. Two we have already mentioned—interest in folklore and in traditional Western magical practices. The other three— Freemasonry, the occult, and Theosophy—came together for Gardner in the Hermetic Order of the Golden Dawn, a society that like the Freemasons was hierarchal and secret. It was through the Order of the Golden Dawn that Gardner met Aleister Crowley, a ceremonial magician who had created a systematic rendition of the Western magical tradition. The influence of the Golden Dawn can be seen in covens run as secret societies in which members swore not to reveal the identities of others, and which include three degrees or ranks of learning, as exists in the Freemasons. The magical and occult teaching of the Golden Dawn, particularly as presented by Crowley, continues to serve as the basis for Wiccan magical practices.

From almost the moment that Wicca became public, sects began to develop. Some groups claimed that they too were hidden Witches whose covens could trace their history back to antiquity; others were clearly splinter groups from Gardner (Hutton 1999). The religion also began to spread beyond England, first in English-speaking nations and then through much of Europe. The religion has not spread significantly to the third world, in part because many of these societies have indigenous pagan religions and magical practices. In parts of Africa and Latin America individuals, most commonly women, who use magic for evil purposes are called witches and are hated by the community and at times murdered (Evans-Pritchard 1937; Stoller and Olkes 1987).[3] Although the term has negative connotations in the developed world as well and some Witches have experienced discrimination, there is little fear of their being killed, and at least among some countercultural subgroups the label is considered "cool."

The religion came to the United States in the 1960s and to Australia in the 1970s during a time of social change. Rosemary and Raymond Buckland, who trained in Gardner's coven, are credited with bringing the religion to the United States. Immigrants from both England and the

United States brought the religion to Australia (Hume 1997). The environmental and women's movements, the growth of individualism, and the questioning of all authority, including that of science, were under way at this time. An elective affinity exists between Wicca and these movements. Women are drawn to the religion because of the worship of the Goddess, those in the environmental movement because of the emphasis on the celebration of nature and its cycles, others by the focus on the individual authority of spiritual experience and on the practice of magic. These social movements in turn helped to transform the religion. This transformation was most marked in the United States, where the women's spirituality movement absorbed and challenged Wicca and where there developed a large enough market to make the publication of Witchcraft books profitable for publishers.

Zsuzsanna Budapest, a Hungarian immigrant, created the first feminist all-women's coven in California in 1971 (Eller 1993). The coven might have gone unnoticed but for the arrest of Budapest on fortune-telling charges. Her story was covered nationally, appearing in *Ms. Magazine* (Griffin 2002), and her notoriety helped spread the ideas of feminist Witchcraft. Budapest is considered by many to be the mother of feminist Witchcraft, which focuses on the veneration of the Goddess to the exclusion of the God and limits its membership to women. Her influence on the larger Witchcraft movement was most significantly through her student Miriam Simos, who writes under her magical name, Starhawk. Starhawk had already been initiated into a Wiccan coven in California when she trained with Budapest. The influence of both feminist and traditional Witchcraft is evident in Starhawk's writings and in the teachings of the Reclaiming Tradition of Witchcraft that she helped found. Both the Reclaiming Tradition and Starhawk's books incorporate feminism, environmentalism, and activism with Witchcraft. They also are inclusive of men and women and venerate both the Goddess and the God. (It was this combination of Witchcraft, feminism, and activism that particularly appealed to Beverly in the opening vignette.) Starhawk was one of the earliest authors to publish on Witchcraft. Her first book, *The Spiral Dance* (1979), has sold more than 300,000 copies (Salomonsen 2002). Although not all practitioners or forms of Witchcraft are feminist, Starhawk's writings have influenced the direction of the religion, most clearly in the United States but to some degree internationally, as she is read worldwide (Eller 1993; Salomonsen 2002; Griffin 2005).

Wicca, as it was first developed by people like Gardner and Starhawk, is an initiatory religion. New members traditionally join a coven and train in esoteric knowledge, including ritual and magical practices. Although there are beliefs that are common among Wiccans, such as a belief in the efficacy of magic, the immanence of the divine, and a "this-worldly" spiritual orientation, the central focus of the religion is not beliefs but experience of the other world, the divine, or the mystical realm. Wiccans are trained to put themselves in an altered state of consciousness through dance, chanting, meditation, drumming, and other practices.

Rituals both commemorate the seasonal cycles—called the wheel of the year—and help people enter an altered state of consciousness to reach the other realm. Witches speak of raising energy during rituals, which can then be used for magical workings. The energy raised can be either sent out into the world or embedded in a talisman that the Witch or her or his friend can carry around. Magic is viewed as the ability to change events in the world at will (Adler 1979). Just as the most common prayers of Christians are for health, so are the most common magical workings of Witches (Crowley 2000). But Witches use magic for an array of other issues, including doing well on exams, finding a job, and dealing with relationships. Despite what some popular spell books advocate, Witches generally consider it unethical to perform spells to make a particular person fall in love with them, as this would be a violation of that person's free will. Many Witches believe that any magical act a person does that hurts or helps another will return to them threefold—making it among other things dangerous to do love spells. Magic in some ways is similar to prayer—in both, one hopes for nonmundane intervention in life. But unlike prayer, in which the individual asks for help, magic gives the person performing it a sense of control. Furthermore, for Witches, magic is more than getting the world to change at will; it is a way of connecting with the divine. Through magic, Witches see themselves as linked to the universe; in some instances they experience direct contact with the deities.

For Witches, the year is divided into eight major holidays, sabbats, which occur approximately every six weeks (Luhrmann 1989) and com-memorate the beginning and height of each season, with a corresponding mythology of the changing relationship of the Goddess and the God. Within this mythology the God is born of the Goddess at Yule, 21 December, grows to manhood and becomes her consort at Beltane, 1 May, and dies at the fall harvest, 21 September, to ensure fertility in the world, only to be reborn again at Yule. The Goddess is eternal but changes throughout the year, from maid to mother to crone. Australian Wiccans have turned the wheel of the year around to match the seasons in the Southern Hemisphere (Hume 1997), celebrating Yule on 21 June, Beltane on 31 October, and fall harvest on 21 March. In addition to the sabbats, rituals are normally performed for esbats, the celebration of the cycle of the moon, most importantly the new and full moons.

Rituals usually follow a standard protocol: the high priestess (and at times also the high priest), carrying an athame—a ritual knife—walks around in a circle large enough to encompass all present, chanting to create sacred space. Usually all those in the circle simultaneously participate in visualization, such as of a sacred circle of flame or blue light where the circle is drawn. The spirits or divinities of the four directions—east, south, west, and north—are called into the circle and asked to lend their powers to the working that is about to occur. The athame is often used to carve a pentacle in the air as each direction or quarter is called. Each direction is associated with a particular element—east with the air, south with fire, west with water, and north with the earth. In the Southern Hemisphere fire is in the north and earth in the south, as the sun is in the northern sky. A symbol of each of these elements—for example, incense, a lit candle, water, and salt—is used to sanctify the circle and all present.[4] After casting the circle the ritual may focus on celebrating the particular sabbat or esbat. Often in group rituals "energy" is raised through dancing and chanting to do a magical working—for example, a healing of the earth or of a particular person. Rituals are often done to celebrate marriages (hand-fastings) or births (wiccanings), or for other personal reasons. The end of the ritual involves a reverse process to opening the circle, in which the quarters are farewelled (Hume 1997; Bado-Fralick 2005).

Witchcraft is sometimes seen as part of the New Age, as the two share a mystical worldview, an emphasis on personal growth as developed in the

1.2   Altar with symbols of the four elements, USA. Photo by Brad Kinne.

human potential movement, and belief in the occult. They also share some practices such as astral projection and meditation (Heelas 1996; York 1995). More recent commentators have questioned the usefulness of the term "New Age," suggesting that it simply refers to contemporary religious experimentation (Sutcliffe 2003). Neopaganism is more clearly a religion than is the New Age (Berger 2003). If there is a New Age movement, it is very diffuse and does not have the clear, shared beliefs and practices of the contemporary Witchcraft movement, such as the ritual schedule of celebrations of the wheel of the year. Witchcraft does share some of the characteristics of New Age spiritualities (Ezzy 2003a), but it is distinctive, a clearly defined movement with its own books, magazines, Internet sites, and groups.

Witchcraft Since the 1990s

During the 1990s Witchcraft underwent a dramatic change. Until 1990, most people became Witches through participating in a coven. Although they may have read about Witchcraft in a book or magazine, books on

Witchcraft were less easy to obtain than they are today. Some young people became Witches; however, very few were teenagers.[5]

Since the mid-1990s covens have continued to train Witches, but individuals increasingly learn about Witchcraft outside the coven setting. Currently in the United States there are more solitary practitioners than there are those who practice in groups (H. Berger et al. 2003). The increase in solitary practitioners has been accelerated by movies such as *The Craft* and television shows such as *Charmed* and *Sabrina the Teenage Witch*, the publication of "how-to" books such as those by Scott Cunningham (1988, 1994), the increasing availability of publicly advertised courses on Witchcraft, and the growth of Internet sites. These changes have resulted in many people learning about and practicing Witchcraft who have no contact with the older coven-trained Witches. The greater availability of information about Witchcraft is democratizing, but it has also encouraged commercialization—either from purchasing books or through links on Internet sites to occult shopping. Although some young Witches we interviewed have been coven trained or are second-generation Witches who have learned the religion from one or both parents, most heard about Witchcraft from the mass media, learned more by reading books, and are self-trained and self-initiated.

While Witchcraft is more organized than the diffuse New Age, it is not as organized as other religious movements such as the Unification Church or the Jehovah's Witnesses. Covens often have a network of links and relationships, but there are no central organizations that define correct Witchcraft belief and practice. Older Witches have relatively little control over the information that is spread about Witchcraft via the media (Ezzy 2006).

The media trend has been fueled by a number of social factors. Lynn Schofield Clark (2003) demonstrates that since 1990 there has been increased interest in, and media attention on, the supernatural, of which Witches are only one example. She attributes this trend to the Evangelical movement's successful use of elements of the supernatural in their movies about the rapture—the secular media absorbed the occult images without the Religious Right's religious message. Possibly the most important film of this genre to pique teenage interest in Witchcraft is *The Craft*, the story of four high school girls who form a coven and develop extraordinary magical abilities, which they successfully use against those who cross them. Furthermore, interest in the occult, which has waxed and waned in Western culture (Magliocco 2004; Ellwood 1979; H. Berger 2005b), has been on the rise since the 1960s. During this time too, a small occult publisher in St. Paul, Minnesota, successfully marketed low-cost books on Witchcraft, among other topics, including popular books by Scott Cunningham (1988, 1994), which provide a blueprint for practicing Witchcraft on one's own.

Young Witches in England, the United States, and Australia share many practices with older Witches. Most celebrate the eight sabbats and the monthly esbats, at least as they are able while living at home or in university residence halls. The notion of magic, which permeates the religion, is shared by the younger and older generation of Witches. However, the separation of teachings from covens is contributing to subtle changes within the religion. Many of the first adherents were drawn to the religion because it spoke to their political and lifestyle choices, for example, environmentalism and feminism. Although these concerns continue to draw people to, and make them comfortable in, the religion, there is a growing trend, particularly among solitary practitioners, to focus on the use of magic and ritual for self-transformation and to be less concerned with social and political issues (H. Berger et al. 2003; Ezzy 2006). On the whole, this is true of the young Witches we met. In part this is a life-stage issue, but it is also an outcome of their route to Witchcraft. Most practice alone or with others their own age. Except for those raised as Witches, few have systematic and regular interactions with older Witches. This is not to suggest that the young people are shallow in their religious practices, but that their focus is on self-transformation. Self-transformation through magical and ritual practices has always been one element in Witchcraft: Witches identify areas of their personalities or lives that require change, and focus on changing those things both magically and in the mundane world. The difference we note, therefore, between the new generation of Witches and those of their parents' generation is one of degree, not of kind. Nonetheless, it is significant.

Many religions claim to change the behaviors and even the personalities of their participants. Malcolm X (1965), for example, successfully prose-lytized inner-city African Americans to the Nation of Islam by initially focusing on getting people off drugs and out of a life of crime. The Nation of Islam, before coming into conflict with the authorities, was praised for its success in getting and keeping people off drugs. Many Christian groups claim to have influenced people's behavior, resulting in their being less promiscuous or self-oriented. Christian Smith with Melinda Lunquist Denton (2005) found that religious teens were less likely than their unreligious contemporaries to participate in antisocial behaviors such as underage drinking. Witchcraft, unlike these other examples, advocates or opposes no set of specific behaviors. The religious practice encourages, and in some instances requires, that individuals explore their personalities, identify problems, and attempt to work on correcting them. This does not mean the religion is value neutral. There is a strong emphasis on being environmentally conscious, if not activist, and strong sanctions against interfering with another's will. But the emphasis in ritual and in all self-transformation techniques is individual discovery and self-development. There is no clear list of behaviors, such as those that exist in Islam, Judaism, or Christianity, that adherents are expected to change or adopt.

The Interviews of Teenage Witches

This book is based on our interviews with ninety individuals between the ages of seventeen and twenty-three who began practicing Witchcraft as teenagers (and in a few cases as preteens) and have practiced for at least one year. Most have been practicing for several years, although two have left the religion. Between October 2001 and September 2004 we conducted thirty interviews in each of three countries: Douglas, an Australian, did all the interviews in that country, as did Helen, an American, in the United States, and we each conducted fifteen interviews in England. To ensure consistency we created the schedule of questions listed in Appendix A. To enable the young people to tell us their own stories, we permitted the discussion to wander in the direction that the young people took us. We feel that this provided the best combination of consistency and freedom.

It became clear early that by requiring those we interviewed to have practiced for at least a year we eliminated the more superficial seekers—those who were in it only for the spells. This may have been further influenced by our call for interviewees stating that we wanted to speak to Witches, as those in the early stages of seeking may not have yet taken that label. In all instances we accepted a young person's self-definition as a Witch.

We found our respondents through several methods. We placed advertisements in student newspapers, made announcements in our classes, asked colleagues to put up notices in their universities and ask students in their classes, and placed notices in U.S. and British occult bookstores. In England and Australia the national Pagan associations provided help. Pagans from these organizations, who knew we were serious scholars, vouched for our research and passed on information about it to young people they knew. In England we also placed notices on two well-known Internet sites, Witchvox.com and Children of Artemis. The former is a U.S. site that also provides pages for Pagans in other nations. We sent personal messages to those young people listed on Witchvox who indicated that they did not object to getting spam. Once we were contacted by a young person, we asked if that person knew anyone else in their age group who was also a Witch.

Our sample is not random, nor is there any method that could possibly provide a random sample of Witches, as they are scattered throughout the countries we studied and are often secretive. Our method did draw young people from a wide variety of backgrounds, from children of well-to-do families—such as Ollie in England, who attends an exclusive boarding school, and Heather in Australia, whose father is a physician and mother a college professor—to others whose parents are on welfare or are factory workers. Some in our sample are attending or planning to attend prestigious universities, while others have dropped out of school and are working. In the United States we interviewed one African American woman and one Latina, numbers consistent with demographic studies of older Witches, which indicate that most are white, well educated, and middle class (H. Berger et al. 2003; Adler 1986; Jorgensen and Russell 1999), and with the demographics of those who join other new religious movements

(NRMs). Although there is some variation among NRMs, most research indicates that recruits are disproportionately well educated and grew up in middle-class homes (Dawson 1998). Bryan Wilson and Karel Dobbelaere (1994) suggest the reason for this demographic is that most NRMs often require that the recruit learn new information through reading, and that they must be willing to explore ideas that contradict their previous beliefs. These are all skills honed in the education system, and middle-class youth are more likely to be college educated.

Since the 1990s, the age at which people first explore this new religion is probably younger for Witches than for members of other NRMs. The current influx of teenagers and even preteens into Witchcraft is an unusual phenomenon. Although research has shown that the young are most likely to join new religious movements, they normally are in their early twenties. Excluding those raised as Pagans, the average age at which our respondents started to explore Witchcraft is fourteen (see Appendix B).[6] "Exploring" is not the same as "becoming"; several noted a two- or three-year gap between their initial exploration and taking the label "Witch." Furthermore, fourteen is not the average age at which people become Witches; as in the past, some people are adults when they join. Nonetheless, the average age of those who joined the Unification Church, colloquially referred to as the Moonies, was twenty-three (Barker 1984); those who joined Krishna Consciousness were largely between the ages of twenty and twenty-five (Rochford 1985). No researcher has reported individuals not born into a new religion joining as teenagers. The average age at which the former generation joined Witchcraft was probably higher than that of either the Unification Church or Krishna Consciousness. This drop in the age at which individuals become Witches is part of a larger change that occurred in the religion in the 1990s, when movies, television shows, books, magazines, and Internet sites spread positive information about Witchcraft far and wide.

It is hard to say exactly how many teenage Witches there are in each of the three countries we studied. In their study of the religious beliefs of adolescents between the ages of thirteen and seventeen in the United States, Smith with Denton (2005) found that 0.3 percent, or approximately 60,660 teenagers, are Witches or Neopagans.[7] This number is probably an underestimate, as some of those they spoke to may have been keeping secret their identity as part of a minority religion. Further, as it is possible to combine the practice of Witchcraft with other religions, some of the young people may simply have picked the more conventional religion to discuss with the interviewers. Also, Smith and Denton exclude teens of eighteen and nineteen, ages when young people are more likely to have left their parental home and are freer to explore religious options. Nonetheless, it is clear that Witchcraft remains a minority religion among U.S. teenagers, as it is among that country's adults. Smith with Denton in the same study (2005, 31), for example, found that 52 percent of U.S. teenagers are Protestant and 23 percent are Catholic. There are more Muslim and Jewish teenagers than Neopagan, 0.5 and 1.5 percent respectively, but more Neopagan than Unitarian Universalist teenagers, at only 0.1 percent.

Witchcraft, however, has a larger impact than its numbers would suggest, as many more young people explore the religion than actually become Witches. If it is hard to estimate the number of Witches in each of the three countries who practice Witchcraft, it is even harder to say how many dabble. Most, although not all, of the young people we spoke to describe exploring the religion with one or more friends who have dropped out. In some instances, we suspect, groups and individuals explore the religion and none go on to actually practice. The impact of the religion, therefore, goes beyond those who become Witches. Furthermore, Witches, particularly teenage Witches, are featured in a number of popular television shows. This has made the religion more visible and is one factor in the increasing number of teenagers exploring it (see Chapter 2). The visibility has also brought a reaction from some Evangelicals, who have defined Witchcraft as a threat. The visibility and the controversy that it has precipitated would alone make teenage Witches an important topic of inquiry. But, additionally, teenagers are swelling the ranks of Witchcraft and have the potential to alter in subtle and not so subtle ways the religion itself (see Chapters 5 and 7). Possibly most importantly, a look at the world of teenage Witches provides insight into contemporary trends in religious identity, into processes of joining new religious movements, and into community among teenagers. As we discuss in the next chapter, teenage Witches provide a model of conversion different from that of other new and older religions. Their reliance on books and the Internet also provides an alternative form of religious and spiritual expression, one that may have implications for other religions.

Each of the young people we interviewed has a unique story and voice, and several are featured in the vignettes throughout the book. The first time we mention or quote one of our informants, we note the country she or he lives in. In Appendix B we list all persons we interviewed, noting their pseudonym, country, age at time of interview, and, when available, the age she or he first began exploring Witchcraft. As we will see, they tend to share some characteristics and often ideas and notions of the divine, spirituality, the afterlife, and magic. Some, like Beverly, are deeply spiritual; others, like Charles, are intrigued by the paranormal aspects of the religion; and still others, like Ruth, are drawn more to the self-help aspects of Witchcraft. Some are more committed to the religion than are others. Although most believe they have found a spiritual path that they will follow for their lifetime, we know that statistically, individuals in the West, particularly those who are young, change religions. Two of the young people we spoke to were ex-Witches who have moved on to other religious traditions, and another is somewhat ambivalent about her commitment. We anticipate that at least some of the remainder will not be Witches in ten or twenty years. Yet contemporary Witchcraft is growing— and teenagers represent one group where it is growing most quickly.

Witchcraft in the Media

The media play a more significant part in Witchcraft than in most other religions. Particularly since the religion migrated to the United States and Australia, books have been central to helping spread the religion. No other new religion has entire shelves devoted to it in mainstream bookstores. Movies and television shows have become increasingly important, particularly since the 1990s, in putting a benign public face on Witchcraft, even if they have trivialized the religion. For many of the young, the Internet is a source of community as well as a way of learning about their religion. Books and the Internet are the two major sources to which young Witches turn to explore the religion. They first hear about Witchcraft from a myriad of sources, but the ubiquitous representations of Witches in the media are the cultural backdrop in which this takes place.

Nearly all the Witches we interviewed are familiar with representations of Witchcraft in television shows such as *Charmed* and *Buffy the Vampire Slayer,* and in movies such as *The Craft.* Only six report that they never watch any television shows about Witchcraft. The most frequently mentioned show is *Charmed,* with two-thirds of those we spoke to saying they had watched it at least once. In its eighth season in 2006, the show depicts three sisters who learn they are Witches and spend each episode fighting evil while dealing with being young U.S. adults. Half the young people mention *Buffy the Vampire Slayer,* in which Buffy is helped in her quest to rid the world of evil vampires by her friend Willow, a young witch and lesbian. Some young people watch these shows "religiously"; others have watched only one or a few episodes.

Evaluations of *Charmed* and *Buffy* by the young Witches vary significantly. At one end of the spectrum are people who think they are good programs that provide them with important information about Witchcraft. For example, because the rituals in *Charmed* are somewhat realistic, the British Witch Victoria tells us: "I've learned a lot through *Charmed.*" Several people feel that *Buffy* and *Charmed* provide positive representations of Witches as "good people" and that this is valuable for the contemporary Witchcraft movement. Female empowerment is a theme noted particularly with reference to Willow by a number of the young people. Willow is described as an ideal of "girl power" or as being "cool," "awesome," and "a good role model for gays." Twenty people mention the television show *Sabrina the Teenage Witch* as a funny show that they watched when they were younger. *Sabrina* features a sixteen-year-old girl who discovers she is a witch after moving in with her two aunts, also witches, and their black cat, Salem, who can talk. Each episode is about Sabrina's coming to terms with being a witch as she comes of age.

Many of the young Witches enjoy the television shows that feature witches for their entertainment value; Witchcraft is secondary. For example, Amber, an Australian, describes watching *Charmed* for its "fun, fantasy, and escapism." The Witches on *Charmed* and *Buffy* are all beautiful young women, a scenario that disturbs several people. Logan, an American, for example, reports that *Charmed* "made me angry because . . . there is the old hag crone who is old and evil or there is the young beautiful half-dressed female . . . [who is] a sexual object, as opposed to having anything in between those two, which is I think where most Witches actually fall." As we will see, most of the young people eschew the feminist label but have feminist concerns and object to women being treated unfairly or as sex objects (see Chapter 5).

A substantial minority are offended by *Charmed*, describing it as "dreadful," "simplistic kids' stuff," "commercial," "dangerous," "fake and stupid," and "fashion-accessory Paganism." Logan described it, somewhat amusingly, as "Hollywood witchcraft—mostly big shining lights and clashing things." Some of the young critics, furthermore, point out that Witches do not fight demons and do not have a conception of "good versus evil" that is often represented on *Charmed*, and that the representations of magical practice are often wrong. Similarly, some people thought Willow provided a distorted and unrealistic image of Witchcraft. The British Witch Tim offers the opinion that "Buffy is good fantasy, but . . . it is based on Judeo-Christian theology. So that's not a good start for Witchcraft, to begin with. Secondly, it's all power, power, power, power. "Give me power!" "I want power," . . . which isn't what Witchcraft is about. [Real Witchcraft] is more self-development than "Give me power" over things. It's good entertainment, but when you take it seriously, it's no good."

Nearly one-third of those we interviewed saw the mainstream movie *The Craft*. Opinions of the movie are similar to those regarding *Charmed* and *Buffy*. A few people note that it stimulated their interest in Witchcraft, for example, the British Witch Bianca reports that after watching *The Craft* she looked for more information on Witchcraft, but that now she finds the movie "appalling" because it portrays Witches as seeking power over people and doesn't contain any images of the Goddess.

Like the older generation of Witches, young Witches are avid readers. With one exception, all had read books about their religion and related mythology and fantasy books, typically obtained from libraries and mainstream and occult bookstores. Some of the young people borrow books from siblings, cousins, and aunts or from friends and classmates. Because of restricted finances, many cannot buy all the books they want and so use the library. Some local and school libraries have a better selection of books on Witchcraft than others, but most young Witches are able to find at least some of the books that interest them. They often choose books on the basis of recommendations on the Internet or from friends.

The most popular author is Scott Cunningham; one-half of Americans, one-third of Australians, and one-eighth of English Witches mention him as an important source.[8] Cunningham published two books, *Wicca: A Guide for the Solitary Practitioner* (1988) and *Living Wicca: A Further Guide for the Solitary Practitioner* (1994), which are among the earliest and most important books to advocate and provide information for individuals to practice Wicca alone and without having been initiated into a coven. Cunningham's books provide the format of rituals, suggesting how these can be performed alone, and describe the basic beliefs and mythology of the religion. Among the rituals he describes is a self-initiation that several of the young people discuss using or modifying. Although not alone, Cunningham is an important figure in the transformation of Wicca from coven training for Witches to the more mass-market mediated form of Witchcraft typical among teenagers.

Silver RavenWolf's work, which is geared toward teenagers and pre-teens, follows Cunningham's in popularity among young Witches. Her books include *To Ride a Silver Broomstick* (1993) and *Teen Witch* (1999). While one or two of the young people we interviewed are critical of Cunningham, more are critical of RavenWolf, suggesting that she was too lightweight or condescending. Others, however, say that one of her books "just all made sense," or was "a good friend of mine," or was "very good" because it doesn't assume anything. RavenWolf, like Cunningham, is an important figure in the popularization of Witchcraft, particularly because of the appeal of her work to young people. Like Cunningham, she provides an overview of Wiccan beliefs, practices, rituals, magical workings, and ethics. She presents some spells geared specifically to young people, such as one to do well on examinations or to deal with a difficult teacher. She throughout emphasizes the need for Witches to work ethically. For example, she notes that it is not acceptable to hex or harm a difficult teacher, only to work a spell to avoid problems with or the notice of that teacher.

The popularity of both RavenWolf's and Cunningham's books among teenagers is significant because not only were these among the first to make Witchcraft accessible to a younger audience (although Cunningham's are not specifically targeted at young people) but also they provide a much more sophisticated discussion of ethics and the mythology and worldview of Witchcraft than have most popular Witchcraft books for teenagers (Ezzy 2003a). Many such books are composed entirely of spells, particularly love spells, with little or no discussion of deities, spirituality, or ethics. As noted earlier, the popularity of Cunningham and RavenWolf among the Witches we interviewed reflects the seriousness of their practice in contrast to the fad-oriented focus on spells that characterizes more ephemeral participants and the books they read.

The young Witches impressed us with the number of serious books on Witchcraft that they have read in addition to the works by these two well-known popular authors, fifteen have read Raymond Buckland; twelve have read Starhawk; seven have read Vivianne Crowley, a professor of psychology at London University. Authors mentioned by two to five Witches include Margot Adler, an NPR reporter and one of the early and influential writers on U.S. Neopaganism; Dion Fortune, an occult practitioner, novelist, and author from early in the twentieth century; Ronald Hutton, a British historian; Gerald Gardner; and Phyllis Curott, a U.S. lawyer and writer. One-third of the Australians, but none of the Americans or English, mention Fiona Horne, an Australian writer who, much like RavenWolf, gears her writings to teenagers and young adults. Fantasy novels, such as those by Terry Pratchet, Anne Rice, Marion Bradley, and Diane Duane, are also mentioned when young people are asked about important Witchcraft books. (As we will see in the next chapter, fantasy literature is one way in which young people become interested in Witchcraft.) Interestingly, none of the young Witches mentioned reading any popular novels that focus on Witchcraft, such as those based on the *Charmed* television show or those in the Sweep series by Cate Tiernan. This may be because we did not ask specifically about this sort of literature and they did not think it important enough to mention, or it may be that they do not read such books.

Unlike the books, which tend to be read in all three countries, young people read local magazines.[9] *Green Egg*, now defunct, and *Circle Network*

News, published by Circle Sanctuary in Wisconsin, are the two most cited in the United States. English Witches read *Wicca and Witchcraft,* a publication geared to the young, and *Pagan Dawn,* the journal of the British Pagan Federation. Australians typically read *Witchcraft Magazine,* a glossy commercial publication distributed at newsstands, or *Pagan Times,* a publication of the Australian Pagan Alliance distributed to subscribers. The geographically based nature of magazine readership suggests the publications' great significance for local networking and community.

But the Internet may be the most important form of mediated community for the young Witches. The extent of use varies—some never go online and others are on for hours a day. Almost all use it as an encyclopedia, searching for information about rituals and the magical qualities of colors, stones, and herbs. A smaller percentage use the Internet as a forum to interact with others, either talking in chat rooms or posting information on bulletin boards to which others respond. A minority of young people describe making contact with other young Witches internationally, but it is more common for young Witches to interact with others in their own nation. Real-time conversations between Australia and the United States did occur in two cases but are made difficult by the time difference. In some cases, young people meet each other in person after interacting on the Internet, or by reading advertisements for open rituals or gatherings organized by local Pagan groups (see Chapter 4).

The Internet for some serves as their main source of information about the religion. Limited budgets and limited ability to travel sometimes make it difficult to obtain books, but either at home or at school they have unlimited computer access. In some instances the Internet also permits the young people to become instant experts—sharing their rituals, practices, and experiences with others. This has both a positive and a negative effect. Positively, it boosts young Witches' self-esteem and makes them feel more in control of their spirituality. Most are still students in their mundane lives and enjoy the role reversal that permits them now to be teachers. Negatively, some of those offering spiritual advice and information are no more and possibly less knowledgeable than the seeker (Cowan 2005). That anyone on the Internet can claim expertise has resulted in some young people being skeptical of what they read there. However, at least one of our respondents is being trained by another young Witch, and the U.S. Witch Aguina claims to be training others on the Internet. We cannot determine the quality of this training—only that it is given by one young Witch to another. Because most young Witches practice alone, the Internet becomes an important source for feeling that they are part of something larger than themselves.

TV shows, movies, books, magazines, and the Internet are, to varying degrees, all "mediated" forms of community. That is, instead of community being based on face-to-face interactions, community is increasingly based on prescribed, prepackaged interactions. Increasingly, the young learn what is hip to wear, say, and become through what they hear, see, and read in the mass media. The mass media is part of the "community" in which the young live. Anthony Cohen (1993, 15) reminds us that "community . . . is where one learns and continues to practice how to be social; . . . it is where one acquires 'culture.'" Although Witches debate the validity and authenticity of various books, movies, and television shows, these mediated forms of culture are part of the milieu in which young people seek out, learn about, and practice Witchcraft. Clark (2002, 749) argues that "entertainment media are one element of a culture that shapes and constrains religious identity construction for contemporary teens and an especially important one for those with few ties to formal religion." As we will see in the next chapter, most of the young U.S. Witches we interviewed come from homes that are religiously affiliated. Only six describe their parents as not participating in a religion. Nonetheless, Clark's insight about the media's influence on religious affiliation is valid for young Witches. The media is an important part of the cultural milieu in which elements of the religion, such as environmentalism, women's rights, cultural relativism, and even magic, come to be normalized.

There has been a backlash against the normalization of Witchcraft, particularly by the Religious Right, which suggests that the young are being lured to Satan. Bill Ellis (2000) contends that this backlash is the result of some members of the Religious Right attempting to gain legitimacy by creating an enemy they can then fight against. Stuart Wright (2005) similarly contends that the fear of Satanism is manufactured by the Religious Right to bolster its social position as many of its members lose ground in the global economy. Whatever the motivation, the backlash is real. Young Witches in all three countries report being mistreated because of their religious affiliation, some being ostracized by old friends, others being pushed and hit. Recently in the United States a divorced Wiccan couple embroiled in a custody battle was enjoined by the judge not to teach their religion to their son (Concoran 2005). The decision was overturned (McNair 2005), but it is indicative of the real discrimination that continues to occur against those practicing Witchcraft.

Our research suggests that young Witches are not seduced into the religion. Most are active seekers who believe that they have found a "home" in Witchcraft. They feel the religion speaks to their spiritual needs, their ethical concerns, and their sense of developing a self and becoming adults at the beginning of the twenty-first century. Nothing in our research suggests that these young people are being harmed by the religion, although it does at times create rifts with parents who disapprove and old friends who oppose it. All the young Witches, like members of other religions, speak about the religion helping them make sense of their world, work through daily problems, and find answers to their existential questions.

Theory

Throughout this book we use studies from sociology, religious studies, and other social sciences to compare what is occurring among teenage Witches and other new religions. Our intent is twofold: first, to illuminate what is different or unique about teenage Witches and to understand what is common among teenagers or religious practitioners; second, to either bring into question or bolster previous research. Our main intent in this book, however, is to use theory to illuminate the world of teenage Witches. We find that the work of Anthony Giddens specifically and postmodernist theory more generally is helpful for understanding the phenomenon of teenage Witches in the developed world. Our interest here is not to argue the fine points of postmodern theory, but to use it to help to understand what has been called a postmodern religion—Witchcraft (Orion 1995; H. Berger 1999; Eilberg-Schwatz 1989). We use the term "postmodernism" in a general sense to refer to the culture of late, or high, modernity, characterized by consumer capitalism (Giddens 1991) and a network or information society (Castells 1996).

Postmodernists argue that contemporary society is marked by several trends, including globalization, the "death of grand narratives," and the relativizing of all truth claims. The first, globalization, is the process through which the world becomes linked. Economies are intrinsically dependent on one another, sharing media, meaning, and knowledge, particularly in what Giddens refers to as expert systems, such as medicine, computer science, or mechanics. Because of globalization, changes tend to be rapid and worldwide. Contemporary Wicca has been spread through globalization and through the growing importance of the media. Movies, television shows, and books about Witchcraft are available in the three countries in our study; all the young people know about them, and most have watched the same television shows and movies and read many of the same books. All knowledge is interpreted through the lens of culture, and more specifically through linguistic categories. Media takes this to a new level, as reality is viewed through the lens of mass communication.

The mass media and relatively inexpensive air travel, telephones, and the Internet all help to expand time and space beyond a particular locality. We all become part of the same time system even if in different zones, marking time within the same system. Space itself is transcended. Local knowledge, local deities, and local customs become part of a world system. It is within this context that Witches are able to borrow deities, rituals, and magical practices from around the world and make them part of their own spirituality.

The second and third trends identified by postmodernists as characteristic of contemporary society are that grand narratives such as Marxism, evolution, and the notion of progress, which attempt to provide an overarching explanation for historic change, have been called into question, and that all truth is relative. The most radical postmodernists suggest that all that can be produced is a series of competing stories that attempt to explain the truth. Giddens (1979, 1987) suggests that science, the hallmark of modern thinking, requires that all knowledge be open to question, revision, and review. In the contemporary world, science itself has become open to question—offering one among other possible "stories" or ways of seeing the world. It is within this context of questioning, and seeing as relative, science, history, and all knowledge that magic is viewed as a reasonable alternative for well-educated Westerners.

Postmodernity has supplanted tradition; radical change has become the norm rather than the exception. On the one hand, we have seen a growth in the scope and power of bureaucracies, from multinational companies and governments to international relief and watchdog organizations. Within these organizations, individuals are cogs, easily replaceable and interchangeable. On the other hand, personal life, the place that most people get a sense of self, has been set free from social institutions. Marriage, courtship, friendship, and sexuality are more and more seen as matters of choice. It is through these choices that individuals in postmodernity define themselves and find meaning.

In postmodernity, as Lorne Dawson and James Beckford contend, religions have changed in form and content. Along with the decline in centrality of traditional religions, there has been a growth of new religious movements that emphasize a holistic worldview and focus on self-transformation. Under the conditions of postmodernity, individuals need to develop flexible selves, which must be invented and reinvented to fit new careers, communities, and situations (Giddens 1991; Gergen, 1991). Both Dawson (2004) and Beckford (1992a,b) suggest that new holistic religious movements provide, among other things, an avenue for this creation of self and development of meaning within societies in which there is greater and greater uncertainty. Many of the rituals and magical practices of contemporary Witches are geared toward people transforming themselves (see Chapter 3). At the same time, Witchcraft attempts to reintroduce tradition—but a created tradition. Many Witches see their religion as in some ways returning to a mythical past when the Goddess as well as the godhead was worshipped, women respected, all people treated well, and nature protected. Most contemporary Witches know that theirs is not an old religion in the sense of having been passed down in a direct line from antiquity but believe that they are returning in some ways to an older sensibility.[10] Young Witches, like the former generation of Witches, see Witchcraft as providing them with a worldview, ethics, and spiritual path that at once speak to their contemporary lives and provide them, if not an anchor, an ethical system that permits them to shape-shift in a shifting world.

Structure of the Book

Throughout the book we capitalize the words "Witch," "Wiccan," "Pagan," "Witchcraft," "Wicca," and "Paganism" when discussing the religion or its practitioners but not when referring to media representations that are describing neither the religion nor indigenous practices in other societies.

We begin our exploration of teenage Witches in Chapter 2 with a discussion of how young people come to Witchcraft. The chapter explores the notion expressed by many Witches that they have "come home" to Witchcraft or always have been a Witch. Cultural orientation through the mass media and individualistic seeking behavior are of primary importance in attracting young people to Witchcraft.

Chapter 3 reviews the ritual, magical, and spiritual practices of young Witches. Although young people use instrumental spells for finding love, doing well on exams, and other mundane problems, the most common rituals are to improve health and self-esteem. The rituals of Witchcraft go beyond spells linking Witches to nature and to the divine. Like all religions, Witchcraft helps its participants create meaning in the face of pain and loss.

Young people's involvement in Witchcraft community is the subject of Chapter 4. The Witchcraft community is dispersed and disorganized. Friendships with other Witches often develop through Internet groups, among school friends, or in local Pagan communities. The chapter also reviews parental responses to youth becoming Witches.

Chapter 5 examines the extent to which feminism and environmentalism are part of the world of teenage Witchcraft. Our research indicates that, although not activists, young Witches are on the whole concerned about gender equity and environmental issues. Chapter 6 reviews the ethics of young Witches. Although they are often individualistic, they are typically not selfish but develop an empathetic concern for others. The concluding chapter reviews the main themes of the book and places them within a theoretical context.

Vignette

Morgan—One Path to Witchcraft

Morgan is nineteen and lives in Texas when she is not attending a prestigious university program on the East Coast of the United States. She prefers to use the term "Pagan" instead of "Witch" when referring publicly to her spiritual path. I use the term "Witch" in friendly conversations with people who I already know. Because I think a lot of the people have a negative connotation with the word and if I am using it on the street then I can't go into the history and my goals, reforming negative opinion towards positive opinion, you know, when I am waiting for [public transportation]. *Morgan is painfully cognizant that the religion she chose is a minority one. She reports that as she has become more involved in this path, she has* made a more conscious effort just to not put forward an image of—What kind of adjective can I use?—badassness. Just because I don't think it is positive for our religion to be seen as a fringe religion, so I don't walk around in a cape. I have actually started wearing black a whole lot less.

Morgan's journey to Witchcraft began with doubts about her religion of birth. I was raised Protestant, and I realized that wasn't for me about sixth grade. I had always been really interested in Greek and Roman mythology and I developed an interest in Egyptian mythology in about the sixth grade. And I was trying to do anything I could just to find out more about Egyptian mythology and I picked up a few books on Egyptian witchcraft and magic, and it was really neat. The first books were in the library, but then just Barnes and Noble. Barnes and Noble is my outlet for Pagan resources. Or at least it was when I was in high school. I picked up those books, and I never practiced anything, but I was reading them. And one

49

day I saw a Silver RavenWolf book on the same shelf and picked it up and I was like, "Wow, this is what I believe." I [had] been on an existential crisis from like sixth to ninth grade. And I was researching different religions trying to figure out what worked for me, and finally I got really frustrated and just wrote down everything I believed, and didn't give it any name or anything, and when I picked up that RavenWolf book, everything fit. Sadly enough, the hokeyist title on earth, it was *Teen Witch*. . . . I just really went for the theology and not the working that a lot of kids get into it for; . . . I don't think I did any spells or anything until I was seventeen.

Morgan's first magical working at the age of seventeen was for health. I had a number of friends who were in very bad health situations, and I made them some sachets, and some herbal bags, and what not. So those were the first real ones [magical workings she did].

Magic has always taken a backseat to the spiritual aspect of Witchcraft for Morgan. She tells us that she found in RavenWolf's Teen Witch (*1999) and* To Ride a Silver Broomstick (*1993) a set of ideas that resonates with her own.* A lot of it was, I definitely believe in reincarnation. I believe that there are spiritual forces around us that we can't see. In the everyday world I have a very strong connection to the four elements [fire, water, earth, and air]. And then the fifth, the spirit. I never put a face on divinity. But I recognize certain attributes that I like to work with at certain times. And I always thought that a masculine and feminine force were necessary in the world. (*These are common themes in the interviews discussed in Chapter 2. A belief in the supernatural, a connection with nature, and an appreciation of the importance of the feminine are all important themes that resonate with and help attract young Witches.*)

After finding RavenWolf's books and discovering a name for what Morgan tells us is her own form of spirituality, she continued to read books on the topic. She found some useful sources, particularly Scott Cunningham, and she was disappointed in some others because they were the fluffy bunny approach. I am not a fluffy bunny. *She also made contact with the owner of the occult bookstore in her hometown.* I was lucky enough to actually have a metaphysical shop in my town. I was really shy, but the woman was very, very open, and she put more of a physical face to living the life. Not just what you get out of books.

Although Morgan does use the Internet, it has never been a central element of her search. I never used anything I found there. I just liked to read, and see what different people did. . . . I try to stay off the chat, it is just a breeding ground for drama. I actually e-mailed a girl the other night because she was brand new to the community and I just wanted to tell her, "Hi, you know, say if you have any questions, I'm not a scary person, you can just ask." Mostly, I just go on to check for [local] events.

I'm very much into the individuality of my particular practice, *although Morgan says other people have always been part of her learning and practice. As is commonly reported in the interviews, Morgan knew other young people in high school with an interest in Witchcraft. Early in her search, friends gave her* tables and correspondences and stuff *and she in turn gave* two of my friends . . . books, and I know that they are still on the path, like they haven't decided. *Although they exchanged information, her high school friends* weren't that committed *and they did not perform any magical rituals together. Although two of these friends are still exploring, Morgan is the only one who has become a Witch. Once she came to university, she joined her university Pagan association and through that connection is undergoing structured learning with a local group.* I'm technically a solitary, but I am actually in the training course for my first-degree initiation into the Cabot tradition. I practice with an open circle right now for my training. . . . I [also] am taking my magical training. *Although she is being trained in a tradition, Morgan insists that she is a solitary practitioner, based on the notion that she remains in control of her own spirituality and that she can take what she wants or needs from her training and integrate it into her sense of what works for her. Furthermore, the Cabot tradition more than most others focuses on individual training, with a one-on-one mentor relationship.*

Morgan also integrates elements of her university coursework into her spirituality. This semester has actually been planned around both academic things towards my thesis, and in doing so, actually strengthening my own belief and understanding of ancient religions. I have been reading a lot about ancient Greek and Roman religion and just the history of witchcraft in early modern Europe. And, I'm looking at different—just ideas, . . . because I am eclectic so I can add things.

In her sophomore year of high school Morgan recalls creating a circle, and they were more worship circles . . . than anything else, where I would just sit and do meditation or a visualization of the cycles turning and the seasons. . . . I think that just really helped connect me to the earth a whole lot more—just witnessing the change [of seasons]. *Since coming to university, Morgan has done some magical working with others, both in her university club and in the group with which she is training.* I have done various things. Charging certain things and making herbal mixtures and what not. I did one with a group of friends for good grades— unfortunately we can't burn things in the dorms and I live in a dorm so [we were limited in the type of ritual we could do]. I always just kept [the talisman I made] on me and the smell was really invigorating, it kept me going. I have done ones for independence, just for inspiration, for focus with academic studies—a lot of mine are for focus.

Although doing magic is not her primary object in rituals, Morgan is sure that it works. I have been doing a lot of reading in clonomechanics and [it suggests that] all animals on this earth, all things in creation, emit a light ray, even in the minutest of quantities—even black holes emit light, though it is a negative light, and all animals including humans are sensitive to light and the pineal gland—and I believe that . . . when you mix certain elements together, like when you bring in a candle, you shift your consciousness, and therefore you shift how your pineal gland responds to those light waves. It is just like any other muscle. The more you work with it, the more you work it out, the stronger it becomes. When you use psychological triggers like candles or robes or incense, you trigger a shift in consciousness, and your pineal gland works stronger, and I think that is what you work with when you work with psychic energy or energy on any level, because magic really is a shifting of energy by your will. And when you shift light, you are shifting energy. That is what I believe. *Dancing Wu Li Masters* [a popular-science book on the "new physics" that discusses energy patterns] is by far what every Witch should read as they are forming their belief about magic.

Divinity is an important element of Morgan's spiritual practice. She describes herself as a polytheistic monotheist, so I believe that there is one Great Spirit, but because we are a male and female race we view things that way. As a women I identify with a Goddess easier, and in particular,

I identify, right now, in most of my days, with Artemis, because I aspire to certain qualities in her or need her inspiration in specific dealings, but if I am feeling a little bit darker or I'm going through a mourning period, I would easily identify with Kali [an Indian goddess of death, destruction and change], or if I was going out for healing, Asclepius [Greek god of medicine and healing], I would identify with that particular masculine version right then. So I think that because men and woman embody both genders, but one is just more dominant, we can work with both, because they are both part of one.

I very much identify with Diana [a Roman goddess of nature and fertility] or, well, actually with Artemis [the Greek equivalent of Diana]. She is a very big part of my life. I have a few statues of her just because she inspires so much in me. I invoked her at a group ritual once, and it was one of the most powerful things I felt. My friend about two minutes earlier had invoked Apollo [a Greek god of the sun and music, the twin brother of Artemis], and we are very strongly connected since then. We're like twins. We finish each other's sentences. He knows what I'm thinking when I look at him. . . . The God is just a force. I don't give any name to it usually—just more the hunter, the horned god.

This summer I was just really confused, just the way things were going, nothing in particular, it was just one of those few weeks when you just feel lost. And I came home three nights consecutively and on different channels the same show was on. And I turned it on at the same time to watch a thing about Bridgit [a Celtic fertility goddess] and children making Bridgit's cross. And that night I was reading a book and Bridgit came up again, and so I had a circle and I prayed with Bridgit and I dedicated some things that I was working on to her work, and her inspiration in me. Bridgit is definitely my mother Goddess that I associate with most.

Morgan's mother does not approve of her involvement with Witchcraft. My mother knows, and that is a whole complicated situation. She is undergoing a change in her whole spirituality, but she is remaining very Christian. She is embracing more Eastern ideas in a Christian way. So at first it was very, very confrontational in my house and over time she is becoming more accepting, but it is still a matter of contention. . . . I have heard that my dad knows. My dad is not an outward person so I have never had a conversation with him. . . . My mom is very religious. My dad is more socially religious. The thoughts of God do not come up every day for him. He enjoys going to church, he enjoys talking to people, hanging out, you know, going to church Christmas Eve, Easter, maybe, not usually—he wouldn't be one of those people who push to go to church every weekend. My brother and his wife know. My brother is fine with it. I mean, he probably still thinks it is like the young rebellious thing, but five years into the Craft, you're really not going to go back. *Morgan believes that she has found the correct religion for herself. She is quite open with all her friends and has even told her former high school teachers in Texas. Morgan and her boyfriend have discussed marriage. Her boyfriend is not a Witch or Neopagan.* He is not religious. He is a very spiritual person, but he does not identify himself with anything in particular, but we have talked about getting married and he is very supportive of me raising our children Pagan.

Morgan is committed to Witchcraft. Even her university studies are based on her interest in ancient pagan religions. She sees Witchcraft as having changed her in small ways. It has definitely pushed me to be happy more in what I choose to do for a career. It has made me more mindful of what I say and how I speak to other people. It has definitely deepened my boyfriend['s] and my relationship. It definitely changed the way I decorate. I'm just more conscious of the images I put around me, and the things I'm drawn to these days have been much more earthy or, you know, statues of different cultures, divinities. I am a lot more confident, definitely.

For Morgan, the essence of Witchcraft is healing. I just think that so much of what we do is healing, whether it is expressed verbally in your circle as healing or not. Because every time we work, we change ourselves, and most of the people I associate with as Witches work positively, and even when they do love spells, which I don't totally agree with, that is putting a positive love in the world. You can heal your friends physically; you're changing them for the better.

Morgan describes herself as an extremely religious person. . . . I don't do a circle every night, I don't walk around with all sorts of pouches and satchels and my sickle or anything, but it is very important to me. *Witchcraft was so important that one factor that influenced which university she chose was whether or not it had an active Pagan club. Morgan feels that through her interactions with others in her club and through the classes she is taking with a local group that her* internal focus—I don't know what terminology is most appropriate to use—but I feel the energy shifting much more physically, and I'm much more aware of it whenever I practice. *She feels this is a combination of* just experience [and] . . . participating in group meditations, . . . group workings. . . . I have been working a little with my class on truly developing those senses and it is just coming more naturally.

Morgan did not suddenly convert to Witchcraft. Rather, she drifted into Witchcraft over a number of years. She began by reading books, speaking to Witches, and checking the Internet and has progressed to participating in a university club and seeking training by an established group. She sees herself as committed to continuing on this path, which means for her continued study, reading, training, and practice. Morgan views Witchcraft not just as a religion but as a way of life. She sees it permeating every aspect of her life, influencing it and making it better by giving her a spirituality that is meaningful to her and that gives her an ability to heal—herself, her environment, and her loved ones.

CHAPTER TWO

Coming Home
to Witchcraft

Morgan, in the foregoing vignette, presents one road to Witchcraft. Others first learn about Witchcraft from a myriad of sources, including television shows, news broadcasts, fantasy books, and computer games. Although Morgan does not speak for all teens, her story shares features common to most of the narratives. Her route to Witchcraft involves a sense of alienation from the religion in which she was raised; her initial information came from books and the Internet, and only subsequently from people; and her first spell was for healing. Unusual although certainly not unique for her generation, she is training in the Cabot tradition in the town in which she attends college, although she insists that she is still a solitary practitioner.[1]

Most young Witches proclaim as Morgan does that they did not so much convert to a new set of beliefs as find a name for the beliefs they always had. While the idea of "coming home" occurs in a variety of religious traditions (Kemp 2000; Shires 2003), it is less common in evangelical religions, such as many forms of Christianity, that emphasize the conversion of a lost soul. As discussed later in the chapter, reports of "coming home" are very common among Witches. For example, Jane, whose father is a lay preacher for the Uniting Church in Australia, reports: "I was about fifteen and I was actually looking for a religion that matched my own beliefs and I stumbled across it on the Internet. . . . 'Cause I went searching for nature religions and that's what popped up." Jodie, another Australian, tells us: "It sort of felt right. Almost, I'd say, familiar, but that's really clichéd and stuff." Charles, whom we met at the beginning of the book, informs us that when he found Wicca: "I just felt—you know, I felt at home." When asked where he got the expression of being at home, he responds: "It was from a woman who calls herself Bride from one of the Internet things [chat rooms]."

The image of "coming home" to a set of beliefs that one has always had is common among Witches of both this and the last generation (Adler 1979; Harvey 1999). Margot Adler (1979, 14), one of the best-known and early authors about Neopaganism, describes this sentiment:

> Neo-Pagan groups rarely proselytize and certain of them are quite selective. There are few converts. In most cases, word of mouth, a discussion between friends, a lecture, a book, or an article provides the entry point. But, these events merely confirm some original private experience, so that the most common feeling of those who have named themselves Pagans is something like "I finally found a group that has the same religious perceptions I always had." A common phrase you hear is "I've come home," or as one woman told me excitedly after a lecture, "I always knew I had a religion, I just never knew it had a name."

Similarly, Harvey (1999, 234) writes that "narratives of conversion ('testimonies' or 'bearing witness') do not occur in Pagan discourse. . . . More typically they [Pagans] discover that the name for their existing sort of spirituality is Paganism. They find that they are not alone in the world but that there are books, groups and World Wide Web sites devoted to the exploration of this spirituality."

The image of individual seekers looking for a name for their spirituality and searching for others who share their beliefs permeates the discourse of becoming a Witch. This image has resulted in a number of scholars concluding that Witches do not convert to Witchcraft (Harvey 1999; Harrington 2004) but merely find a name for their preexisting spirituality. Although conversion—that is, the idea of adopting a completely new set of beliefs—does not adequately describe what occurs in becoming a Witch, the process must nonetheless be viewed as culturally mediated. The emphasis on seekership and the notion of coming home paint the process of becoming a Witch as individualized, implying that it derives completely from some internal compass that has not been influenced by the larger culture. But exploration of Witchcraft, like all aspects of behavior in modernity, must be understood within a cultural context in which mediated forms of community, such as books and mass media, distribute information and help form opinions and options. Many of the concepts of Witchcraft, such as belief in the supernatural, reincarnation, Karma, and gender equality and a reverence for nature, are widespread within the cultural milieu. This is not to suggest that the route to Witchcraft is completely culturally determined. To the contrary, we would suggest a two-pronged process of cultural orientation and individual seekership. *Cultural orientation* to Witchcraft is mediated by the mass culture of contemporary society. The concept of *individual seekership* underscores that becoming a Witch involves individual decisions and choices.

Mass media provides the cultural background that facilitates cultural orientation to Witchcraft, which occurs at two levels. At one level, individuals are oriented to many of the central ideas and themes of Witchcraft by non-Witchcraft culture. These more general aspects of culture include the feminist movement, environmentalism, the magical realism of novels and television, acceptance of the paranormal, and the emphasis on individualistic discovery and reflexivity central to much contemporary culture (Giddens 1991). At a second level, and more specifically, positive representations of Witches and Witchcraft in movies such as *The Craft* and television shows such as *Charmed* orient young people positively to Witchcraft. Cultural orientation is assisted by the widespread availability of positive information about Witchcraft in bookshops, libraries, and on the Internet. These broad cultural factors on their own do not result in conversion to Witchcraft, but they do provide a cultural context in which seekers can feel as though they have "come home" to Witchcraft.

The phrase "coming home" and all that it implies can itself be understood as a conversion narrative, that is, a culturally constructed rhetorical device through which individuals attempt to explain to themselves and others why they changed religions or joined a religion after being unaffiliated. McGuire (2002, 76) reminds us that "the individual who converts *reinterprets past experiences* in relationship to the new meaning system. . . . The convert constructs the story of conversion, drawing on a socially available set of plausible explanations, or rhetoric." Jodie and Charles both acknowledge that their own narratives are in part socially constructed, the former by noting that her description is a cliché, the latter by attributing the expression "being at home" to someone he communicated with on the Internet. This is not to say that these narratives are false or planted in the young Witches' minds by some nefarious individuals or groups. Rather, we all interpret our personal experiences through cultural filters. The narratives of the young, like those of their elders, describe their sense of coming to Witchcraft through their beliefs and in many cases their experiences with the spiritual world. Religious adherents of all faiths are often offended by the idea that their beliefs are shaped by cultural and social processes. However, an understanding of the cultural and social sources of religious belief does not necessarily undermine religious belief and spiritual practice.[2]

Scholars who study Witchcraft, like those who practice it, normally eschew the term "conversion" when discussing people becoming Witches; the process of becoming a Witch is markedly dissimilar to that of conversion to a more structured religion, such as the Unification Church or the Catholic Church, although the two share some elements. Most importantly, it differs from more typical conversion in that teenage Witches generally do not join a group but become Witches either on their own or with other novices. The mass media therefore becomes particularly important in the process of both learning about and being a Witch.

It is not only the cultural milieu that draws youth to Witchcraft. Those who choose to become Witches typically describe themselves as "seeking" or "looking" for a religion or spirituality. Young Witches are not alone in being seekers. As Wade Roof (1999) demonstrates, at least in the United States, religious seekership has been the norm since the baby-boomer generation came of age. For the young Witches, as for their parents' generation, there is a desire for a more individualized and less authoritarian spirituality. Many express dissatisfaction with Christianity or Judaism because they believe these religions do not properly acknowledge the feminine divine or show enough respect for nature. The feeling of "coming home" that many find in Witchcraft to some extent reflects their adopting many of the central values of Witchcraft before they join the religion. But of course many people who adopt feminist, environmental, and individualistic cultural orientations do not become Witches but find "homes" in other communities and places.

Roads to Witchcraft

The roads young people travel to become Witches vary significantly, although there are some common themes. Most of the young people we spoke to became Witches based on their reading of books or Web sites before they physically met another Witch. Some just happen upon the information when they are doing other things and feel the religion speaks to them. Some are actively searching for information about Witchcraft. Their reason for seeking further information ranges from having seen positive images of young Witches in the mass media, to being called a Witch by classmates or others, to attempting to make sense of paranormal experiences they are having.[3]

Five of the young people we spoke to were raised as Pagans—two Americans, one Englishwoman, and two Australians. There are others whose parents were involved to a greater or lesser degree in Paganism or the New Age, but the young people believe they found the religion for themselves. For example, Jen, an American, learned only after she expressed an interest in the religion that her parents were Pagans. "I went to Salem [Massachusetts]. And I don't know what it was, whether it was just the energy or what I saw in the shops, but for some reason . . . my little eight-year-old mind decided I wanted to be a Witch." At the age of ten Jen confided her interest in being a Witch to her mother: "My mom told me, 'Your dad's [a Wiccan], go talk to your father.'" Jen's father subsequently brought her to his group at the local Unitarian Universalist church. Like Beverly, whom we met at the beginning of the book, Jen started exploring Witchcraft through a Covenant of Unitarian Universalist Pagans (CUUPS) group. After her parents' divorce when Jen was twelve, she moved with her mother to another state and left her father's group, which she occasionally attends when she visits him. Jen continued to explore the religion both in books and on the Internet and occasionally joins in ritual with her mother's women-only Dianic group.

Most young Witches begin learning about Witchcraft through reading—books and Internet Web pages. In some cases they find the books or the Internet sites when they are actually looking for something else. For example, Percy, an Englishman, was introduced to Witchcraft through American friends he met in a chat room for folksinger Sinead O'Connor fans. As Percy tell us:

[Sinead O'Connor] was touring at that time in America and some of those people were going to go to one of the concerts and I got some money together and ended up going to America—New Jersey. . . . I'd been talking to these people for roughly a year on and off and it just so happened that a lot of them were either Pagans or Wiccans . . . of one description or another and when I got out there and started chatting to these people (I was friends with them anyway and so forth), there was one particular person whose name is Hope who—her and I had a thing going and it got a bit more passionate whilst we were out there as well. A bit of that holiday romance. . . . And she happened to have been a Wicca practitioner for about ten years and whilst I was reading some of her books and so forth out there, and then I began to realize that this was just something I'd actually always had an interest in and, you know, I'd always been reading about Pagan things or things related to the occult and particularly interested in mythology. Mythology is something I've always read up on. . . .

So when I came back to the U.K. for about two, three, four months I was dithering around thinking, "Is this really for me? Is this really what I'm interested in?" And then I began to look at Web sites and I found a particular Web site which is religioustolerance .org and they take a standpoint that there's no right or wrong and they try to outline as many religions as possible from a neutral standpoint and they're just telling you about the religion. So I was reading about their pages on Wicca there and Pagan in particular and I said, "Well, yeah, actually I agree with all that."

Percy's description of his journey to Witchcraft shares many elements that we see throughout our interviews. He speaks of a lifelong interest in Witchcraft, which he views as a continuation of his earlier interest in the occult and mythology. His journey is multifaceted; it includes the Internet, friends, a romantic partner, books, and his previous interest in the occult and mythology. He is somewhat unusual in that his point of entry was a chat room unrelated to Witchcraft, religion, or the occult. But he is not unique. Charles first learned about Witchcraft in a chat room about the reality television show *Big Brother*, and Laurel, an Australian, learned about Witchcraft in an online discussion group about fantasy novels—not surprising, since several of the young women in our sample cite interest in fantasy novels as part of the backdrop to their interest in Witchcraft. As we will see, only a few young people became Witches as a consequence of close friendships with other Witches. However, eleven young people we talked with heard about Witchcraft from friends, acquaintances, older siblings, or relatives—often cousins, but sometimes aunts or friends of their mother's or friends of other relatives.

Many young Witches do not describe even the limited interaction and friendship that Percy and Charles had with Witches. Many young people discovered Witchcraft through books, independent of personal relationships with other Witches. For example, Brianna, an American, "stumbled upon a book when I was looking through the school library. . . . I decided I wanted to do a report on it for my English class; . . . I went to the public library, and they didn't have any [helpful] books at all. So I went to bookstores like Borders, Barnes and Noble, and looked through the sections and I just picked up books at random and started reading them. I looked up all kinds of Web sites on the Internet and went through them."

Erica, an Australian, similarly describes happening upon books: "I was actually really interested in mythology and that's probably where it stems from, but I just really had an intense interest in Greek and Celtic mythology, and a lot of books about those also incorporate a lot of stuff about Witchcraft and Paganism." The first book Erica recalls reading is Homer's *Odyssey*. Like Morgan and Percy, she was drawn to Witchcraft through her interest in mythology. Although Erica's initial foray into mythology was through reading a classic work, she notes that some of the books she found in the mythology section included material about Witchcraft. She subsequently read books specifically on Witchcraft, beginning with one by Gerald Gardner.

Morgan and Erica are among eleven young people we interviewed who say that they began their exploration of Witchcraft from an interest in mythology, history, or folklore. Whatever the point of entry, the young people typically learned about Witchcraft from a number of different sources. The transition was also normally gradual. Simon, an Australian, illustrates this: "Now it [Witchcraft] wasn't something I became interested in all at once, it was a progressive sort of thing. Ever since I was about eight or nine I was really interested in herbal remedies and things like that. . . . And it kind of grew out of an interest in folk traditions and what people used to do and also my own sense of feeling there's something more that can come from a spiritual feeling. . . . And earliest, I guess that I just got books out of the public library system on New Age books. They had a lot of books in it with healing methods and things." From books on healing Simon continued on to explore Witchcraft.

It is common for young Witches to have a hard time pinpointing when they became Witches. For some, the point at which they self-define as a Witch is when they are initiated, most commonly self-initiated. This usually occurs after they have been reading about and practicing Witchcraft for a year or longer. For others there is a more vague point at which they move from dabbling and studying to actually practicing Witchcraft, but they are never initiated and are often uncertain exactly when the switch occurred from seeker to practitioner, although they know it did take place. Asked when they first started practicing, some of the young people seem almost surprised by the question, saying as Beverly and Morgan do that they were really always Witches—they just found a name for it. For others it is unclear; they begin by reading, maybe trying a spell or two, and then at some point become serious about the religion and start to define themselves as Witches.

Keeping in mind that the route to Witchcraft among those we interviewed always involves input from several different sources, and except in one case always involves books, the most common point of entry in all three nations is an interest in the occult or New Age. Several of the young people come from families that are to varying degrees involved in the New Age. For example, Patricia, an Australian, began exploring Witchcraft at the age of thirteen: "Around three, four years previous to that I was exposed to Native American Indian teachings through my mother and father and so I was already open to the whole spiritual aspect of life and everything." Patricia's mother "was part of the first Native American Indian circle that was held [in a local town]. . . . She used to work with pendulum and tarot before she got into the Native American Indian teachings. . . . And then I was exposed to Witchcraft through television and books and people I knew and then when I sort of learnt a little bit about that through reading and stuff I realized that it resonated within me." Cailin, an American, informs us that her mother is "Christian but she is very into the occult and, I mean, she teaches tarot and astrology classes; . . . she is a published tarot author and an interfaith minister and a hypnotherapist and a crystal therapist." Other young people's interest in the occult is not directly derived from their families. Cherry, an Englishwoman, tells us: "I was interested in mythology and Paganism in general, that kind of thing—New Age Spirituality—but [I became interested in] Witchcraft itself [when] I went to a New Age Convention in a town . . . in Buckinghamshire and there were a couple of Witches there. I think they were Wiccan, but they gave a couple of talks on the basics—the Wiccan Rede and that kind of thing." Others report picking up a pack of tarot cards or in one case:

My sister for her birthday got one of those really daggy spell kits and, and my sister goes, "Oh, I don't know what to do. Denise, do you want to join in?" I went, "OK, it looks a bit like fun." It was something I had in the back of my mind that was kind of interesting and she got a couple of friends over and we all dressed up and we all had a bit of a do outside and we got candles and we made— What was it?—strawberries covered in chocolate, and we kind of made a bit of a festival about it and it was one of those really tacky love spells that she got for her birthday. I don't know if she would've gone out and bought one herself, but it was a present.

Eight of the young people tell us that a movie or television show provided their first exposure to Witchcraft. For example, when we asked the Englishman Li what first drew him to this religion, he responded: "It is such a cliché; it was probably through the media, through films. . . . *The Craft.* Then I started reading up on it and realized that it is nothing like that at all. What was in the books seemed a lot better than the glamorous version of the film." Cliff, who became a Witch as a high school senior in the United States, speaks about the importance of the news media to his quest. "I was a member of the Methodist church and extremely active, and I disagreed in fundamental ways with some of the teachings that were going on and so I had heard about Paganism through like TV and books and things and so I started exploring it on my own and I eventually just stopped going to the Methodist church." When queried about which television programs had grabbed his interest he responded: "Around Halloween you always get the real Witches and stuff like that on TV or the occasional things on Discovery Channel."

Some young people are encouraged to explore alternative spiritual paths and religious cultures by open-minded parents and teachers. This reflects the more general cultural emphasis on choice and making up one's mind for oneself (Giddens 1991). For example, Seamus, an American, was started on his quest toward Witchcraft by his religious-education teacher:

I did twelve years of Catholic school. And my eighth-grade religion teacher who was a very devout Catholic, but also a very wise and intelligent woman, asked the whole class a question. She goes, "Raise your hand if you know someone that isn't Catholic," and half the class raised their hand. She goes, "Put your hand down if that person is Jewish," and everybody put their hand down. And so she looked at us and she [said]: "So basically the only spiritualities that you guys [are] aware of or exposed to are both Judeo/Christian, you know, pretty similar," blah, blah, blah. . . . And so she told us all that she is going to prepare us for confirmation because that was her job and that was what she was supposed to do. But she really thinks that you should be twenty-one, twenty-five, before you decide how you are going to live the rest of your life, that kind of thing. She told us all that the next time we were in the library just to look up something on another faith or another religion, just so you know what is out there and then you can really decide that Catholicism was for you.

So I was in the library, like, I don't know, a couple of days later, and I started just randomly looking up religions, and I came across Buddhism, which I thought was really confusing, and then I came across Hinduism, which I liked a lot, but I wasn't exactly Indian so I didn't really connect to it. Then I came across Wicca, and all of a sudden, I kind of —I started reading everything in it, and it was like everything that I thought on my own was true, a lot of beliefs that I already held about reincarnation and things like that all of a sudden now had a meaning . . . and I was really, really overjoyed and amazed that all of this stuff that I believed was already commonly held by other people.

Clarissa, an Australian, similarly began her road to Witchcraft through a class. "I was studying comparative religion in high school, looking at rites of passage, and wandered into a bookshop and found a book about Pagan rites of passage. It appealed because it was something I was looking at from a different perspective and [I] picked that up and thought, 'Oh, this is rather interesting,' and went from there."

Although most Witches have searched for information about Witchcraft on the Internet, only a few young people discovered the religion online. Ollie tells us that "a couple of years ago I actually found out that what I believed was called Witchcraft." Asked how he had discovered Witchcraft, he said through an online spiritual test. "It was a site called Spirits on Line and . . . at the end of it they ask apparently completely unrelated questions and they say, 'You are probably or your answers have indicated that you are [a Witch].' And I thought, 'Well, this is potentially mad and I'm not quite sure how this all works.' And then spent the rest of the night and the next couple of weeks just reading and finding stuff on the Internet and all the time it was just—'I'm getting this. I'm really getting this.'" Other forms of popular culture are also sources of information about Witchcraft that spark young people to search for more. For example, Tim reports first thinking about Witchcraft as a consequence of a computer game he was playing.

Several of the young people spoke of coming to Witchcraft through paranormal experiences they or their parents have had. For example, Bonnie, an American, relates:

I was born wearing a cowl, like a piece of skin over your face; as I was growing up, people were always telling me, "You're a witch" whenever they would find that out. And I never really understood what that was and at the end of seventh grade, I was actually thrown out of Catholic school and the nun, the principal of the school, told my father . . . : "I'm sorry, but your daughter can do things I'm not supposed to believe in. So she's gotta go," basically. . . . Weird things had always been happening to me regarding energy forces. . . . My mother had told me when I was a baby I was in what is now the spare room in my parents' house, all the way in the back of the house, right next to my parents' bedroom. I was sleeping, and the door was shut to that room, windows were locked, all that good stuff, and in the middle of the night I woke up screaming, and my parents came running in and I had this enormous handprint on my face. Like somebody had slapped me. It was an adult-sized handprint. And nobody could have gotten in or out of the room, I mean there is only one door in and my parents were in the living room, which was a few feet away, the whole time. It was never explained. . . . Sometimes I don't even really notice I do it anymore. I will say something and it will happen a split second later. Or weird things—I will complete other peoples' sentences before they even really get to saying them.

Other stories of paranormal experience are less dramatic than Bonnie's, but many involve contact with the spirit world, sometimes by other family members. For instance, Jane tells us: "We used to live in Perth when she [her sister] was little and our grandmother had just died and she was—her spirit was—still in the house and my sister always knew that the spirit was there."

In some instances young people believe that paranormal experiences indicate they were born Witches. An American woman, Jacqueline, tells us that "it's kind of like a family thing. My mom was a Witch too, and all of my siblings are too." She then confides that her father doesn't know about it and that she learned about Wicca primarily through the Internet. Questioned about this apparent inconsistency, she offers: "There is actually two kinds of Wiccans. One are natural witches, that's what I am, that's what all my siblings are, and my mom too. And the other people choose to become Wiccans." According to Jacqueline, what makes her family natural Witches is "my mom and my siblings and I all can feel, like, ghosts around and some of us can even talk to them. My siblings are strong enough to actually see a few."

Paranormal events are common in the West. Most Americans when surveyed in the 1980s claimed that they have had at least one paranormal experience (H. Berger et al., 2003). Interest in the occult has waxed and waned in Western society (Magliocco 2004; H. Berger 2005b). Since the 1970s it has been on the upswing, as witnessed by the number of newspapers that carry horoscopes in the United States, England, and Australia, among other Western nations (York 2005). But, most people who have paranormal experiences do not become Witches or join the New Age. People can define these experiences within the context of their mainstream religion—such as an awareness of angels or of people contacting them from heaven. Or they can present a rationalist interpretation, much as Scrooge does in *A Christmas Carol*, declaring when confronted by Marley's ghost that the apparition was just a bad dream caused by a bit of undigested meat.

For some young people these paranormal experiences are a central element of their narratives of becoming Witches. The religion affirms and provides an explanation for what has occurred to them. This is similar to the role that paranormal experiences play in conversion to some other New Religious Movements (Howell 1997). For others, these experiences are described as less pivotal in their decision to become Witches, but nonetheless part of the context whose beliefs resonate with them.

In summary, books, television shows, movies, and the Internet provide a background cultural orientation that facilitates young people's learning about Witchcraft. While friends and other people are sometimes important in stimulating interest in Witchcraft, it is more common for young people to begin seeking information without any friendship with other Witches. Experiences of the paranormal are part of some Witches' conversion narratives, consistent with the older accounts of conversion. It is also clear that the Western emphasis on reflexivity and individual decision making encourages young people to explore alternative religions such as Witchcraft. There is no hint that young people are seduced or emotionally manipulated into becoming Witches. All the narratives emphasize choice and individual seekership.

Converting or Coming Home?

Religious accounts of conversion typically ignore the social dimensions and cultural sources of conversion. For example, Dawson (1998, 25) describes the stereotypical conversion narrative, using St. Paul as the prototype:

> Paul, a Palestinian Jew, we are told, was on the road to Damascus to persecute Christians when he was suddenly smitten blind by a brilliant flash of light from which Jesus spoke to him. Three days later his blindness was healed by a pious Christian from Damascus sent to restore his sight by Jesus. Paul then converted and was baptized into the new faith. . . . Much like Paul's experience, conversions are traditionally thought (1) to be sudden and often dramatic, (2) to be emotional and even irrational, (3) to be single events, (4) to create total life changes that last a life time, (5) to be individual experiences, and not a collective phenomenon, and (6) to be something the convert passively receives as a result of the action of some seemingly external agency.

In contrast, sociological accounts since the 1970s emphasize the social dimensions of the conversion experience. Beginning with John Lofland's 1966 study of the Unification Church, colloquially referred to as the Moonies, sociologists began to question the religious accounts of conversion, contending that in most instances they are not sudden or single events but involve a social process.[4] Although he later modified the model, in his original study Lofland suggests that individuals who join new religious movement (NRMs) are those who suffer some major life crisis and are open to solving that crisis through religious means. At this turning point in their lives they meet members of the religion, form affective ties with them—at the same time weakening external ties—and ultimately join the group. Further scholarship specifically on NRMs has brought into question several aspects of Lofland's model. Snow and Phillips (1980) suggest that those who join such groups do not have a higher level of anxiety or more crises than the general population. Richardson (1992) notes that the weakening of external ties, particularly to family, occurs only when groups are in tension with parental values. But the studies on the whole confirm that friendship networks are the most common form of recruitment. Neither proselytizing nor passive forms of recruitment, such as printed literature, appear to serve as significant techniques, although Richardson (1992) does observe that friendship networks tend to be more important for women than for men. In short, sociological studies emphasize that conversion to religious movements is not simply a product of a life-transforming encounter with the divine but also involves a social process, and particularly includes the development of friendships with members of the NRM to which a person converts.

Tanya Luhrmann's 1989 study of the early Witchcraft movement in England further transforms this model of the conversion process. She argues that people adopt the beliefs of Witchcraft through "interpretive drift." As individuals read books, practice magic, and interact with other Witches, their worldview gradually shifts to accept magical ideas and beliefs. Although Luhrmann (315) notes that interaction with other Witches "certainly helps," she argues that "the crucial element of the persuasiveness of magical ideas is the private phenomenological experience within the practice of magic." In other words, Luhrmann's study of Witchcraft suggests that strong friendships and interaction may not be as important a part of becoming a Witch as these are in conversion to other religions. She also underlines that learning to think of oneself as a Witch is a gradual process of "interpretive drift," rather than the radical transformation experience of St Paul. Our research supports Luhrmann's account and extends it by putting this process within a larger cultural context.

Our research further indicates that many of the factors identified by Lofland as typical of conversion to NRMs do not apply to young Witches. First, a "major life crisis" or turning point is not present in the accounts of most young Witches. Of those we spoke to, fifty-three (59 percent), do not state that they were particularly stressed at the time that they became Witches. Sixteen indicate they had some stress such as being shy or suffering from lack of self-esteem. Twenty-eight discussed serious emotional problems. In several cases they spoke of feeling suicidal, having been hospitalized for depression or taking medication for depression, having had a drug problem, having parents or a parent who were abusive, having either a parent or a grandparent die or suffer from a serious debilitating illness, in one case being raped in high school, and in another being treated poorly by classmates after sleeping with another student. U.S. youth were more likely to mention emotional distress than were either English or Australian youth.

We did not directly ask most of those we interviewed if they were suffering from depression or other problems but were dependent on them to tell us, so it is possible that the distress rate is somewhat higher among these young people than we know. But the distress level among those who become Witches does not appear to be higher than that among the general population. Suicide, suicide attempts, and depression are common problems among contemporary youth. Child abuse, rape, and bullying in school are also acknowledged problems in all three countries. Although, as we will see in the next chapter, young people do use magic to deal with their social and personal problems, our study suggests that there is no indication that stress is what causes most young people to seek out Witchcraft. Of course, a personal crisis is what set some on the path of seekership, but this does not appear to be true for the majority of teens. Furthermore, others in their age group suffer from some of the same problems and do not choose to become Witches.

Second, in regard to the factors identified by Lofland as typical of conversion to NRMs, only twelve of our ninety respondents (13 percent) claim to have learned about Witchcraft from someone in their social circle. Of these only two, June and Dane, fit the more traditional model of integration into a religion through friends. June, an Australian, was first introduced to Witchcraft by two friends from high school. These two young women were interested in teaching others about their spiritual path and getting them to participate. However, they knew only slightly more than June did about the religion, and they were not part of an established coven or of a larger organization.

Dane, an American and the only other person who was introduced by a knowledgeable friend, describes his route:

A couple of years before I was formally introduced to it [Witchcraft] by a mentor friend, I used to spend a lot of time at libraries reading. I was a real nerd when I was a kid. I picked up a lot of books on the New Age/Occult section and just started reading through it and I happened upon it once or twice, but it didn't stick out so much, but as time went along and I was reading more books, it kind of became an interest for me. There were books on Buddhism, meditation, and reprints of old Levi books, magic, Kabbalah. I was young—early, early teens, like thirteen. Like late thirteen, fourteen years old. I was living in California at the time. . . . And this one man I met, he was into it and I started to ask him about it and he suggested some books for me to get.I think he was only about seventeen or eighteen years old. He was in high school. He had his own . . . Neopagan, Wiccan scene in the area, but his mentors were in their thirties. There was one woman, a high priestess, that he would hang out with a lot. . . . I would hang out with him a lot and a couple of good friends were into it and I just started to read my books and [began] getting more into it. . . . I would go there a lot and picking up books and reading there, and buying books when I had the money. I was reading more about it.

I started to do my own little rituals. When I had the space and time for it, when my parents weren't around. . . . I would make, I guess, a jury-rigged [jerry-rigged] altar of sorts. I would cast a circle. I would use the hand method. Again, I was young. I didn't have a whole lot of access to support. Trying to call the Goddess and God down. Asking them to guide me, for protection and stuff like that. There was a lot of things going on in my family at the time that was causing a lot of strain for myself. In retrospect, I realize that it was the family crises that were causing a lot of personal strain, but at the time I was really out of sorts and I needed some guidance. So I was asking for guidance, divine inspiration, so to speak.

June and Dane both fit, to varying degrees, the typical recruitment process of NRMs, as they came to Witchcraft through friendship networks.

Dane, furthermore, describes himself as a seeker who had been reading on a variety of alternative spiritual paths before meeting in middle school the high school student he still remembers as a man. Dane discloses that at the time he was under a strain—his father was coming out as a gay man and his parents' marriage was dissolving.

The other eleven who comment that they learned about Witchcraft from friends or acquaintances were more like Heather:

> I had a couple of friends that I was going to school—well, more acquaintances really. I didn't know them that well and they were interested in it [Witchcraft] and I really didn't know anything about it, but I sort of found the whole idea kind of intriguing. So I looked at one of the books that one of them had and sort of went into a New Age kind of bookstore and basically picked up the first thing on the shelf with "Wicca" in the title. I had no idea what it was or anything and I read it from cover to cover and thought, "Well, this is rather interesting," and, yeah, basically went from there.

Marilyn, an Englishwoman, became interested because her boyfriend was practicing magic. Fritz, an American in the midst of a crisis, was helped by a woman who is a Witch. He felt she was so kind that he became interested in her spirituality. Others were given magazines by fellow high school or middle school students whom they are not sure were even Witches. Mary, an Australian, first learned about Witchcraft from a group of young women in her high school but quickly found that they knew little more than she did. These examples demonstrate that even Witches who are recruited to the religion by others do not on the whole follow the pattern suggested by studies of other NRMs—they did not join a well-established group of adepts.

Although initial interest in Witchcraft is not typically a product of social interaction with other Witches, many of the young people eventually have social interactions with other Witches and Pagans (see Chapter 4). Social interaction with other Witches cements or reinforces Witchcraft self-identity, even if that interaction is with other beginners, as many of the young Witches note.

Consistent with, and an extension of, Luhrmann's account, the process of "becoming a Witch" begins with individuals reading and practicing on their own. This does not mean that cultural and social factors are not important. Rather, it reflects the increasing influence of technologically mediated forms of culture such as the television, movies, the Internet, and books. As we have seen, it is through these that most young people are first culturally oriented toward Witchcraft, and then begin to learn about and practice the religion.

Until the 1990s and the upsurge in interest in Witches, it was more common for Witchcraft to be taught in covens. From the 1960s and 1970s when Witchcraft was imported to the United States and Australia, books were of growing importance to the spread of information about Witchcraft, but most people who initially learned about the religion from a book found a coven in which to be trained (Luhrmann 1989; Ezzy and Berger forthcoming). The growth in the number of books on the subject and particularly those geared toward the solitary practitioner, such as Scott Cunningham's works (1988, 1994), helped increase the number of solitary practitioners (H. Berger 2005a). This increase was further helped along by the Internet, which made finding information on Witchcraft easier, particularly for the young, who may not have money to buy books and may not be near a library with books on the subject. The road to becoming a Witch was always somewhat different from the path toward joining more centralized religions. Contemporary recruitment to Witchcraft, particularly among teenagers, crystallizes this difference and suggests an alternative recruitment method that may have significant implications for conversion theory in general.

Since the 1990s there has been a growth in Witchcraft books and Internet sites geared to teenagers, particularly teenage girls (Ezzy 2001). These grew in number after the release of *The Craft*, which as we have mentioned, was a movie that featured four teenage girls who used Witchcraft to seek revenge on their high school nemeses. The success of the movie engendered U.S. television shows that feature teenage Witches, broadcast in the United Kingdom and Australia as well as in the United States. All the young people we spoke to know about the shows and most have watched them at least once. As noted earlier, only a few came to Witchcraft via this movie or the television shows, and even those are quick to note that the shows are unrealistic, something they appreciate as soon as they begin to explore the religion itself. But such movies and television shows are part of the social world in which the young live. Mish, an Englishwoman, confides: "It used to be, like when I was at school [prior to university], if I said I'm a Witch, you know, it was black cape and pointy hat. Now you say I'm a Witch, they tease me for playing with candles, . . . purely because of Buffy." Another English Witch suggests that although unrealistic, these media Witches make it easier for real-life Witches, as one has to explain less about the religion.

In from *Angels to Aliens: Teenagers, the Media, and the Supernatural,* Clark (2003) argues that the media aimed at teenagers is imbued with supernatural or occult images—angels, visitations from aliens, and contact with the dead. She notes that this has not resulted in most teenagers joining covens—or, we would add, becoming solitary practitioners. As we have indicated, most who see television shows, find books, or hear about Witchcraft do not explore it, and most of those who do explore Witchcraft do not become Witches. Throughout our research we have heard young Witches tell us that they began exploring with others who lost interest when they found that they did not gain the magical abilities described in the *Harry Potter* series or seen in *Charmed* or *Sabrina the Teenage Witch.* Nonetheless, Clark argues, the media portrayals of the occult influence young people, making them more open to alternative ways of viewing reality and to the possibility that magic is real. Relying on the work of Stuart Hoover (1997), she suggests that the media provides a "symbolic inventory" of ways to interpret reality and most importantly the paranormal.

Clark convincingly demonstrates that the influx into the media of supernatural images comes not from the New Age but from the Evangelical movement, which so successfully incorporated fantastic images of the rapture into their own films and books geared toward teenagers. The gory and magical aspects were then integrated into the mass media in a nondenominational form. This has helped to create a world in which the magical, the mystical, and the paranormal are viewed as at least possibilities. Like Clark, we want to emphasize that the media is not responsible for young people's becoming Witches. Nor has anything that we learned in this research suggested that those who have chosen to become Witches are harmed by their experience—in fact, in some instances they are helped to deal with life crises and the demands of growing up and developing a "self" at the beginning of the twenty-first century. But the mass media must be understood as one part of the cultural background, one that provides a symbolic inventory that young people use in their decision making, even if they are unaware of its influence. The acceptance among the young of the possibility that there is an alternative reality helps to create part of a cultural context in which young people make choices about their spiritual and religious practices. As Patricia opines: "When Sabrina was on and even though the shows don't really truly depict the true essence of Witchcraft, they still had the elements within them that could trigger Witchcraft within people. It activates that yearning to know more and stuff." Although television and movies are an important part of the media background, it is only one part. For young Witches, the Internet and books are, if anything, more important.

Unlike the findings on recruitment to other new religions, social networks within Witchcraft are seen as less important than the availability of books, the Internet, and magazines. But social networks are not unimportant. Many of the young people begin exploring Witchcraft in groups, often of two or three friends. However, the significance of these friends is often linked to the mass media, and not to established groups of Witches. For example, Iris, an Australian, reports that at age fifteen: "I watched *The Craft* and I got a bit of an interest there, except I didn't really sort of get into it then—it was a couple of weeks later when my friend said she was also interested and we went down the library and started looking up books and things like that." Iris's friend subsequently lost interest, but Iris did not. Although the paths to Witchcraft are remarkably similar for girls and boys, boys are slightly more likely to begin their search alone, and girls to research in groups or pairs. Both genders use the Internet, but boys are somewhat more likely than girls to begin their exploration on the Internet and then move to reading books. Nonetheless, most boys, like most girls, begin with books.

Witches have a sense—often a strong sense—that the religion is innate to them. But this sense of always having been a Witch must be put within the context of a culture that orients young people to many of the central ideas of Witchcraft. People "come home" to Witchcraft at least in

2.1 *Teen Witch* by Silver RavenWolf.
Photo by Helen A. Berger.

part because elements of the religion have become mainstream. Witches do not proselytize in the traditional manner, but they do spread information about their religion through beginner books and Web sites. Beginner books on Witchcraft are mass produced and widely available. Although the authors' intent in writing these may be to spread the word about their own religious practice because they feel it is such a good one that they want to share it with others, the publishers' intent is market driven. Some of these beginner books, particularly those that come in pink or lavender covers that are geared to teenage girls, tend to focus on doing spells—most commonly love spells—to the exclusion of the more mystical aspects of the religion. These books, mass marketed not by a religious organization or group but by publishing houses (some, like Llewellyn, geared toward the paranormal), must be seen as among the cultural resources that facilitate recruitment to Witchcraft. The purpose of publishing these books is not to gain converts but to make money.

Ironically, Witchcraft—often referred to as the "old religion" by its members, many of whom see their practices as a counterbalance to the ills of modernity—is being spread through market-mediated sources. This has important implications for the religion. The young are more likely to be solitary practitioners and to be eclectic. In their 2003 study of U.S. Neopagans, Helen Berger and her colleagues found that about one-third are concerned about the growing popularization of Witchcraft, fearing it is watering down the religion and will have long-term negative effects. This fear is greater among older Neopagans than younger ones. Clearly the form of recruitment into Witchcraft by the young influences their practice and their participation in the larger Neopagan community.

The mass market for beginner books on Witchcraft must itself be understood as a product of young people's interest in Witchcraft, stimulated both by mass-media images of Witchcraft and by trends of the late twentieth and early twenty-first centuries—most notably, concerns about gender equality, the environment, acceptance of the paranormal, the growth

2.2 Young Witch with broom, UK. Photo by Neil Keane.

of individualism, and with it a desire for a more self-directed spirituality. To use Weber's (1930) term, there is an elective affinity between Witchcraft and the values of one strand of contemporary Western societies. In other words, the growth and appeal of Witchcraft derive from an interweaving of broader structural processes and individual choices.

We do not want to overemphasize the role of the mass media in recruitment. It provides one prong of the two-pronged process we have mentioned. The other prong is seekership on the young people's part. Many more young people see television shows and movies or happen upon something about Witchcraft on the Internet and do nothing than go on to search out information, and only a portion of those who do search out more information feel that the religion resonates with them.

Who Becomes a Witch?

Clark (2003) offers a five-part typology of teenagers' responses to alternative realities: those who mix an alternative reality with traditional religions, those who experiment with it, those who try to separate it from their religious practices, those who resist it, and those who are more interested in the supernatural than in organized religion. An interest in Witchcraft is not the only or even the most common result. Is there indeed something different about those who become Witches? Our answer is a guarded yes, guarded because we have not done a comparison with teenagers who are not Witches.

Our comparison therefore must be based on the work done by Clark (2003) and Smith with Denton (2005), who investigate only U.S. teenagers. Although it is impossible to generalize to all the young Witches, they appear to have two qualities that differentiate them from their peers. Both Clark's and Smith and Denton's research suggest that most young Americans are not involved in the New Age. Clark insists that the interest among the young in alternatives is an outgrowth not of the New Age but of the Evangelical movement. Smith with Denton similarly note that most of the young people they interviewed can neither define nor give an example of "spirituality."

In contrast, as we noted previously, an experience with, or reading about, the occult or New Age is a common precursor to entry into Witchcraft. The extent of involvement varied from direct parental involvement in the New Age (or, as we saw with Morgan's mother, spiritual experiments with "Eastern spirituality" within the context of Christianity); to the young people's coming across the materials themselves in bookstores, libraries, or amusement parks; to their having received tarot cards, books, or spell kits as gifts. Often their first forays into the occult are playful and only later result in their seeking out information on Witchcraft. In many ways books, tarot, and spell kits are the material culture of a more general and widely distributed cultural milieu that celebrates and commodifies occult and paranormal ideas. So it is not surprising that many of the young people have some prior experience with occult or New Age ideas or paraphernalia. Ellis (2003, 7) argues that "one motive for becoming interested in the occult is to participate directly in the mythic realm, in spite of organized religion's efforts to institutionalize it." Witchcraft, as noted earlier, is an experiential religion that focuses on individuals gaining access to the mythic realm.

The young Witches also share a sense of themselves as always having been different. For example, Jason, an American, tells us why he first became interested in Witchcraft:

Well, somehow in middle school I got this reputation [as] a scary kid, just because I was weird and a lot of people thought I was into black magic right off the bat, when I really wasn't. I was basically atheistic. This one friend of mine, he kept asking me to teach him how to do stuff, and I kept telling him I didn't know any real magic because I am just a normal guy. So basically, just out of curiosity because he and some other people I knew kept mentioning all these things about black magic and all this stuff—again, I was sort of into all that scary stuff at the time—and I went on the Internet and checked out some Web pages on magic and that is how I sort of got introduced into Wicca. I found out how completely wrong everything that they said was, like there is no real black magic nor white magic.

Repeatedly, the young people say that they felt different from others. This sense of being different often reflected their membership in cultural minorities or unusual experiences such as the death of their mother, or being the only person at school from their area. Some say, as Dane does, that they are nerds because they like to read. A number of the young people are into or on the fringe of the Goth movement, a subculture whose members wear black, listen to particular types of music, and attend Goth nightclubs (Hodkinson 2002). They are quick to note that Goth is distinct from the Witchcraft movement, but that there are some overlaps. About half the young men we spoke to are openly gay or bisexual, or had been thought to be gay in high school even if they are not. Not all young people who think of themselves as different become Witches, but those who do become Witches often see themselves as different. Furthermore, and possibly more importantly, on the whole they like the idea of being different. While being different can be unpleasant, conforming to the norm can also create considerable tension and discomfort. The young people embrace not fitting into the crowd in high school. Witchcraft provides a group in which they do fit. This sense of finding a group of people similar to them, even if that group is only on the Internet or meets infrequently at Pagan gatherings, is one aspect of "coming home" to Witchcraft. The religion, among other things, provides a venue in which being different is acceptable and even seen as positive.

It is impossible to say whether this sense of being different is distinctive of the experience of young Witches, or whether it is shared by the older generation. Other studies of Witchcraft that examine which people become Witches do not mention this aspect (Harrington 2004; Luhrmann 1989).

Most young Witches are avid readers. We were repeatedly impressed with the books they have read, some by quite sophisticated authors such as Vivianne Crowley (1996), Margot Adler (1979, 1986), Starhawk (1979), Raymond Buckland (1986), and Gerald Gardner (1954). Research on NRMs suggests that their members tend to be better educated than their contempories. Witches and Neopagans are on the whole well educated (H. Berger et al. 2003; Adler 1986; Orion 1995; Jorgensen and Russell 1999). As part of our recruitment for our study was at universities, our sample may be skewed, but it does suggest that these young Witches tend, like their predecessors, to be well educated and more inclined to read than their peers.

Nonetheless, the young Witches we interviewed come from all walks of life. We asked what their parents did for a living as an indicator of social class. Judging by parental occupation, most appear to be middle class or upper middle class. At least one Englishman is upper class, attends a prestigious preparatory school, and spoke about his family's riding to the hounds, a recreational pursuit requiring considerable wealth. Others' families are working class or poor. One African American woman describes herself as coming from the inner city and poverty. Several young people's parents work in factories or are unemployed due to illness or disability. One young Englishman's mother is on drugs and he is forced to work to support himself. He has dropped out of school and hopes to go back once he has enough money.

The religious affiliation of the parents of our interviewees, when it is mentioned, is predominantly Christian. Of the 172 parents whose religion we know, over one-third (sixty-one parents) are not religious or are atheist or agnostic. Of the remainder, 23 percent (forty parents) are Protestant, including Baptists, Methodists, Episcopalians (or Anglicans), and Presbyterians; and 22 percent (thirty-eight parents) are Catholic. Two parents are Mormon, one a Jehovah's Witness, and one Russian Orthodox. Two people report both their parents are Jewish and two others say that one of their parents is Jewish. Three had one parent who is a Buddhist; one parent is Zoroastrian. While many have friends who are Hindu or Muslim, none have family who were part of these religious traditions. Four have Pagan parents, with a further four identifying their parents as "hippy" or "spiritual" (see Appendix 2).

There are national differences in the extent of religious involvement of parents. U.S. youth are most likely to consider their parents religious or somewhat religious, a rather arbitrary distinction; for example, parents who went to church regularly mainly for social reasons are included in the "somewhat religious" category. Among U.S. youth, ten reported that their parents are religious, thirteen that they are somewhat religious, and three that their parents are either Neopagans or New Age. Only four said that their parents are not religious. Among the Australians, ten described their parents as not religious, six as very religious, twelve as somewhat religious, and two as Neopagan or New Age. The English youth reported the least religious parents of the three groups: seventeen described their families as not religious, five as only somewhat religious, five as religious, and three as either New Age or Neopagans. The difference, we think, reflects larger national differences in religiosity. Some ministers and others concerned with youth leaving traditional religions for Witchcraft or other new religions have pointed to a lack of religious upbringing or lack of parental involvement in their churches and synagogues. Our research suggests that this is not the case. Cross-nationally, involvement or lack of involvement in religious organizations has no apparent influence on young people's participation in Witchcraft.

For some of the young people, participation in Witchcraft may be a form of rebellion, but on the whole this did not seem to be the case. Rachel, an American who describes herself as a "daddy's girl," stopped practicing Witchcraft for a while and tried to return to Judaism because she felt it would please her father, who had converted to Judaism when he married Rachel's Jewish mother. Rachel currently attempts to integrate her Witchcraft with Judaism, claiming that the former provides the mother figure and the latter the father figure in her theology. In several cases the young people have prompted both or one parent's interest in Witchcraft. Several tell us that they work hard to teach their parents about the religion so that they will approve, or at least feel comfortable with it. Those whose parents disapprove or who fear their parents would disapprove if they were told are saddened by this.

Conclusion

Lorne Dawson (2003) summarizes the research on NRMs, pointing out that recruitment is typically through friendship networks, in which the neophyte has growing affective ties with people in the group and weakening friendships with those outside it. Individuals are usually seekers, that is, they are actively looking for a new religious expression and have few ideological alignments. Their reason for joining is both because of the growing friendships they have formed and because the new religion provides them with some benefits. Witches do not fit this model. Most do not come to the religion through friendship networks, but to the contrary find out about Witchcraft primarily through books and secondarily through the Internet. Young Witches do not join because of growing affective ties with other Witches, and they typically maintain their friendships outside the religion. Young Witches over and over speak about being proud of having a broad spectrum of friends, only some of whom are Witches or Neopagans. Most that have a romantic partner are not involved with another Witch or Neopagan. They say that they do not care what religion their partner practices and only want someone who is tolerant and supportive of their own spiritual quest. Most are seekers who have a preexisting alignment to the occult or the New Age. Like all converts, they view their religion as beneficial. Young Witches tell us that Witchcraft empowers them and provides them with a worldview that is consistent with their own and rituals that are meaningful to them.

Young Witches and older Witches both speak not of converting but of always having been Witches, based on their feeling that Witchcraft resonates with their longstanding beliefs. We do not think that this claim is false, although it is part of the Witchcraft conversion narrative, but it is an indication that most of those who become Witches have already accepted many beliefs generally held by a segment of contemporary society. Among the cultural chords with which Witchcraft resonates are individualism, gender equity, personal empowerment, environmentalism, and a belief in an alternative reality or other world that is magical. The mass media in the form of books, television shows, movies, and the Internet all help create a milieu in which many of these cultural chords appear normative. As we have noted, becoming a Witch is a two-pronged process: a cultural milieu that makes Witchcraft and magic appear possible and individual seekership. Of these seekers, only a small percentage of those exposed to the media pursue information about Witchcraft, and of those an even smaller percentage become Witches. Those who seek it out tend to have a previous interest in the occult, view themselves as different, and—possibly more important—enjoy being different.

To a lesser or greater degree, the broad strokes of Witchcraft beliefs resonate with those of one segment of the larger society, but its practitioners are the ultimate authorities of their own religious experience. It is a religion that eschews dogma, permitting adherents to create their own version of the religion. However, the variations created by this individuality are not as great as might be thought. The young Witches we interviewed read the same books and surf the same Internet sites. Nonetheless, they are not required to do or believe anything. For most, however, the Goddess provides an image of both the female divine and the sanctity of nature. For most Witches, magic is real, learned, and to be practiced within some guidelines.

Before 1990, more people came to Witchcraft through friendship groups, joined covens, and were trained in particular traditions. Although some of the young Witches we interviewed are involved in coven work or are participating in structured courses with more established Witches, most are not involved with established covens. The result is that most of the young Witches are eclectic, and most of what they know about Witchcraft is mediated by books and the Internet.

Recruitment to Witchcraft offers a very different model from that provided by other NRMs, one much more dependent, first, on seekers finding the information on their own in books and on the Internet, and second, on the religion's many aspects that resonate with and feel familiar to those who seek it out. More centralized religions, particularly those that require communal living, are unlikely to recruit members on this basis. But others that are loose and less structured may to varying degrees follow a similar two-pronged model: cultural orientation based on mass media and the Internet, and seekership among those who are ideologically predisposed to the religion's message. Young Witches thus are not seduced into the religion; they are seekers pursuing a spirituality that speaks to their own needs and helps them grow as individuals. Their sense of finding a religion that reflects these needs is real, but that sense must be understood within a social context.

Vignette

Karen—Magic, Ritual, and Self-Transformation

Karen, a nineteen-year-old Australian Witch, is studying biology in her first year of university and lives in the suburbs of a large city. She became interested in Witchcraft when she was fourteen after she found the occult section in the school library. And I thought, "Wow, that looks really interesting," and I read one book, and I read another book and another book, and I ended up reading the whole section and . . . I was just so fascinated and I kept going back for more and more. *The books were mostly historical, including a number about the Salem Witch trials.* There wasn't really anything to do with Wicca there. I thought, "Damn, I've got to go out and find something about the actual practice just to see what it's about," and I read more and more books from the local city library.

Although she has been reading about Witchcraft for five years, Karen began performing rituals only a little over a year ago. I'd been reading so much and I didn't really doubt what I was reading, but I thought it might be a good time to see [if] maybe I can better my life, maybe help people if they want it, help myself if I try some of these things. So that's when I started doing the healing rituals to see if it would actually help, and it did. So I continued on and kept on because it made my life pretty good.

One of her first spells was a healing spell. I was quite ill at the time. I was going through a lot of flu, after flu, after flu. Using the different correspondences you get from Scott Cunningham's books and Cassandra Carter, I just performed a self-healing ritual. And it worked [laughs]. I feel really good now. So that was really good.

Other rituals Karen has performed include earth healing and a self-love spell to help boost her self-esteem after she was diagnosed with depression. She also regularly performs the sabbats, writing and designing her own rituals and focusing on what they mean to her. What I do is I read as many [accounts of the ritual] as I can from all my books that I've got and discover what the patterns are, like what really goes on in each sabbat. Then I'll put together my words—what I want to say and relate it to the typical story line of the [ritual] . . . [then I write down] actions that accompany it, as well. I just make it up as I go [laughs].

All my ritual work is done at about one in the morning when everyone's gone to bed [laughs]. Firstly I write what it is I want to do, my aims, what I'd like to say. Then I go through the correspondences, like what color candles I need. Underneath my altar I've got everything in boxes, so usually I don't have to go out and buy anything because I bought it all in bulk [laughs]. . . . So I'll collect everything I need and I'll set it all up. I've always got the decorations of the season on my altar permanently anyway, so that just sits there in vases if they're flowers or pine nuts or whatever they are. At the moment I've bunnies for Easter [laughs].

Over time Karen has developed a regular structure to her rituals. She practices skyclad, that is, naked, because I feel that it connects you a bit more. *She always wears a small silver pentacle on a silver chain. Her boyfriend recently gave her a chalice for her birthday and she has an athame, candleholders, and a pentacle for the earth. She also has an* amethyst cluster because I feel that it clears the negative energies out of the circle.

In my book [of Shadows] I have a set casting of the circle how I do it. I do it the same every time. I cast a circle and invoke the quarters as I go and I start in the south. A lot of people will disagree, but that's where I start. So I invoke the Goddess and the God. Depending on what the purpose of the spell is, I will invoke a different deity. My way to describe it would be that each deity is a representation of the personality of the God and Goddess. For example, Kali is the Hindu Goddess of destruction and yet life giver at the same time. So say you want to destroy something, like maybe a negative feeling within you, you call on Kali and that's how I do that.

Once I've got everyone here [laughs], I would proceed with the spell and the candle lighting and all that sort of thing. I can't light incense or anything because my mom's got very chronic allergies, so the incense is replaced by the feathers that sit on the altar. I can't [burn] herbs because I'm not allowed to have open flames in the house. Mom and Dad don't know about the candles. I try to keep it as simple as I can because of Mom. . . . As I go, I say the words that I've written down. Usually I celebrate a simple feast at the end. I'll have orange juice or wine or whatever it is, sometimes mineral water, that sort of thing. And at the end I always leave a little bit. The same with the food, whatever I've got there, whether it's nuts for fertility or whatever, and I'll always keep some on the ground as an offering and say a little thank you to the Goddess at the end. That's my basic outline.

Asked how magic works, Karen responds that whether it's mixing the ingredients, burning candles, saying the words, it's putting your will, what you want—even thinking about it puts your will into motion and manifestation. And I guess it manipulates the energies around the earth or something and it just manifests—it sort of travels along in a chain until it happens. That's how I think it works anyway. It seems to make sense that way.

Karen was a little concerned about reporting that she has also performed a money spell, because the interviewer might think her selfish. After being reassured, Karen briefly described the spell. I did a prosperity spell for my parents. I asked my mom first and she said, "Please help us out." They were going through a very tough time and it worked because they're fine now, but maybe it was a coincidence, maybe not, you never know, but that was [a spell] I did. *She repeated the spell once a week during the waxing moon and continued to perform it for six months.*

Karen has no formal training in Witchcraft, either by correspondence, over the Internet, or in person. She has taught herself. Recently she has been working through the exercises in a book called Witchcraft *by Ly de Angeles.* That's actually got a lot of visualization exercises and meditations and guided meditations and things like that. I've been working through that, trying to learn how to meditate. I'm still trying to get the hang of it.

Karen's ritual practice has been entirely solitary. Although she wants to work with other people, she has never had the opportunity to participate in group rituals. I've done it all on my own because I didn't know about the Pagans in the Pub until a friend told me. . . . So it's all just reading and experimenting and finding out for myself. I have no support [laughs]. Just experimenting and seeing how things work. *She has a couple of other favorite books that she purchased about two years ago.* I love, love Scott Cunningham. I absolutely love him. He puts everything so simply and makes you feel better about yourself. Saying, "You can do it. You don't have to be initiated by a coven or anything like that. You can do it yourself," and he gives you the confidence, I feel. . . . I [carefully read] *To Ride a Silver Broomstick* [by RavenWolf] and I find myself referring back to that again and again and again. I find it to be absolutely brilliant. . . . Everything is put very simply and it's very basic too. So I guess when I was a beginner it was a very good book. The same as Scott Cunningham, as well.

Karen also regularly buys the commercially available Witchcraft Magazine for the moon times and the phases and which sign the moon [is in]. That's what I need. . . . They've got a lot of good articles in there too. . . . They've had some on Shamanism and things like that. It's really interesting to read about. *She began using the Internet about a year ago, typically for a few hours a week, and regularly reads material on Witchvox and finds useful information on the Web site of a local esoteric bookshop.* They've got some herb definitions; . . . I printed out the entire herb page, which is very thorough, because I didn't know very much about herbs at the time, so I have a list of what all the herbs do. Just every now and then I'll bump across a site and I'll . . . print it all out.

At one Internet site she posted a message inviting people to contact her. I didn't get anyone e-mailing me back, so I thought I'd e-mail the three girls [listed as living in my city] and then they all e-mailed me back and it turned out I knew them all . . . and we kept e-mailing back and forth and back and forth, and that's when we decided to become friends [laughs]. *All her other friends know Karen is a Witch:* I told one and she told the rest of them [laughs]. . . . They're absolutely fine with it. . . . They're usually pretty good about it. They don't give me shit or anything like that.

Karen was diagnosed with depression when she was fifteen, but the doctors did not prescribe any medication because she was taking medication for other conditions—various other tablets and they didn't really want to mix the antidepressants with them . . . so they suggested the natural things like

St. John's wort, and I didn't really find that made a difference. *Since she has been practicing Witchcraft, Karen reports that her depression and self-esteem have significantly improved:* I have become a nicer, more open, accepting person, I guess you could say. Not as angry [laughs]. I used to be a very angry person. I wasn't a very happy child; . . . I was constantly told by [my] parents how much they hated me and how much they loved my brother. It was like that for years, and they're a lot better now. I don't know whether it's because I've changed, maybe, and it's changed my relationship with them. I didn't have any friends because, once again, the self-esteem was always at a rock bottom, and so I guess now that it's up again I can relate to people more and I have friends.

The repeated denigration by her parents was a major problem for Karen. I just tried to put my parents away, you know, because they just made me feel terrible all the time. So I put them out of my life—not out of my life, because I live with them, but out of my emotions. They can't dictate the way I should feel about myself. So I got rid of them and thought, "Bugger them, I'm gonna pick myself up, I'm gonna make some friends, and I'm going to enjoy my life." Why should I live the way they want me to be? Down in the dumps or whatever it was. So it [Witchcraft] did improve my relationship with people a lot because now I can talk to someone, whereas I used to probably sit in a corner and never associate with anybody.

I was brought up semi-Christian; . . . every Sunday we'd go to church and eventually my family just got sick of it and we stopped. . . . I didn't feel comfortable in the Christian religion. . . . It didn't make sense that someone could tell us what to do and someone who was so good would send us to hell if we had sex before marriage or if we drank or whatever it is. I didn't feel that was fair. With Wicca or Witchcraft or Pagans it's more earthly, nature [oriented]. It's really attractive to me. . . . It just sort of makes me feel part of nature. Part of nature—that's probably the easiest way I can describe it.

We used to have Sunday school. God, it was so boring [laughs]. . . . Mom only went because it's the thing to do. You have to go to church on a Sunday. Dad used to be a Sunday school teacher when he was younger, before we were born, but he gave that away. To be perfectly honest, I don't know if they believe in God. I really don't. Mom doesn't seem to at all. She only did it because you have to kind of thing. Dad I have no idea. I don't really speak to my dad.

Karen's father is an electrical engineer with his office at home. Her mother is a professional share trader who also works at home. Although Karen shares a house with both her parents and her younger brother, she doesn't speak to her father. He was the worst one when it came to telling me how horrible I was and every now and then—it wasn't serious, I never had any broken bones or anything—he'd just decide to throw me a couple of swings to the head, that sort of thing. Then I took up karate and he did [come at me] one day and I took one of those funny stands and I said, "Don't you effing come near me." And he backed off. And I said, "I'll kick your head in" [giggles], and he backed off. So he never ever tried again because I stood up for myself for the first time. That was [when I was fifteen] when I started karate. That was another thing that helped my self-esteem go up because I could kick someone if I wanted to [laughs].

Witchcraft [has] made me feel a lot better about myself. . . . It just made me feel like I belong somewhere. I have a purpose for being here. I have a purpose for living and I can be myself. I don't have to worry about what anybody else thinks. . . . I can open up and talk to people instead of being pushed down to be a little nobody like my parents made me feel. [Witchcraft] helped me to open up and talk to people. Because the self-esteem is so low, you don't want to talk to people, you don't want to get to know anyone. And now that it's up again, I love to meet people. I love to make new friends.

Karen has been with her current boyfriend for more than three years. Her boyfriend's mother used to be a Bible-bashing Catholic. . . . It was awful going 'round there. [I felt:] "You're not welcome here because you're not Catholic." And then, almost as if overnight, she came up to me and said, "I'm giving it up." "What?" "Catholicism. I'm giving it up. I've realized it's a load of bullshit." That's what she said: "And I'm not interested and I'd like to start studying a similar path as to what you've been studying." I'm just going, "Wow! Come with me. Lets go back to basics" [laughs], but that was amazing when she did that.

[Witchcraft] clarifies everything. It makes sense. I've always had doubts about the God. Is God real, is Satan real, all that sort of thing. But

the fact that the God and the Goddess are actually part of nature themselves rather than some supreme being sitting up there dictating. Because
I feel they're actually part of us and everything, it makes me feel more
comfortable, like they're actually there; . . . it really makes me feel included
in something, rather than being dictated [to] by some God who is going
to send me to hell if I do something wrong.

*Karen believes that she can feel the presence of the Goddess or God, but not
that they actually speak to her:* I think they're everywhere within nature itself, within me, within you, just within a plant, it's within everything, I believe, all the time. You don't have to say, "Hey, come here," or anything like
that, it's just there. That's how I feel, anyway. If I walk through a park or
something, you just feel this wonderful feeling because there's trees and
stuff everywhere. It just feels really good.

*One of Karen's most profound spiritual experiences occurred during a ritual
sabbat celebration:* Well, I'll tell you a bizarre story. Maybe it's just my head
playing tricks on me, but don't laugh. . . . My first Samhain ritual—or
Sowain, however you say it, I'm not sure—involved a guided meditation.[1]
You imagine the veils parting because [the veils between the normal world
and the spiritual world] are thinnest at that time of year, and I met up with
my loved ones on the other side. [In my guided visualization my grandpa
was] saying, "Hi, how's it going?" [In response I was saying,] "I'm going
fine" and all this sort of thing. And it sounds stupid but I was only ex-
pecting my grandpa to show up because he's the only one I really know
that's died and—once again you're probably going to think I'm absolutely
nuts . . . but all the animals, my family pets that have passed away, they all
came running up behind him, so it freaked me out.

And apart from saying, "Oh, hi, how's it going?" Pa muttered something like, "Oh, Perce is doing fine. He couldn't make it right now," and I
said "Oh, OK," and then he said, "We've gotta go now. We'll see you next
year, bye-bye," and the veils went back. I had no idea [who Perce was]. I
had absolutely no idea and the next day I said to mom, "Mom, who the
hell is Perce?" and she said "Perce?" [I said,] "Did Pa know a guy called
Perce?" And she said, "Oh, Perce was his brother. His brother passed away
just after he did." I had no idea, because Perce lived [in another state]. So
that freaked me out. Maybe I subconsciously heard his name somewhere,

I don't know, but the fact that he mentioned the name Perce, that just spun me out [laughs]. . . . So I guess you could say, yeah, I do believe in some sort of afterlife, because when something bizarre like that happens to you, you can't deny it. I'd also like to think that there was something nice.

For Karen, Witchcraft provides a set of ritual practices that are an important part of her growing up. Through rituals she works to improve her self-esteem, heal health problems, and improve her family's financial situation. Witchcraft also gives Karen a worldview in which she is a valued person. Her magical practice provides her with a sense of relationship with nature and gives her a profound and comforting understanding of the afterlife.

CHAPTER THREE

The Magical Self

Witchcraft is both a religion of nature (Crowley 1998) and a religion of self-transformation (Greenwood 1998, 2000a). These two aspects are clearly reflected in the ritual practices of young Witches. Rituals enable young Witches to transform their self-understanding, improve their self-esteem, and deal with the emotional challenges presented by teenage relationships. Spells for love, money, and health focus on the transformation of individual circumstances, but young Witches also engage in a number of ritual practices that take them beyond individualistic concerns to focus on environmental issues, experience divinity, and offer support and assistance to others in need.

Many of the practices that young Witches participate in are widespread in Western society outside of Witchcraft. Reading tarot cards, consulting horoscopes, experiencing premonitions, and sensing contact with the dead are common (Goode 2000). Most Americans report that they have had at least one paranormal experience, with a large proportion claiming to have had more than one (Berger et al. 2003). What distinguishes these experiences among young Witches is their place in their own religious practice and worldview. As Greenwood (2000a, 23) contends: "Western magical practices are best described as magico-religious: they combine elements of both magic (control) and religion (veneration of deities)." Both aspects are present in the practices of young Witches. In contrast, popular spell books and some television shows often emphasize the instrumental use of magic to control events (Ezzy 2003a).

As Greenwood points out, the religious dimensions of Witchcraft are often intertwined with magical instrumental concerns. For young Witches, the religious and spiritual dimensions of Witchcraft, such as contact with the other world or feeling part of the natural cycles, are typically more important to their practice than instrumental magic, for example, doing magic to find a job or do well on an exam. Veneration of the deities, one aspect of the religious practice of young Witches, can be understood, following Wouter Hanegraaff (1999, 147), as among those practices that ritually maintain "contact between the everyday world and a more general meta-empirical framework of meaning." Even spells and rituals that appear to be instrumental reenchant the everyday world with spiritual and religious significance. Self-love spells enable young people to see themselves within a religious worldview in which they are worthy and valued. Money spells may be used to provide divine financial assistance, but they also reframe the significance and meaning of economic activities. The ritual celebration of the wheel of the year leads to a different understanding of the world of trees, landscapes, and weather patterns.

Through Witchcraft a young person actively reshapes thoughts, worldview, and sense of self. Hanegraaff's definition of religion overemphasizes the cognitive significance of ritual practice. Witchcraft is not only about belief and understanding, but also centrally concerned with experiences and feelings. The rituals of Witchcraft "work" for these young people because they shape their embodied experiences and felt selves as much as they shape cognitive frameworks and interpretations. As Catherine Bell (1992, 116) observes: "Ritual does what it does through . . . [its influence] on the bodies of those involved in the rite." Young Witches use ritual techniques as a way of attaining identity integration and embodied self-understanding.

Ritual and Magical Practices

Circle casting is the heart of Witchcraft ritual practice. It is a way of making a space sacred and containing magical energy during a ritual. Circle casting, as we saw in Chapter 1, involves using a ritual knife (also called an athame) or a wand to draw a circle around the ritual space. Incense, a candle, and consecrated water may also be taken around the circle. This is followed by calling the quarters, or invoking spiritual guardians or watch-towers, at the four directions of south, east, north, and west. The athame is often used to carve a pentacle in the air at each direction. Associated with these physical actions are various forms of visualization, such as visualizing a sacred circle of flame where the circle has been drawn. The end of the ritual involves the reverse process to casting the circle: the quarters are farewelled and thanked for their participation (Hume 1997). Magical work typically occurs between the circle casting and the circle opening. Circle casting can be used as part of seasonal celebrations, full-moon rites, spell working, meditation, and for a variety of other purposes.

Approximately half the teenage Witches report they have an athame, and when asked what they do with it, many say they use it to cast their circle and call the quarters. This suggests that these young Witches are following the circle-casting practices outlined in Witchcraft guidebooks. A smaller number report that when casting a circle they do little outward ritual such as spoken invocations or physical movements and instead "cast a circle mentally"—focusing on visualizations. Karen, in the vignette that precedes this chapter, provides a clear account of circle casting. Other young Witches offer shorter descriptions. For example, Carolyn, an Australian Witch, reports: "You always cast a circle when you want magic because it's dangerous not to. So I cast a circle and draw [the circle first, then] call in the quarters and then call the Lady and the Lord."

Early rituals are often done word for word out of a Witchcraft book. For example, Bianca remarks: "I just did a circle in my garden with some friends and invoked the quarters and the God and the Goddess just out of the book, really." However, as they become more confident in their ritual practice, young Witches typically begin to experiment with different methods of circle casting, sometimes writing their own invocations for the quarters and finding methods of circle casting that suit their particular circumstances. The use of incense and candles, for example, may not be permitted in university accommodations. Similarly, loud invocations may not be appropriate in the middle of the night if practicing in a bedroom. The development of an individual style of circle casting reflects the individualistic and nondogmatic nature of teenage Witchcraft.

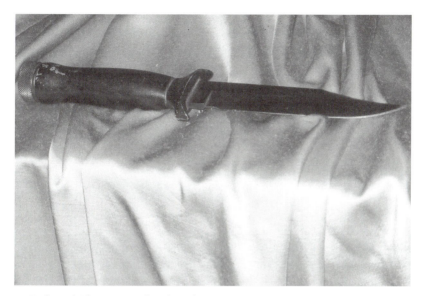

3.1 Traditional Athame, USA. Photo by Helen A. Berger.

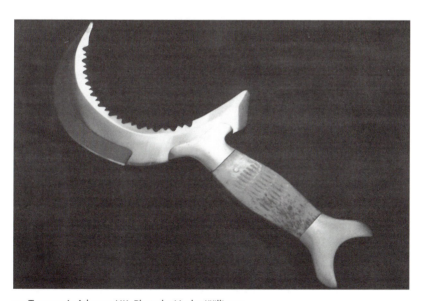

3.2 Teenager's Athame, UK. Photo by Hayley Williams.

Many young Witches describe their individual ritual practice as more meditative and quiet. For example, Bruce, an Australian, reports: "I guess the first thing that I would've done was casting circles and just sitting there, just being in that state." While group rituals often involve movement and actions, quiet meditation is a common individual activity that is central to the spiritual practice of many young Witches. Group rituals tend to be more elaborately organized, with different people calling each of the quarters, participants wearing robes or occasionally going skyclad, and perhaps drumming and dancing. A number of young Witches mention the different "energy" that is generated by the social and interactive nature of group rituals (see Chapter 4).

If circle casting is the basic ritual practice, then celebrating sabbats and esbats provides the basic ritual calendar. When young Witches practice on their own, these celebrations typically do not involve complex rituals—sometimes not even casting a circle. The Australian Witch Susan's account of her celebration of a recent sabbat is the most common form of observance: "Last sabbat, which would've been the spring equinox, [I celebrated] basically just with a candle and meditated." The important aspect of the sabbats for young Witches is an awareness of the seasons and a sense of connection with the earth. The sabbats are celebrated in various ways. One Englishwoman visited Stonehenge for the summer solstice, and another regularly went for a hike in the forest. Stella, an Australian, sums up the motivation behind the celebration of the sabbats: "I normally just honor the seasons. I like doing rituals just to say that I'm honoring them." Similarly, Carolyn says that for her, the sabbats are about "change and celebration and connecting with nature, as well. I think at the sabbat you're connecting with nature and the Lord and the Lady and the different aspects of life. Just celebrating and embracing the good with the bad. It's all that polarity."

Some young Witches do not celebrate all the sabbats, perhaps focusing on Beltane and Samhain as the two major festivals, or celebrating full-moon esbats.[1] Some move their celebrations to a convenient weekend if they conflict with other obligations, such as exams. It is the spirit of the occasion that is the focus of practice, rather than prescribed rituals and dates. For Australian Witches in the Southern Hemisphere the seasons, and hence the sabbats, are reversed (Hume 1997). Most U.S. and British books on Witchcraft list dates only for the Northern Hemisphere, and many Web sites contain a similar Northern Hemisphere orientation that a few Australians say they find frustrating. Kathy, an Australian, likes the Australian Witch Fiona Horne's book: "I can relate to it a bit more because it's Southern Hemisphere orientated and that seems to make a lot of difference."

Approximately one-third of the young Witches pray to Pagan deities. Most commonly these are generically described as the God and Goddess, or the Lord and Lady. More specific deities, such as Athena, Mercury, and Kali, are also addressed in prayer. In contrast to most young Witches, whose prayers address a God or Goddess, Chris, an English Witch, prays "to the spirits of the fire, water, the earth and the air; . . . rather than linking it to, say, Greek, Roman, and/or Nordic gods, I have a tendency not to give names and aspects to gods, I just go forth with the basic four elements." Similar to the prayers of Christians, some young Witches' prayers give thanks for a good year or a successful day. However, most prayers seem to involve petitioning the deity to help or intervene in some way. One person prayed that her hard work studying for exams would pay off, and another prayed for a sick friend.

Unlike Christianity or contemporary Heathenry (Blain 2002), Witchcraft does not have an integrated or clearly agreed-upon mythology of the spiritual world. Most Christians use the idea of a triune God: Father, Son, and Holy Spirit. Heathens address the Northern pantheon, including Odin, Freya, and Thor. For both Heathens and Christians there are texts that provide stories about the actions of their respective deities. In contrast, Witchcraft has neither an integrated pantheon nor agreed-upon texts that provide stories of the actions of relevant deities. This is true for the practices of both the new and older generations of Witches. Young Witches describe invoking or praying to the gods and goddesses and to spirits from Hindu, Irish, Egyptian, Viking, Australian Aboriginal, North American Indian, and other mythologies. Some people pray to "the God and Goddess" or simply "the Goddess" or to the Lord and Lady in a generic sense. Some understand deities as real spiritual beings, others see them as symbolic of aspects of the self, and others are not particularly interested in deity at all. This diversity among young Witches reflects a similar diversity among older Witches, although it is perhaps greater among young Witches because of their weaker connections to established communities of practice. As we saw in Chapter 1, this pastiche of deities from multiple cultures—among other factors, such as its questioning instrumental rationality, playfulness, and openness to alternative interpretations of the divine—has led scholars to view Witchcraft as a postmodern religion (see H. Berger 1999; Eilberg-Schwatz 1989).

In addition to prayer or rituals honoring the deities, meditation is one of the most commonly reported spiritual practices, mentioned by nearly three-quarters of the young Witches. It is often combined with burning a candle and sometimes with circle casting, yoga practices, chanting, and spending time outside in natural surroundings. Time spent meditating varies from a few minutes to two hours at a sitting. Some young Witches meditate daily, for ten minutes or half an hour; others meditate as the need arises, perhaps biweekly or monthly. For example, Jodie reports: "I've been trying to get back into my meditation just every night before I go to sleep for, say, ten minutes just to calm myself down. My favorite one is the tree of worries, where you go into a garden and pin all your worries and stuff onto a tree and then the tree is like the universe and when you're pinning them onto the tree you're just letting them go into the universe and not having to worry about them any more."

Young Witches learn meditation skills from a variety of sources. Some read about meditation, visualization, and path working in Witchcraft books and on the Internet. Others learn meditation skills through Witchcraft training, attending classes with other religious practitioners such as Spiritualists, Buddhists, yoga practitioners, or visiting occult shops. Those who work in groups often develop more complex meditations and visualizations.

Meditations can involve structured visualizations with complex mythology and imagery. Simon, for example, describes a visualization involving a descent into a large cavern with a lake where "all sorts of things happen." Other meditation practices are less structured, emphasizing sitting, contemplating, and reflecting on issues, plans, or problems. Carolyn, for example, reports that her meditations involve mantras: "Basically you just sit down and you be quiet and you focus on your breathing. And you can repeat a mantra over and over, like a positive affirmation. . . . [For example, your mantra might be] 'I'm becoming more confident and happy' or 'I'm a loved and loving person.'" There is significant variation in the focus of young Witches' meditations, including the year to come, the wheel of the year turning, connecting to Mother Earth, trying to identify experiences in past lives, focusing on the directions of the four quarters or elements, astral projection, restructuring thought processes, talking to fairies, meditating on the chakras, concentrating on breathing, path workings, working to find spirit guides or totem animals, contacting the dead, and healing for themselves.

Relaxation and focus are the two main consequences young Witches report receiving from meditation. In their own words, meditation results in their being "more aware of myself," "calmer," able to sort out problems, make important decisions, resolve emotional tensions, and "see things from a different perspective." Meditation is often linked to practices that increase self-awareness, such as keeping a journal. Patricia says that in her meditation practice she is "mainly working with candles and stuff. I never really followed any specific meditation guides or anything like that. It was mainly just sitting at my altar and . . . I'd do the silent meditation, but then I'd get to a point where I'd just start talking to the universe and so I'd just be answering my own questions and sorting stuff out in my life, and I found that as I developed I picked up on energy a lot and so I'd sit at my altar working with the energies that were around me and doing visualizations of energy patterns and movement." Patricia's comments suggest that meditation takes some young Witches beyond the cognitive question-and-answer approach to their problems and challenges. It provides symbolic techniques that engage emotional and visual aspects of self-understanding. Patricia's working with energy patterns can also be understood as a symbolic technique for making sense of one's place in the world through nonverbal forms of self-understanding.

In *Seeing Voices*, Oliver Sacks (1989) contends that sign language is not simply translated vocal language, but the use of spatial symbols that provide a different way of understanding. In a similar way, meditative techniques involving "visualizations of energy patterns" may provide symbolic resources for reinterpreting the self and one's place in the universe. Medical and psychological studies demonstrate the value of meditation for the relief of stress and for assisting various medical conditions (Astin 1997; Alexander et al. 1991). Young Witches report that meditation is efficacious in dealing with their stress and helps relieve minor health problems such as headaches. However, it is also a path to religious experiences, such as meeting spiritual beings; a method for magical spells, a way of dealing with interpersonal issues; and a source of transformations in self-understanding.

A variety of other magical practices are used for similar purposes. More than one-third of the young Witches perform candle magic, which involves selecting candles of particular colors that correspond to the purpose of the spell. For example, Melissa, an American, says: "I do a lot of candle magic. I usually will burn a certain candle for a certain purpose. Like my aunt had cancer. So I did a healing spell. So I would light a white candle, and I would make a petition and let it burn down." Young Witches may also carve magical symbols such as runes into the candle, and then burn the candle and meditate while the candle is burning. The spell may also be timed to coincide with a particular day of the week or astrological event. In addition to meditation, candle magic may involve visualization. Some people see candle magic as a way of petitioning the gods; others describe their magical practice as a way of shaping their own thoughts, feelings, and actions.

Young Witches use tarot, runes, and pendulums for divination, the process of finding things out about the world, self, others, and perhaps the future. As such, the use of these tools is emblematic of the process of reinterpretation of self that is central to much Witchcraft practice. Tarot, runes, and pendulums are learned in various ways. Often the first experience is with a friend who does a reading for the young Witch, who then becomes interested in the practice. Several people were taught the tarot by family members, some of whom are Witches.

Tarot readings are often linked to extrasensory perception or premonitions. A number of Witches describe using the tarot to make decisions or to divine things about people for whom they are doing a reading. Some Witches think that they cannot predict the future with the tarot and use it only as a tool for understanding issues or situations in which they find themselves. Leanne, an English Witch, learned from her grandmother a circular layout using thirteen tarot cards. Her account is typical:

> I use the tarot mainly for horoscopes, but not exactly. I use it to help me see a way out of a problem. A lot of my Witchcraft is personal. It's not for other people. It's for me. So it's to help me find a way out of my problems. . . . [For example,] my brother recently left home. He got into drugs and I wanted to see if there was a way I could help him. One of the ways I was thinking of was actually moving out with him to give him a home rather than him going to live with my grandmother, and I got a no [from the tarot]. It told me not to do it and if you actually looked at the separate cards, basically it was say-ing if I moved out with him he'd carry on doing what he was doing. . . . When I finally came to that decision, it made me feel I was validated in making it. I wasn't just thinking, "Oh, it's too much trouble, I'm not going to do it." There was something else saying to me that this wasn't the right thing to do at the moment.

Tarot, runes, or a pendulum are commonly used to assist with decision making. Some people do readings only for themselves; others do readings for family, friends, or acquaintances; and one person conducts readings over the Internet in chat rooms. Several people work as paid tarot read-ers, with some conducting in-person readings and others conducting read-ings on tarot phone lines.

The most common uses of tarot cards by young Witches are for deci-sion making and self-understanding. Kathy suggests that magic works by allowing you to "communicate to your subconscious." Our intent is not to explore theories of the subconscious; however, it is clear that for these young people divinatory practices are important for facilitating self-understanding and decision making.

Premonitions, voices, and intuitive guidance are part of the experience of young Witches, although only approximately one-third of them report these types of experiences and for many they are not a regular occurrence. Such experiences are typically not the intentional product of ritual practice.

It is extremely rare for a young Witch to summon a spirit, for example. The most common experiences are subtler and often come outside ritual practice. Heather's account is a good example: "[I don't have premonitions] in the sense of having a dream or a really distinct vision or a message or something. But sometimes I feel like there's something directing me in a very big way. Like things just happen, synchronicities, if you like. . . . [There's a sense] of being directed. While I don't have a voice in my head saying, 'Be careful, such and such is about to happen,' sometimes I do things and then something will happen and I'll just think, 'How did I know to do that?'"

The sense of being in touch with something beyond oneself is sometimes a product of spending time in natural settings and listening to the world around one. June's account is interesting because she struggles to find words to express the experience she has sitting under a tree in rural Australia and listening to the sounds of nature. "Well, a couple of weeks ago I was on my parents' property and I walked down to the river and I sat with my back up against a tree and I just closed my eyes and I was just listening to the sounds around me. And I kind of heard voices on the breeze. They weren't people's voices. They weren't saying anything, but they were saying—but that was just, really, I don't know, really uncanny."

As mentioned earlier, many of the experiences and practices that Witches participate in are common throughout society, such as being in contact with the dead, having premonitions, and reading tarot cards. As Greenwood suggests, what distinguishes these practices among Witches is that they occur within a magico-religious framework.

Magical, Ritual, and Spiritual Purpose

The ritual practice of Witchcraft is oriented toward three main purposes. One is religious, providing a connection between the everyday world and a meaning system. This includes a sense of connection with nature, an experience of divinity, and the creation of plausibility structures—that is, the creation of meaning in the face of things that might create chaos, such as death. A second purpose of Witchcraft rituals is reframing self-understandings and providing a sense of meaning, purpose, and self-worth. This includes rituals to enhance self-confidence and self-esteem; deal with

3.3 Young Witch casting a
circle. Photo by Brad Kinne.

emotional traumas, depression, and suicidal thoughts; and find a sense of
peace and harmony. A third purpose is the instrumental resolution of
everyday issues that confront teenagers, such as coping with troubles at
school and at home, finding love, helping others to find love, dealing with
health issues of their own and their loved ones, and managing finances
and employment. These three purposes overlap and shade into each other,
but they nonetheless provide a useful way of categorizing the purpose of
magic for young Witches.

The Everyday World and Meaning Systems

Most young Witches point to the development of a "connection with nature" as an important part of their spirituality. For example, Li asserts that
Witchcraft involves "magic—in part that's done in the circle" but "a lot of

the time is just going out and being at one with nature." For some, connecting with nature may simply involve collecting crystals of various types and learning about their healing energies. Others spend more time in local parks and woodlands. But their understanding of nature is most clearly shaped by the central ritual festivals of Witchcraft—the eight sabbats of the wheel of the year. The seasonal nature of these festivals leads most young Witches to a greater awareness of what is happening in the natural world. The sabbat of Beltane, for example, celebrates the new life associated with spring and the beginning of summer. It is often a jovial ritual associated with fertility and sexual imagery and symbolism. Similarly, the sabbat of Samhain celebrates the height of autumn. It is a time of remembrance of those who have died, sometimes with macabre imagery.

Many of the young Witches describe encountering the divine when outdoors or in some other "natural" surroundings. For example, Susan describes her dedication ritual "to the God and Goddess. You just basically go out into a park and meditate and see if anything is said to you and then you dedicate yourself to the God and the Goddess for, I think, a year and a day is a typical thing and then just renewing every year." Others also described dedications to the God and Goddess, or to particular deities, or to the path of Witchcraft—some of these occurred outdoors and others indoors.

A number of young Witches emphasize that their practice provides them with a sense of purpose, meaning, and direction in life. Approximately one-third of interviewees describe rituals in which the primary aim was experiencing or contacting deity or the divine in some form. When discussing their spiritual experiences or the essence of Witchcraft, young Witches often refer to a sense of being "connected." This is not simply an intellectual reinterpretation of the world, although the worldview of Witchcraft provides a cognitive framework within which the young Witches interpret their experiences. Rituals and unplanned spiritual experiences give young people a sense or feeling that they are not alone, and that they are part of a larger whole. For example, Marilyn links her mystical experience with this broader change in self-understanding:

Before, I was following books and I was more, like, reciting poetry rather than actually feeling my connection with the gods and the

Goddess. Now I don't do much spell work actually—it is purely more spiritual than practical that I do; . . . I get sensations, so it is really, really hard to explain. It starts in my hands, and my hands go very, very tingly, and warm as well, and it is mainly in my hands that I have ever felt anything; I mean, I do feel it in my body now, but to begin with, it just started in my hands. And also I feel a bit light-headed. And I just—I feel connected, is the only way I can describe it. I feel a presence there. Sometimes when I was younger and I was in nature, I had the same sensation without doing any workings and without knowing that Witchcraft was even around, without know-ing about Paganism. I didn't understand it at the time. But I under-stand now. I feel connected to the presence of God or Goddess in nature. I think that is the best way to describe it; . . . I'm not so much interested in doing spell work. I'm more interested in connecting with Deity and celebrating myself, and my life, and my femaleness, and being thankful for what I have in my life.

Marilyn's and Susan's accounts underline the vague or indeterminate nature of deity in Witchcraft. Although a few Witches work with speci-fic deities and explore specific mythological traditions in more detail, they are the exception. Nonetheless, the practices of young Witches are clearly "religious" in Hanegraaff's sense of the term. The rituals often have pro-found effects on young persons' sense of self and their understanding of their place in the world. The rituals also help to create meaning for them.

Peter Berger (1967, 1969) and Clifford Geertz (1966) both speak of re-ligion as helping in the important societal work of creating meaning out of what otherwise might become chaos. Both scholars remind us that it is part of the human enterprise to create meaning—what Alfred Shutz (1964) refers to as the creation of a life-world in which events make sense. This life-world is threatened by crises that may bring into question the so-cially constructed meaning system. For instance, people must explain and come to terms with death—their own prospective death and the death of others, particularly loved ones—as well as with other losses, such as of a job or marriage. Both Berger and Geertz assert that religion helps main-tain meaning systems for people during life crises.

Melissa Raphael (1996) argues that no form of goddess worship, including Witchcraft, can provide this ultimate meaning (see Chapter 6). Raphael fears that the divine as Mother Nature does not provide transcendence, which she believes is necessary to create ultimate meaning. But contrary to Raphael's fear, young Witches speak of their religion as providing them with meaning, often noting that they left Christianity because it failed to help them make sense of death or other crises. Water, an Englishman, for example, describes the religious crisis that brought him to Witchcraft:

> Shortly before I was born, my mum was diagnosed with MS and through my childhood she got progressively worse and so she was confined to a wheelchair. My father passed away about then as well [when Water had his religious crisis] because of alcohol problems. So it was a really tough time. It was really difficult to concentrate in school, so I just simply wasn't right. I felt there was no balance there at all. . . .
>
> The way that I had always been taught about Christianity was that these things happen for a reason. Why? Why? It just didn't make sense. Through Paganism, through Wicca, I was able to come up with more of a reason. I know that it was just simply nature's way. It was just nature's cycle. These things happen. In order for good things to happen, bad things have to happen as well. That's nature's balance. That's the way it works, and that just felt a lot more feasible to me than simply: "It's God's will." That doesn't help at all. So I was able to develop much more of a sense of balance in my life through that kind of understanding. Halloween last year, . . . I sat down and had a really good deep meditation and I could just feel the presence of my father. It sounds really weird, but I could feel his presence kind of in the air and things kind of fell into place then.

Water and Beverly, among others, speak of feeling that the Christian faith they were raised in did not offer them adequate answers to the ultimate questions. It is their sense of Witchcraft's providing these answers that draws these young people to the religion. While Christianity does answer these questions, the answers do not resonate with these young people. Some may be poorly trained in or misunderstand Christianity, but Beverly comes from a family of ministers and appears to be theologically sophisticated. Nonetheless, she, like Water, finds appealing the notion of life as part of a cycle in which all that dies is transformed but remains part of the web of life; it appears more logical to her than the notion of the dead going to heaven.

It is not just Witchcraft's cosmology that appeals to these young people; it is also its confirmation of their sense of being in contact with the dead, which provides a sense of meaning and closure around a person's death. Karen, like Water and Beverly, finds peace in her sense of being in contact with her deceased relative. Barbato (2000) argues that conceptualizing these sorts of death-related paranormal experiences within religious frameworks is more respectful, and produces better mental health outcomes, than dismissing them or trying to explain them away through biological reductions. Witchcraft is often referred to as a religion in which people's experiences with the divine take precedence over doctrine or even ritual. For many young Witches, the religion not only legitimates and confirms their sense of having a relationship with their dead relatives but also gives them rituals that help elicit a sense of connection with the spirit world. Heather, for example, found comfort in the spirit world during an illness: "I was really sick . . . and I invoked the Goddess or evoked her and I just felt like Isis was with me wrapping her wings around me all sort of warm and feathery and I felt this incredible sense of peace. It was amazing. I just felt warm and comfortable and safe and there was no pain at all and I just went to sleep with this enormous grin on my face and I woke up the next morning dancing off the walls. It's happened again [since]—it's not the only time that I've had that experience."

Not all the youths' encounters with the other world are benign. Ross, an Australian, confides: "[Witchcraft] helps me take control of what's happening; . . . I've had experiences where I've been attacked by spirits . . . and I can see black shapes leaping on me and waking up with bruises in the middle of my back—really scary stuff. Being able to push that energy away from me by counteracting it with my own energy makes me feel more safe. Rather than being pushed around by all these forces and energies, being able to take control I think is very, very important." Ross provides the only negative or frightening account of the young people's spiritual encounters. He finds that Witchcraft helps him, but nonetheless he has entered a world that is sometimes dangerous.

For most of the young Witches, experiences with the spirit world or the divine help them feel comforted in times of angst and provide them with meaning. Although they all speak of Witchcraft's beliefs being meaningful to them, it was not only the beliefs that appealed to them but also their perception of having entered an alternative universe in which their extraordinary experiences are confirmed and encouraged. Witchcraft thus creates meaning through its cosmology and also through its rituals, magical practices, and legitimization of these young people's spiritual experiences.

Peter Berger and his colleagues (1973) contend that the pluralization, migration, and uncertainty of contemporary society have led to a "homeless mind." Modernity, they argue, has undermined the traditional function of religion to provide a sense of meaning and "home" in the world. Our research demonstrates that young people discover a new sense of being "home" in the religious worldview and ritual practice of Witchcraft. This sense of meaning may in part derive from the religion's emphasis on experience over theology.

Rituals and the Self

Almost all the young Witches speak about rituals helping them develop a good sense of self-esteem. For example, Jackie, an Australian, reports: "I think the Craft has made me a more confident person. Much more happier with who I am. Generally I've a more positive outlook on life. It's like suddenly you see the world as a whole and you can see your place in it and while it can be humbling, it can be inspiring as well." The two parts of Jackie's observation are important. A sense of self-confidence comes out of, or is associated with, the development of a broader understanding of one's place in the world. The religious purpose of Witchcraft provides a sense of connection to nature and an experience of the divine. These ritual mechanisms provide a framework of meaning that transcends the self and provide ways for making sense of one's place in the world. This in turn leads to a stronger sense of self-esteem, meaning, and purpose to life.

The transformation of self-understanding is one of the most noted effects of Witchcraft. Nearly every participant mentions that Witchcraft makes them more confident, that is, increases their self-worth and self-respect, makes them less shy, reduces their self-hatred, makes them happier with themselves, reduces their sense of powerlessness, makes them less afraid, provides a sense of self-purpose, and results in their valuing themselves more. This transformation was mainly achieved through the rituals and practices described early in this chapter. For example, Leanne observes: "I really think that being able to concentrate on something bigger than me—I mean, with my parents' divorce there wasn't a lot I could do, I was so young, but as I got older it was so much easier for me to accept things because there was this bigger picture and I always knew that. I did a lot of happiness spells and things like that to make people happier and I'm not sure if it worked or not, but they made me feel better knowing that there was something I could do. But I don't use it as a crutch. I will try everything else I can do before I will do a spell."

A set of practices that provides a greater sense of meaning and purpose facilitate increased individual responsibility and reflexivity. Many rituals encourage young Witches to reflect on their lives, their choices, and their actions. As a consequence they obtain a greater sense of self-control and agency. Leanne goes on to explain this relationship between ritual practice, self-reflection, and the negotiation of life's challenges: "[I do rituals] not only for my own problems. It's to understand myself better, to understand what I want from life. I think Witchcraft helps me achieve that because it gives me—like, when I'm meditating if I've had a bad day, I will sometimes find it really hard to settle down and do it, but if I make myself do it I actually find myself better equipped to deal with a problem that I've had, or if I've had an argument with a friend or something like that. It just makes life easier because you're focused."

As we have seen, Witchcraft beliefs and practices are not prescribed by a central text or organization; individuals are the ultimate authorities on their spiritual quests. For example, Iris contends: "Witchcraft . . . encourages you to think about things. It's not like you have this one book, the

Bible, for example, and this is the way everything is done. It gives you a chance to think about all different aspects and all different things and decide which one is the right one for you."

It is clear that these young people are using rituals, meditation, and visualizations as techniques for working with central identity issues, and that the techniques encourage reflexivity and self-awareness within a cosmology that places authority with the individual. Cailin has filled shelves with journals "analyzing myself . . . and figuring out every detail of my mind and my spirituality." Similarly Monica, an Australian, went through a "crazy" period as a teenager that ended when her roommate, who was also a Witch, encouraged her to do a ritual: "I wrote down all the points of what had been happening, what was going on, what I could do about it—each one. And I brought them all together and I just meditated for about half an hour and it just all went. There was this whole big cleared space in my head and I came out going [clapping hands together], "Solved it.'"

Witchcraft provides a technology of the self, that is, a series of techniques and practices that enable the individual to reflexively manipulate her or his thoughts, actions, and sense of self. This notion that the self is a lifelong project of discovery and change is one that developed in the twentieth century and that became more defined and developed in the later years of that century and the beginning of the twenty-first century. In the more traditional societies that existed in much of the United States and Europe in the eighteenth century, most individuals lived in the same communities in which they were born, men went into the same occupation as their fathers, and people attended the same church their parents did. Tradition was even stronger in the Middle Ages. But with the advent of modernity, more people began moving, some Europeans emigrating to the United States and Australia and leaving their extended kin largely behind; this mobile lifestyle has accelerated in the twentieth and twenty-first centuries. Choice and self-development have becomes central preoccupations. Giddens (1991, 215) contends that "self-identity today is a reflective achievement. The narrative of self-identity has to be shaped, altered and reflexively sustained in relation to changing circumstances of social life, on a local and global scale."

Many of the techniques of self that the young Witches participate in are not unique to Witchcraft. Meditation, an aspect of some Eastern religions, has become absorbed into the mainstream. Self-affirmation and self-reflection are commonly recommended in self-help books. In Witchcraft as well as in other religions in which they are embedded, however, these techniques also furnish the participants with a series of rituals and a cosmology in which the project of the self becomes a spiritual activity.[2]

Through the rituals and practices of Witchcraft, young people are actively reshaping as an embodied social activity not only their self-understanding, but also their selves. The rituals of Witchcraft work for these young people because they shape their embodied experiences and felt selves, as much as their cognitive frameworks and interpretations. Young Witches are using magic as a way of dealing with a number of difficult identity and interpersonal problems. However, it is the integrally religious purpose of connecting with nature and the divine that frames these more instrumental concerns (see Chapter 5). Witchcraft rituals reenchant everyday life through reincorporating religious mythologies and spiritual experiences into rituals that address central everyday concerns in these young people's lives.

The centrality of the identity issues that the young Witches are dealing with is graphically illustrated by three young Witches who attempted suicide at some earlier stage. We did not specifically ask about suicide attempts, and these revelations often occur later in the interviews after a sense of trust has developed between the young person and the interviewer. Less dramatically, sixteen of the young Witches had significant depression episodes in their recent past; of these, five had been diagnosed with clinical depression and prescribed medication. All these young people feel that Witchcraft has helped them deal with their emotional problems, for example, they report that they no longer need to take drugs for their depression or that they are no longer suicidal. However, there is a possibility that someone with serious psychological problems will use Witchcraft or another religion to avoid getting the help they need. We are not psychologists, but this may be the case with Ross and two women we interviewed who appeared to be agitated. Such cases are the minority. Most of the young people appear happy, filled with life, and hopeful for their futures.

Young people who identified with marginalized identities, such as Goth, gay, or lesbian, find Witchcraft gives them a worldview in which their difference is accepted. However, social isolation can be generated by quite minor differences in a person's biography. Ruth, for example, felt different when she moved from a small town to a larger one. Although the identity struggles that confront some young people are very serious, for others, self-love spells are of a more mundane kind. For example, when asked about his early Witchcraft practices, Bruce reports: "The most dominant thing in memory would probably be a spell to make you love yourself. It probably sounds like I was really depressed, [but] I wasn't. [I did a spell for] just general self-confidence."

At the other end of the emotional scale, a number of Witches report that they are less angry as a consequence of their Witchcraft practices. Meditation, prayer, and a new sense of purpose provide resources to deal creatively with their anger. Jodie reports: "I used to be really angry. I don't know what at. My mum and I used to fight a lot and so I was pretty angry and stuff from that. But once I started getting into Wicca, I found I could almost cope 'cause I could almost talk to the Goddess and God just in my mind and that would calm me down."

Research demonstrates a close link between mental health and social relationships (Karp 1996). For some young people, Witchcraft provides new friendships and social support. However, more than half the Witches we interviewed are practicing on their own and have few other friends that are Witches. Although they may feel themselves part of an amorphous community of those who read the same books and search the same Web sites, we think that meditation and rituals that encourage greater reflexivity are more important. These techniques provide practices through which young people can resolve many of their problems and issues. Spells often focus on helping the individual change attitudes and feelings. Individuals are encouraged to become self-empowered and develop a sense of accomplishment through changing themselves and their lives. Witchcraft also provides a broader cosmological worldview that makes sense of the "finitude, fragility and mortality of the human condition" (P. Berger et al. 1973, 166). Many young people report that the embodied practice of rituals, the reflexive self-awareness they generate, and the broader worldview of Witchcraft contribute to their improved mental health and sense of self.

Instrumental Magic

The Witchcraft described in mass-marketed and introductory spell books emphasizes an instrumentalism often devoid of religious purpose and oriented toward finding love and making money (Ezzy 2003). Although these instrumental orientations are present in the practice of young Witches, they are less important than would be indicated by their predominance in the popular, glossy spell books. Among these young people, ritual practices and spiritual experiences oriented toward the religious goals of connection with nature, an experience of deity, and finding meaning, purpose, and self-worth are typically more than twice as common as instrumental spells. Instrumental spells also appear to be more commonly performed early in the spiritual practice of young Witches, with religious goals and self-development taking on greater significance as practice becomes more developed.

Spells focused on relationships are described by approximately one-quarter of the young Witches. These included spells to help with a failed relationship, to find a new love, to deal with a problematic boyfriend, to increase one's sexual desire, to encourage truth, and to escape a "semi-abusive" relationship. Only five report performing love spells to make specific individuals fall in love with them, and these are typically performed early in a young Witch's spiritual path. For example, Laurel informs us: "Someone gave me a love spell when I first [began], but it didn't work and I wasn't very impressed. It was from one of those really stupid "one hundred love spells" [books]. They're really stupid things."

The few people that performed love spells to make specific individuals fall in love with them report that these were almost always unsuccessful and sometimes resulted in disaster. Jackie summarizes her experience: "I did dabble a little bit in love spells, although, yeah [giggles], they tend blow up in your face, so I don't do those any more." Attempting to make a particular person fall in love with you is considered unethical (see Chapter 6). A few young Witches have been asked to perform love spells for friends or family and refused to perform them. They describe the dangers of such spells and suggest that it might be more appropriate if the person making the request simply found out more about the desired person by talking to him or her.

The most common love spells are designed to make young Witches more loveable themselves, not to control others. Almost one-quarter of the young Witches perform spells meant to "bring love into my life" in a general sense. For example, Cailin reports:

> The first thing that really got me was [when] I decided to just do a spell to, in general, bring love into my life. I was just lonely at that period in my life. I just wanted somebody. I did a pretty elaborate spell, not for anybody in particular because you are not supposed to do things like that, but in general to bring somebody. And about three months later I met somebody that I wound up being with for two years. I had written a list of literally over one hundred adjectives to physically, emotionally, mentally describe this person and he was like every single one of those things. There was no way [it could be anything but magic].

Both men and women perform these spells. Kevin, an American, informs us that he has performed a beauty spell that had "amazing results." He blessed both himself and his "beauty products." Although it did not change his appearance, "it did change my mindset, and it made me more confident in my appearance and in who I was. . . . And it was interesting because very shortly after I cast the spell I would be getting glances from girls in the hallway, and to a teenage guy that's prime." It is easy to misunderstand the importance of these accounts through trivializing the significance of relationships to teenage self-esteem.

A number of young people describe rituals that allow them to express their hurt and anger over a broken relationship. For example, the Australian Yvette notes:

> There was one time when I wanted to get over a guy and it was really bringing me down. I couldn't stop thinking about him and I de-

cided to write a poem about it and—it was like a chant, as well, with
the rhythm, and I cast a circle as well and I lit a blue candle for healing and burnt it as I read it . . . to help me move on to greener pas-
tures, so to speak. I am totally over him now. . . . The spell helped
me to realize that I didn't need him anymore and helped me to move
on and start talking to my friends again and not be so mopey. . . . I
wrote it down in my Book of Shadows after I finished it. So I was
really proud of myself that I did one myself.

Similarly, the American Vanessa cast spells to escape a "semi-abusive
relationship." She says: "I just visualized myself as an independent, strong
chick and just went from there." Such comments underline the profound
influence on self-esteem of Witchcraft rituals linked to relationships. For
young people, self-image and relationships are intimately intertwined,
and magic provides a way of creatively working with these. Most of the
young people emphasize that the rituals help them change their own attitudes, and it is this change in attitude that has a positive effect. Both
Kevin and Vanessa emphasize that the rituals helped them change how
they felt and viewed themselves and hence helped change their behavior.
    More than a dozen of the Witches report performing spells to improve
their health. None use spells as a replacement for medical treatment for
serious medical conditions. Spells are typically performed for minor or
temporary illnesses such as colds or menstrual pain, and often as an ad-
junct to mainstream medical treatment. Several people report that healing
spells are the most common spells they perform—both for themselves
and for others.
    Similar to Thomas Csordas's (1994) observation of charismatic healers,
young Witches rarely see Witchcraft as teaching them to embrace suffering or self-mortification. Rather, young Witches typically think that correct Witchcraft practice enables them to relieve their suffering and be
healed. The use of visualization and meditation combined with alternative
healing practices, such as the preparation of herbal tea, is an important aspect of many of the young Witches' accounts of healing. At least a dozen
report that they collect books on herbalism or study herbal remedies. A few
describe making herbal pouches as part of their magical work to improve

their own and others' health. For example, Cliff used a herbal sachet as part of a spell to help his grandmother: "I did healing spells for my grandmother a lot because she was occasionally ill when I was growing up. . . . I made her little healing sachets of herbs to go underneath her pillow and I remember her saying distinctly she loved them because they helped put her to sleep."

Young Witches are just as likely to practice magic to improve their own health as to help others with health problems. One performed a spell for a friend who was having trouble trying to get pregnant; another tried to help remove a friend's scar. Doreen, an Australian, describes making a doll of her father who lives some distance away and conducting healing rituals by putting "my energy into this representation of him."

Healing rituals are often designed to assist with the emotional dimensions of an illness. Both the healer and the person for whom the healing is performed often report that it improved the way they feel about things, as well as the actual illness. Healing rituals are an important part of the religious practice of these young Witches, and in this they reflect the importance of healing in most religious traditions (Csordas 1994).

More than fifteen Witches report performing spells to improve their own financial situation, and five report spells to improve the financial situations of others. Mary, for example, tells us: "The first [ritual] that I really remember was a money spell because I wanted to buy an athame. . . . It was a simple candle spell—green candle, oils—and it really, really worked. I got a check from my grandfather for a thousand dollars; . . . I was pretty stoked." However, a number of young Witches are ambivalent about performing spells that could be considered selfish and focus on spells to improve other people's financial circumstances. Aguina says: "I don't do money spells for myself; . . . I don't feel as though, because I have the power to do these spells, that I should give myself all this stuff. It is not something I do. I help others with my spells."

Money is not central to the rituals of most Witches. Aguina's ambivalence about money spells reflects an interesting characteristic of Witchcraft. Although much of the practice of the young Witches is focused on self-transformation, they are not typically selfish or self-centered. There is no evidence of the prosperity doctrine sometimes found among charismatics (Csordas 1994) and occasionally in evidence in popular spell books (Ezzy 2004) that promises religious practice will provide substantial wealth.

Seven young Witches describe spells to help them find work, and twelve describe spells to help them succeed with their schoolwork. This distribution of spells probably reflects the relatively young age of the interviewees. Most are still in school or have recently left, and although many who are still in the education system have part-time jobs, the stress of exams and schoolwork clearly remain an important issue.

At least six Witches report using spells to deal with difficult situations at school or work, and another five describe spells to deal with verbally abusive parents. One young man has a squeaky voice and put a binding spell on classmates who were teasing him about it.[3] Others bound malicious associates or "nasty" work colleagues. Louise, a nineteen-year-old English Witch, provides a detailed account of some trouble she experienced at school. It brings together a number of themes, including relationships, self-esteem, and the practice of magic:

I think the first real proper ritual was for two things—the first thing was to cheer myself up; I was starting to get quite depressed. And had an awful lot of stress at the time, this was about age sixteen. So I started getting bullied really badly. It got to the stage where I was being kicked. I think the main thing was because I had a sexual relationship with a boy at college [preparatory school]. It broke up between him and I, it was perfectly amicable, it just hadn't worked out, we were just very different people. But his friends jumped on it. I think part of it was jealousy. That it was him that I had chosen and not any of them. And the insults were "slut," "tart," and it just escalated to the point where there was so many rumors going on, I mean really horrible things. It was almost into a primary-school level . . . and it got to the stage where one day one of the boys just walked up to me and kicked me out of his way. At that point I decided enough was enough. But I also really didn't want my parents to find out what had caused everything to take off. . . . So I cast a spell. I wanted to just make it go away. Just calm things down at the school so that Dad wouldn't intervene, and so it was a two-pronged ritual—the other thing was to cheer myself up in the process. And as if by magic, things did smooth over. The boys stopped taunting me. They kept away from me. The boy who kicked me . . . disappeared.

As Louise's account demonstrates, there is a strong link between abuse and low self-esteem. For example, Zoë, an Englishwoman, says: "My parents used to fight a lot, so I did spells for happier homes." Pete, an American, reports doing spells to try to deal with a verbally and physically abusive father. Dane describes seeking guidance and direction on how to respond to family crises that are causing him considerable stress.

Again, it is important not to underestimate the significance of relationships at school and at home for young people. As Karen's account in the preceding vignette demonstrates, abusive parents and social isolation can have a major negative impact on young people. Witchcraft provides these young people with a way to deal with their emotional responses to such situations. Witchcraft also provides spells and magical practices that the young people see as a constructive way of trying to resolve the situation.

Conclusion

Witchcraft for these teenagers is centrally a religion of the self, but clearly not a religion of selfishness. As well as celebrating the self, it provides them with self-confidence, it empowers them, it gives them the freedom to make-up their own rituals, it gives them control. Witchcraft also leads them to a greater awareness of that which is beyond themselves, including nature, deity, and other people. Celebrating the self takes them beyond the self.

Some sociological commentators have suggested that the contemporary trend toward increased reflexivity and individualism is leading to increased selfishness and instrumentalism in relationships (Elias 1991; d'Epinay 1991; Lasch 1979). Christopher Lasch (1984), for example, appears to devalue any form of individualism, claiming it results in medioc-

rity and the ignorance of broader social and political issues. More specifically, in studies of contemporary religion, some argue that the individual-
ist self-ethic leaves largely unaddressed the question of moral obligation
at the levels of community, society, and the globe. York (2001, 367), for instance, contends that "the ramifications of this ethical no-man's land can
be enormous and questionable." However, the self-ethic of Witchcraft
does not necessarily lead to an "ethical no-man's land." Rather, it provides
a different site for ethical struggles.

Drawing on the work of Charles Taylor (1989, 1992), we argue that the
individualism and emphasis on self-fulfillment characteristic of modern
life has value. Taylor's conception of authenticity locates individual cre-
ativity and choice within a socially constructed and communally constrained self. Consistent with Taylor's argument, the findings reported in
this chapter demonstrate that reflexivity and the turn to the self do not
necessarily lead to narcissism. Rather, where reflexive self-awareness becomes a moment for individuals to discover, and be in touch with, their
selves, this process enables the discovery of authenticity as that which is
unique to the individual. Authenticity leads, in turn, to a broader appreciation of and consideration for other people and concerns beyond the self.

The rituals, visualizations, affirmations, and practices of young Witches
provide technologies for creating meaning and a sense of self-identity.
These practices are primarily oriented toward the self. However, as Paul
Heelas (1996, 220) notes, New Age techniques "open up new perspectives
and possibilities with regard to what it is to be a person." The practices of
young Witches are a clear example of how religion is being transformed
into a cultural resource (Lyon 2000; Besecke 2001). When young Witches
seek to make sense of themselves and deal with difficult identity problems, they draw on Witchcraft rituals and the techniques they provide. In
the process they reenchant everyday life through reincorporating spiritual
mythologies and providing experiences of the mysterious.

Vignette

Victoria—Creating Pagan Community

Victoria is nineteen years old, studying criminology and philosophy in her first year at a British university. Although her parents are British, she was born in New York but moved back to Britain when she was five. She maintains dual nationality. She tells a fascinating story of the role of community in her path to and practice of Witchcraft. Mediated community, particularly in the form of books, is central to her becoming a Witch, but it is the movies that are important to her searching for and creating community. Even though she initially identifies as a Pagan, it is clear later in the interview that her practice and understanding is very much part of contemporary Witchcraft.

[I call myself a] Pagan. I wouldn't define it specifically as "Wiccan" or "Witch," on the basis of people's stereotypes if I say those two words usually—usually because of that rather than anything else. . . . Unfortunately, I think I do conform to the stereotype, but not purposely, which is a problem really. But it is the whole Witch that dresses in black, the Gothic out at night kind of thing. . . . I seem to conform to that somehow or other. I'm not sure I specifically intend to. I think it also scares people a bit. I think people are a bit wary of stuff like that. But they are also intrigued by it. So they are the first ones to criticize it, but then they say, "Will you read my tarot cards? Can you do a palm reading?" They are the first ones to come to you for that. But if you mention the word "Wicca," or "Witch" especially, there is a definite, "Oh, what's that about then?" I think a lot of people assume that you say it but you don't actually mean it.

I think "Pagan" is more a term of religion. If you say "Pagan," they believe that you are very religious about it rather than to say, "I'm a Witch."

122

I think when you say that you're a Witch you kind of lose that religion, you just gain the magic. Whereas if you say "Pagan" you gain the religious term, rather than just "I do magic." I think I first got into the whole interest in Paganism through my dad when I was about thirteen because he had a set of tarot cards that his mother had had, and they had been in the family. And he said to me, "Oh, I think we should [use them]." . . . So I got into it by that. *Victoria doesn't know if her grandmother was a Pagan or how she came to have the tarot cards. She was seven when her grandmother died.*

Although her father encouraged her to use the tarot cards, he remains ambivalent. My parents aren't embarrassed by the fact that I'm into these kind of things, but my dad doesn't say very much about it. My mom comes with me to all the fairs and we have a lot of mind, body, soul fairs that travel around the U.K. and she will come with me and do the aura readings and palm readings and we always go to those. But my dad kind of just thinks it's one of those things, I think. Unfortunately, I am still in the bracket of going through a phase, I think. Haven't quite escaped that yet.

Similar to a number of other Witches, a fascination with magical popular culture was another thread that encouraged Victoria's growing interest in Paganism. I have always been interested as a child in fairies more than anything in the world. I was really keen on fairies. I still am today, but I was extremely keen on the whole idea of fairies and all of that. My room was covered in fairies. You can get all the books on all these different kinds of fairies, flower fairies and things, and I think my dad noticed I was getting into that. But then through that, I got into earth spirits and that kind of thing.

Victoria's interest in fairies led her to discover Scott Cunningham's books on contemporary Witchcraft in a bookstore when she was sixteen. It was just by absolute chance I happened to come across it [Cunningham's book]. It was just a normal bookstore and I went in and I was looking for books on fairies because I love all the artwork of fairies and I was just looking, and it [Cunningham's book] was different because it was earth spirits, and I thought, "Oh, it is not just fairies, then." And so that then made me think, "So what else is [discussed by Cunningham]?" because he has written about a lot of things. I then realized there is a bit about that and fire spirit and a bit about this and then I got really keenly into the herbs and things like that.

I'm a keen reader as it is. The one thing I think that brought it all about for me was that I started reading books by Scott Cunningham. I read the *Earth Spirit*. I read that, and that was the one that gave it to me because that was the whole link. That was probably the key link between fairies and the religion. It brought it together and I realized that you could actually not believe in fairies but have an interest in fairies and acknowledge the root of them and where they came from and why people believe in them and what they supposedly were meant to resemble, what symbol and stuff like that, and so I think it was the interest in fairies that led to the reading and Scott Cunningham, he is pretty well known anyway, I mean he has written a lot of books on a lot of subjects, so from thinking, "Oh," he was the first author I ever read.

While Victoria sometimes speaks as if there was one thing that led her into Witchcraft, she mentions a number of things that "first" sparked her interest. Most of them are aspects of popular culture. It is probably a combination of all of them that initiated and sustained her interest in Witchcraft. I read Phyllis Curott's book and I blame it on Phyllis Curott [laughs]. I read her first book, the *Book of Shadows*, and absolutely then realized what I was doing. I was never really one that sat around a candle watching *The Craft*, trying to change my image and all of that from the film. I was never really very much into spell crafting [casting] to begin with. It was more interest in the deities and the origins of Paganism. It was always more of an interest rather than an active practicing. I was more being interested in it and reading about it. So it was more buying books rather than buying candles and spell kits and that kind of thing. And so, after reading her book, I realized that what I was interested in wasn't just an interest. You didn't have to just be something I did every now and again, it could be something I lived. I could actually wake up every morning and feel that way, and feel that I was part of that.

I started reading all about into the supernatural and all that kind of aspect of things, the unexplained and all of that. And I would say I was about sixteen. It was about the time, I hate to say, that *The Craft* came out, the film. . . . It could have been that that pointed me in the direction, but I don't know. You saw people actively doing it with other people, which I think was the thing that got to me. It wasn't solitary practitioners, it was groups, girls that were together. And I thought, "My goodness, I haven't said anything to anyone else, maybe there is other people that haven't said anything to anyone else." So I went on the Internet, and [started] advertising for people in the area that were also interested in that.

Victoria uses the Internet to find information about books, and to find and create community with other Pagans. She has never used Pagan chat rooms. The Internet came about because I decided that literally to look up Scott Cunningham, other authors, if you [go] into Amazon, you type in Scott Cunningham, it gives you similar authors and that kind of thing, which is where I found Phyllis Curott, and I found her book there and that was the end of it, really. It all came fitting into place really. So the Internet came in on the basis that you realize how many people there are out there that are [into a] similar kind of thing, and the networking site Witchvox is a perfect example, the Witches Voice. It networks everybody, and I was eighteen [and] I had decided I was ready to try and share my beliefs. I felt that I understood what I was talking about and I knew what I felt. I wasn't wavering about as much, I had pretty much found my place.

Victoria found Witchvox.com and began to contact other Witches. It is a pretty major site, that one. And I started to advertise, and I got about five e-mails back from people in the area and I thought, "My goodness!" I advertised originally as a teen group. . . . So in the end there were about five of us and this was when I was about eighteen and they were about sixteen to about twenty [years old]. . . . We met where I live in [her town]. We met in the big garden there. . . . It was nice because it was just like a group of friends. There was no strings attached. It wasn't like, you have to talk about Paganism right now, because we were all the same age, we were interested in similar things. . . . My friend Jasmine, she is sixteen now, she was fifteen at the time, and I had to speak to her parents before she came because I didn't want her to come without her parents knowing what she was coming into. And her parents were a bit wary, but now they seem to be different. But she has become a quite good friend of me, and she would always ask questions and that kind of thing.

After this initial meeting Victoria began to advertise among older Pagans, which resulted in a moot. A moot is when people are getting together and chatting as opposed to a circle, which is more of a group of people that are practicing [ritual] together. *In England and Australia many Pagan groups organize moots, and Victoria's moot became linked to a large Pagan association that organizes moots in the area.* We continued to advertise it, and we got a lot of people coming that were older and I loved that more than anything. . . . [People in their] twenties, thirties, forties [started coming]. . . . It became an actual moot and the Pagan Union took interest in the group because it was running quite smoothly and we were all getting on extremely well. We were holding rituals in the parks and stuff, and it was really nice. That is how I then got involved with the Pagan Union; . . . I had never been involved in group work in that respect. I had always been extremely wary about it. I didn't know if my beliefs were strong enough and if I knew enough to call quarters and to hold rituals and things like that. So I became quite wary of that, but from going there and meeting these people that were all older and I thought, "My goodness, they have been living this way for so long now. They have all handfasted, they have had Wicca names for their children, it is an absolute lifestyle," and it was so refreshing to see that this wasn't just something I was thinking now. I could take this now with me and go through life with it.

Meeting other Pagans at the moot had a significant impact on Victoria. It showed me that you didn't have to believe in it all our life to suddenly take it on. You didn't have to have been instilled with it. You can find it at any time in life. . . . [There were] businesswomen. That was the thing that got me. My dad always said it was a very New Age religion, it is a hippies, free love, kind of peace religion. But these were people that were executives and it wasn't like that. They were coming from work in their suits and they weren't that kind of thing, they weren't artists, and they weren't poets, and they weren't writers, and it wasn't just that. It didn't confine itself to that.

Although her moot, and the Pagan Union, are enjoyable experiences for Victoria, another group was not a positive experience. One group which is a bit further up from us was fully formed. It was an open moot, and then they had a closed circle afterwards by members of the circle. It was for rituals and initiations and things; . . . I never really felt it there. That always pushed me away a little bit.

Her own group also had some problems when an older couple began attending the moots. They wanted to take over the group and turn it into a ritual group. The [older couple] were presenting the male and the female divine and asking people to use them to access the divine through them, and it involved rituals of odd natures. I was never really involved in it fortunately, because it was during my exams. So we lost a few people to them. There were two girls that were about twenty-three and they had been coming and they wanted rituals so badly whereas we were quite happy with it being more of a moot and a chat and being able to talk to people of similar interests and stuff. But they were really pushing to go down the ritual route and have a closed circle and . . . these two girls ended up going with them [the older couple], but we then realized that it was a little bit odd what they were doing, so we obviously stopped them coming.

Victoria had to move some distance to attend university. She could no longer attend her old moots and joined the Pagan Society that had recently formed at her university. When I came up here, I just ran [to join] the Pagan Society and then obviously I'm president of that now. Last year they started it up, and this is the second year that I have taken over for it. So, yeah, it is a new society, but I think that is quite a good thing really. *At first Victoria was a little disappointed with the University Pagan Society.* We have a lot of guys that are in the society who are very much into chaos magic and that kind of thing, and the dark half, Crowley and animal magic. And we have one guy we have dressed up as a bat. And around university he'll have ears and wings, because it is the nature of the animal—he's an animal guide. It really pushes me away from it because I realize that there are people out there that are taking it so, like, floozily and, in my opinion, not realizing what they are doing.

We have an occult library through the society, we have our own library. . . . But I found that there is a lot of people that are very solitary within the society and everyone is willing to do rituals. But we never do rituals for purposes. They are very vague rituals. We had one at the beginning of the year that was a Samhain ritual and it was just a welcoming all the people to the new year. It was useful because it was at the same kind of time of the university year, so we were quite lucky with that. . . . That was really the only purposeful one we have had. The rest of them, they are just very vague, they are very nothing, I don't feel anything when I partake in the rituals here at all. I don't feel connected or nothing because basically

I try not to be because I don't really wish to kind of enter the same kind of circle with the certain people who are here. . . . They are looking for "What can I project?" rather than "What can I bring?" I find that difficult with the society because it isn't a Wiccan society. It is a Pagan society.

Even though Victoria has been an important part of a number of Pagan groups, she still thinks of herself as a solitary practitioner. This is consistent with the individualistic nature of Witchcraft. I definitely would call myself a solitary practitioner, because I live with my religion, I live alongside it. I do rituals every day with myself alone. That definitely acknowledges me as a solitary practitioner. But because I am now away from the group that I was with, because I am up here rather than home, I miss—I don't partake in those kind of things in the rituals. But when I [am home], we have the big rituals . . . usually for solstices and that kind of thing. They are not everyday rituals. They are not "bring it to me" rituals. They are "this is how we are" rituals. When I am in the group, I am still me and then I am giving myself, but I am not everybody. . . . So I see it as I am a solitary practitioner within a group ritual, but I'm not a group practitioner at all because I don't work with people regularly enough to be considered a nonsolitary practitioner, I think.

As noted, Victoria likes Goth clothes and jewelry. This, combined with various other Pagan items she has in her room, means that people often ask her about her religious beliefs. My friends know I'm Pagan because of my room. . . . My mat is a pentagram, and that is for rituals, which is why I do that, and I have [an altar cloth] on my bedspread. And I got a lot of herbs and a lot of trinkets and things full of weird chemicals and things like that. So I think they know in that respect. But I always get asked, "Do you worship the devil?"—from my necklace or from my ring, all the time. [They think] I'm a Satanist. All the time. I don't get offended by it, but I get upset by it, because I think, "Are you mocking what I believe in, or do you actually think that? Are you that misguided to think that anything with a star and a circle resembles Satan just because of the goat of Mendes?"[1] I find it kind of difficult to deal with that, because for me, it is such a belief and such a way of life rather than me dabbling in magic. . . . But I hate the fact that people probably think that about me. I don't like that. I don't go, "Hi, I'm a Pagan," at all. But I don't wear these things to make people know I'm a Pagan either. I wear this because one of the girls I met through the group, . . . I remember her through that, and also through my religion.

People know because people ask me to do tarot readings. All my friends ask me to do those; . . . I should start charging, I think, because I am always asked to do those [laughs]. *When asked how successful she is at tarot reading, Victoria tells us that she* predicted a pregnancy in the beginning of the year. When I first got to university [and] . . . I had my tarot cards, I was asked to [by] my friend [to do a reading] and we found this pregnancy. . . . I was always thinking, "Oh, my goodness, what have I just done, what have I told her?" But when it happened, everyone was like, "Oh, my goodness, do you remember when you said that during the reading that she was going to get pregnant?" . . . I am a bit wary of what I say, what I reveal and what I don't.

Victoria's experience of Pagan community is a common one. Her initial information about Witchcraft came from books, movies, and the Internet. These are forms of community mediated by technology and the mass media. Through contacts made on the Internet she created her own local community of Witches and she developed friendships with other Pagans, some of whom have become close friends. Not all her experiences are positive. Some groups seem exclusionist, some people try to use the groups for their own aggrandizement, and others are simply "different" types of Pagans. Victoria herself is more comfortable with Witchcraft beliefs and rituals. Her experience of Pagan community transforms her understanding of her own beliefs and practice. Through meeting others she develops an understanding of Witchcraft as a genuine religious tradition and a lifestyle that she could go through life with.

CHAPTER FOUR

Within *the* Circle: Community *and* Family

Beverly, Morgan, and others we have met throughout this book maintain that they are solitary practitioners, although they may gather with others for rituals, belong to a coven, or join a student organization. Individualism, a hallmark of contemporary Western society, is an element of their self-concept and helps define their spirituality. Nonetheless, all are members of a spiritual community, a family circle, a group of friends, and a network of work and school associates. The spiritual community within Witchcraft is different from that organized by churches, mosques, or synagogues, or by leaders of more centralized new religious movements. The community is "emergent," that is, it often is amorphous or informal. A group of school friends watches *The Craft* and decides to meet at one of their homes. An enthusiastic young Witch contacts other young Witches in her area via the Internet and they start meeting in a local coffee shop. Posters are placed on notice boards and a university Pagan society is formed. A computer-savvy young Witch begins an e-group for Witches in the local area. Occasionally the focus of community is around events organized by established Witchcraft traditions, but even in this case, the community that forms is typically not coordinated by others but emerges out of the actions of the young people themselves.

Not all young Witches find a community of other Pagan practitioners. Seven of the young Witches we interviewed do not have any friends who are Witches. Tanya, an Englishwoman, observes: "It just does seem a very lonely path. Incredibly lonely because it's so difficult to get in contact with other people." Fewer than half are completely immersed in community, but most have some interaction with other Witches even if it is not regular or sustained. Being part of a network of Witches serves to affirm their religious identity, and to help them find the confidence to combat discrimination or misunderstandings they feel they experience as members of a minority religion. Although many parents are supportive or understanding of these young people's chosen religion, others are fearful, dismissive, or abusive of their children who practice Witchcraft. Young Witches are often cautious about whom they tell about their beliefs and practices due to negative experiences they have had coming out of the "broom closet."

Here we explore several different forms of community: face-to-face communities that the young people develop in school and through Witchcraft networks, online community, and a community of belief and practice among those reading the same books and magazines. We also examine the role of disclosure and secrecy of their Witchcraft identity to peers, family, and the larger social network.

Witchcraft Community in Schools

Much has been written about social pressures exerted on the young to conform among their peers. Witchcraft can serve as either a form of conformity with a group of friends who explore it together or a form of rebellion or nonconformity. More than a third of the young people we spoke to met others in their middle or high school who are also Witches. These friends became important, confirming their Witchcraft identity. For example, Koehl, an American, became friends with another Witch: "She was in one of my classes actually. She saw the pentacle that I was wearing around my neck and we started a little conversation about it."

Not all the friendships are equal in importance. They vary in longevity and intimacy. Some young Witches report meeting only for a short time with others who are "superficially interested" in Witchcraft. The friends then drift away and the young person continues to explore Witchcraft on her or his own. For some, Witchcraft is a fad that permits them to present themselves as different or hip. Patricia for instance, recounts:

I had two friends with me in high school. [The three of us] were all born on the seventeenth of the month and we made up fire, air, and water. We had this whole obsession about finding the fourth person to make the circle type thing because we already made like a three. So we'd walk around the school being *The Craft*. We'd have the whole better-than-thou persona about us, but whenever we worked [ritual] together and I started talking about the more intimate, the more depth, of Witchcraft and rituality, they'd just shut down and want to talk about guys and stuff. . . . I'd just start talking about the symbolism of the animals around us, and what crystals mean; . . . they wouldn't take it in or wouldn't really understand it. . . . [They were interested in] the whole casting spells and being able to do things, this whole power thing, trying to be better than everyone else because we are so cool. . . . [They tried to] do the love spell thing . . . though it never worked. . . . It was just a fad, really.

Patricia says that after this group of friends dissipated, she met some other Witches in her later years in high school who have become her close friends, a scenario that repeats itself in other young Witches' stories. A few who meet in high school jointly search for and meet older, initiated Witches. For example, Rachel reports that she and a group of friends, all of whom were exploring the religion together, once did a ritual with an older Witch. Morgan, featured in an earlier vignette, spoke to and received helpful information from the owner of the occult bookstore where she shopped. Although not unique to these two women, contact with older Witches was unusual for high school or middle school students. Most of these young people practice and learn about Witchcraft among themselves—reading the same books and magazines.

Witches in Australia are more than twice as likely as their U.S. or English counterparts to report meeting other Witches in high school. Australian youth appear to be more open about alternative beliefs at school and therefore find it easier to meet others who are exploring alternative spiritualities. This difference may be explained by the fact that U.S. youth who tell their schoolmates about their religious practice are more likely to describe being harassed in school than those in Australia. Some, particularly those who live in the Bible Belt, report they fear being open about their religious beliefs at school. British culture appears to be more private, with aspects of the self more hidden. This is reflected in the fact that British Witches are much more likely than either U.S. or Australian Witches to report doing invisibility spells to avoid being noticed in public places.

Finding other friends who are Witches often has a significant influence on young people. Jodie confides: "Well, she [her friend] started it [exploring Witchcraft] and then I followed her after that. We would branch out and read different things independently, but we'd also talk about it together. I went to a private Catholic school, so having a friend who I could talk about that kind of stuff with was definitely very beneficial because I wasn't stuck thinking, 'Oh, my God, I'm having all these feelings and I'm going to go to hell,' that kind of thing." Similarly, Morgan, speaking about her university club, reports that "having a Wiccan group, whether you practice together or not, is just amazing for opportunities—socially, communication-wise—and it gives you a home."

Finding other friends who are Witches significantly reduces the sense of social isolation and provides young Witches with a sense that their religion is legitimate. Morgan tells us that finding friends was important for "just the support of having people know what you're talking about." University Pagan societies are often places where young Witches find groups of friends, boyfriends, and girlfriends and make contacts with the broader Pagan community outside the university through speakers who are sometimes invited to come and talk. They are also places where students feel safe. Louise describes a sabbat ritual she performed with her university club: "I did my first group ritual with [people from the Pagan Society] just a few weeks ago. We did a very brief ritual for Beltane. And that was quite nice, but it did feel odd to be with a group. Most of us had never done a ritual in group before. . . . It was simply to celebrate the fact that it was Beltane. There was a nice feeling about it. It was a very friendly, simple ritual, slightly comic as well, because it was like, What do we do now?

What do you do now? Should we cast a circle now? It was nice." It also provided the group with a sense of safety in numbers. As Louise explains: "The feeling of solidarity that we have with the Pagan Society together [means that] the others can persecute us all they like, we don't really care what they think anyway."

Participation in Pagan or Wiccan societies or clubs at universities is often important in helping young people solidify their practices and feel comfortable with their self-identification as Witches, and a small minority of those we spoke to have joined covens to be trained. Still, the notion of being solitary practitioners, even if they join with others to learn about Witchcraft and to celebrate the sabbats and esbats, permeates their discourse.

Witchcraft Community and Networking

Young Witches attend public social events, such as pub moots, open circles, workshops, and Pagan festivals, which provide important forums for developing friendships with other Witches and for the formation of "community." Established Witchcraft traditions often coordinate these events and provide young Witches with experiences of group ritual. Pagan friendships and community also form at occult bookstores and through alternative subcultures, such as Goth, and Pagan relatives or family friends. The Internet is also of import, as we will see.

In Australia and Britain, Pagan organizations arrange pub moots or Pagans in the Pub. These are typically held in local pubs or hotels, are open for anyone to attend, and involve socializing and often a group discussion around a topic chosen by a coordinator. Pub moots are advertised on Web sites, e-mail networking lists, in local magazines and newsletters, and on the bulletin boards of local occult bookstores. For new Witches they are often an important point of initial contact with the broader Pagan community. One-third of both Australian and British Witches have attended a pub moot and many attend their local moots regularly. Several Witches note that they are aware of pub moots but are unable to attend because they are too young to go to a pub.

The first time a young Witch attends a pub moot is often an overwhelming and intimidating experience. Some report that the people at the moot are older and that they felt awkward talking to people not their own age. Others felt quite comfortable and enjoyed the moots, particularly when they had friends who also attended. Cheryl, an Australian, notes that she became friends with an older Witch at a shop who told her about a local moot. The moot is where she has met most of her Witchcraft friends, many of whom are her own age; one in particular is her main source of information about Witchcraft. "I mean, I go and buy books and just read them and that's where I get most of my information. [I also get my information] from Pagans in the Pub and talking especially to Morag, she's really a good source of information."

While moots can be an opportunity for networking between older and young Witches, it can also be a place where the barrier of age becomes obvious. For example, the Australian Jodie reports that when she and a friend went to their first pub moot, "it was really overwhelming 'cause there were a lot of older people there. So we kind of stuck together and just sort of sat amongst ourselves. There was another nineteen-year-old there as well and we started talking to her, but we didn't really talk to the older people. I guess they already had their own groups formed." Karen puts it more strongly, suggesting that the older Witches "discriminate against" younger people. Karen feels "put down upon by these third-degree initiates." There is significant variation in the relationships between older and young Witches, with some constructive and other more antagonistic relations.

In the United States, young people make contacts with Witches in their local area in open circles and workshops. For example, Fritz reports that he has met quite a few local Pagans: "There are some local organizations in the area and they sometimes put on workshops and the like." Similarly, Brianna tells us that she drove some distance to attend an open ritual organized by a coven: "I have done a ritual with this coven . . . and that was just a really exciting experience, because I got to be with other actual Witches that have been practicing for many years and see what it is really like." Although Brianna never met these Witches again, her first group ritual had a significant impact on her.

4.1 Pagan Pride Day in Massachusetts. Photo by Helen A. Berger.

Approximately one-quarter of the young Witches we spoke to in the United States, Australia, and England have attended a Pagan festival. Some last for several days and involve rituals and workshops, with accommodation and meals provided, such as those described by Sarah Pike (2001) in the United States and Lynn Hume (1997) in Australia. Others are shorter events, such as the Witchfest organized by the Children of Artemis in Great Britain, which typically involves a day of workshops and other events that provide the opportunity for some young Witches to meet new friends and have their spiritual beliefs reinforced. Haley, an Englishwoman, recounts her experience of attending Witchfest: "I think when you go to some of the lectures [about Witchcraft] and . . . you sit in an audience with people who are all agreeing with you and applauding or just sitting there thinking, 'That's so true,' I think it does kind of give you more confidence and it kind of gives you more pride in what you actually believe in and really makes you kind of want to do things and go, 'Rah, I'm a Witch' [laughs]. It's a beautiful thing." As Haley suggests, group participation often changes the self-understanding and practice of these young Witches. These groups provide a form of secondary socialization, reinforcing and helping to further develop young people's identity as Witches. However, unlike the stage of "intensive interaction" described by John Lofland (1966) for total conversion to the "Doomsday Cult," interaction with other Witches is often ephemeral; it remains important nonetheless, as it helps to provide a community of believers.

Some of the young Witches have links with organized Witchcraft groups or traditions. Some have joined, or are considering joining, these groups, either on their own or with one or two friends. In both the United States and England at least one young person has joined a traditional Witchcraft coven. The absence of any young person who joined a traditional Witchcraft coven in Australia is probably a reflection of the relatively smaller significance of established Witchcraft traditions in that country. There are currently fewer than twenty initiated Gardnerians in the whole of Australia.[1] Youth in Australia, like their counterparts in the United States and England, however, did join other groups.

The minority who are being formally trained in a coven feel the coven has a profound impact on their understanding of their spiritual practice. The U.S. Witch Melissa's account is typical:

I'm actually part of a group that . . . I joined last year. That group has been an amazing influence on me. They are such great people, and I am starting my steps for initiation and it is just great, great. . . . They are an eclectic group. We will have ritual every other Friday and we will do an Egyptian ritual or a Norse ritual. So it is really fun because we're not set on one thing. I actually get to learn a little bit about different traditions so it works out really well; . . . [the members'] ages range from twenty-two to fifty. There is about ten of us in there. . . . The high priestess is forty-four and the high priest is fifty. . . . They are sort of my spiritual family. That's what I call them.

More than a dozen young Witches report that they practice rituals with a group in which ritual practice has grown out of discussions among the friends. In these cases it seems that community, friendship, and ritual practice all overlap. In some cases these ritual groups are ongoing friendship groups that formed in high school, university, or through friends of the family.

Nearly a fifth of the young Witches indicate that they have met other Witches at occult bookstores. For some this simply involves regular extended conversations with the person behind the counter, asking advice about books and products. Other bookstores have workshops and conduct open rituals, and a number of young Witches attend these. Some strike up conversations with other people in the shop and go on to befriend them. Louise met her fiancé in a local shop: "I met him while I was buying a compass to call the quarters; . . . he happened to ask if this is feng shui, and I told him no, it is [for] calling the quarters because I'm a Witch, and it led to a conversation about it and we ended up going for a drink."

Approximately one in ten of the young Witches we interviewed are, or have been, involved in the Goth subculture. A few have met other Pagans at Goth events. Others suggest that Goth and Witchcraft are completely separate. Some people find acceptance of their Witchcraft identity in alternative subcultures that included Goths, homosexuals, musicians, and punks. More than half a dozen Witches describe friendships with family friends who are also Pagans. Mothers, fathers, brothers, sisters, or cousins who are Witches or followed other Pagan traditions often introduced young people into Pagan networks. Jacqueline notes that her brother is a Witch and that she keeps contact with his ex-girlfriend, also a Witch, asking her advice on ritual practice. Other young people meet peers who are Witches in a variety of places, including a piercing shop, a local bar, on CB radio, and at work. Aguina, an African American, for example, recounts that when she was working part-time as a cleaner at a fast-food shop, she met her high priestess: "[I was wearing] a pentagram, and she saw it, and she was like, 'I have one too.' Then we switched names and numbers."

Young people who are integrated into a network of Witches tend to know both contemporaries and older practitioners. Seven young Witches, however, know only peers, and four are acquainted only with older Witches. The former are most likely to be those who made friends in middle or high school with peers who were Witches. The latter most commonly have made their contact with others through their parents or their parents' friends or by joining an established coven.

Witchcraft on the Internet

The early ethnographies about Witchcraft (Berger 1999; Luhrmann 1989; Hume 1997) barely mention the Internet. In contrast, in our study, the Internet is one of the most important spaces where Witches meet. Only seven of the ninety Witches we interviewed never use the Internet for Witchcraft-related activities. The Internet's potential to transform religions, making them more democratic, international, and individualized, has been noted by scholars and social analysts (O'Leary and Basher 1996; Cobb 1998; Helland 2000; Zaleski 1997). The profound impact of the Internet on Paganism has been described by academics (Cowan 2005) and by a number of practitioners (Nightmare 2001; Telesco and Knight 2001; Davis 1995).

The Internet can be seen as the most recent addition to what Giddens (1991) refers to as time-space distanciation, that is, the compressing of time and space through modern technology such as television and radio, and through relatively affordable air travel. In the twentieth-century cliché, the world has become smaller, increasing the spread of ideas along with the fear of pandemics. The transmission of Witchcraft and other forms of Neopaganism and the creation of community on the Web is a continuation of an earlier trend in the religion—its dissemination through books and magazines. For example, in the United States *Green Egg*, a magazine published by the Church of all Worlds from 1968 to 2001, not only provided information about the religion but also offered a forum in which Neopagans, by writing letters to the editor, could participate in open debates, helping to create a community among diverse practitioners (Adler 1979; Melton 1978). The Internet has accelerated this process by decreasing the time and effort required for individuals to respond to one another and making forums more international. However, one must be wary of exaggerating the impact of the Internet on internationalizing a movement or a religion. Although individuals can access Web sites internationally and some of the young Witches did contact sites in other countries, many accessed sites in their own nation. English is the native tongue of all those we interviewed and therefore there is no language barrier to their accessing and participating in Web sites of each other's countries.

This would not be true of Witches in non-English-speaking countries, some of whom may be discouraged from accessing English-language sites by the language barrier. The young Witches we spoke to do post and write to people in other English-speaking countries, but real-time talk is difficult because of the time differences.

The demographics of the young Witches match those most likely to have and use Internet access, and for many, the Internet is their primary site for forming friendships and relationships. Internet usage is consistently higher for young people than for older generations (Skinner et al. 2003) and for middle-class individuals, particularly in developed nations (Cowan 2005). Unlike research that indicates that males have higher Internet usage than females, we find no gender differences. Teenage Witches use the Internet for an average of just over an hour a day on Witchcraft-related activities.[2] Usage varies from half an hour a week to the four hours a day reported by Tina, an English Witch, who says: "Yeah, I'm properly addicted."

Young people's Internet use waxes and wanes. A few relay that they used the Internet to search for information when they became interested in Witchcraft, and that as their understanding of Witchcraft progressed, books and face-to-face contacts became more important and the Internet became a less significant source of information. Others report an increase in use as they gain access to the Internet either when they attend university or when their parents buy a computer or make the computer more available to them. Others found that demands on their time change. Laurel reports that she used to chat a lot, but when she began university studies and part-time work there was little time left for the Internet.

Only a few Internet sites like Witchvox.com both contain information and facilitate networking. In most instances these two functions are found on separate sites. Some sites facilitate real-time conversations, described as "chat."

The Internet as an Information Source

Most young Witches report that they regularly search on the Internet for information about Witchcraft, and several that the Internet is their primary source of information. Some claim that the anonymity of the Internet makes them feel safe. They often print out information found on Web sites, with some young Witches developing sizeable archives. Lovette, an Englishwoman, discloses that the Internet was her "lifesaver; . . . I do a lot of research on plants, herbs, astrology, . . . [and] folklore and [folk]tales as well." Similarly, Jen reports that she looks up correspondences, moon phases, and spell sheets, such as a mirror spell she found recently. Several Witches conduct research on deities and mythology that they then use to inform their practice. Much of the information the young people are interested in, such as information about deities, can be found on Web sites that are not Wiccan or even related to Witchcraft.

Several young Witches disclose that they do not trust the information on the Web, preferring books as more reliable sources of information. Those who have strong contacts with family or local Witches are more likely to distrust the information on the Internet. Some who are aware that information on the Web is not vetted are cautious in the sites they use. Leslie, an Englishwoman, relates that she knows she can trust the information on the Pagan Federation site, as the Pagan Federation is a well-known and respected Pagan organization. Assuming that sites linked to Pagan Federation must also be trustworthy, she feels confident moving to those sites.

Chloe, an Englishwoman, uses books to discriminate between Web sites when she is researching a topic: "I look in books, and then I go on the Internet to browse and see what there is. The things that look more authoritative, then I might hit them and have a look at them. It is something that I am wary of now rather than just reading everything and believing all, because there is a lot of stuff on the Internet. And especially if you're a teen Witch, a lot of it is hype and sensational stuff. So I am quite wary of the Internet now. I do still use it."

Even though a number of the young people, like Chloe, note that they are concerned about the quality of information they find on the Internet, the sheer wealth of information makes it a substantial resource for developing individualistic spirituality. Amber tells us that she uses the Internet for

a lot of Google searches, just putting in words [such as] "Witchcraft" [and] see what pops up. If there was something I was interested in, I'd just type it. . . . and [then] I'd just go through all these Web sites and read more on herbs and spells and . . . tools, sabbats, books. [I'd use that information] to practice, myself. . . . I love the Internet, . . . not just its wealth of resource[s], but [that] some will conflict [with] each other. I was looking up something today, for example, on the planet Mercury. What colors are associated with Mercury? I've got a feeling myself [that] the color of Mercury might be purple . . . but then I was reading other people's ideas of what the correspondence would be and I've got red and yellows and pinks and blues from everyone else, and so it's that wealth of information that I can sift through and I get different ideas from everyone else; . . . I can take what I want from that. It's like going to a supermarket and being overwhelmed with choice and going, "Yeah, actually, that feels right." I like the fact that it's not dogmatic. . . . [Asked if this openness results in confusion, Amber is emphatic:] No, definitely not. I feel that everyone is different. When you ask people to define what Witchcraft is, you'll get as many different answers as there are people. And that's to me what it is about, finding the path that's right for you. It's all a similar path and we all [are] on a very similar path, but we all take different roads getting to our destination, really.

Amber's reference to a "supermarket" that overwhelms with choice is reminiscent of Roof's (1999) analysis of the "spiritual marketplace," in which individuals are able to pick and choose which religion to participate in or which aspects of various religions to incorporate into their own spiritual practice. Earlier, we discussed Giddens's (1991, 5) argument that in contemporary society, self-identity "becomes a reflexively organized endeavor," but one that is affected by the media and larger social forces. Amber speaks of creating her own spirituality, which she believes is unique and in which she is an active participant—but her choices are made from the marketplace of spiritual ideas provided by the Internet and books. These mediate her experience and interpretation of the "other world."

Internet as Community
The importance of the Internet for helping create community among young Witches varies from those for whom it is the sole form of commu-

nity building to others for whom it is of little import. There are four ways that the young Witches create community on the Internet. First, sites such as Witchvox.com provide a space to post information about oneself, allowing others to e-mail one privately. Second, sites such as ukpagan.com require people to sign on as members; they may then post messages on e-bulletin boards. Others who visit the site read these messages and may post replies. Third, e-groups or e-lists such as those at Yahoo or AOL permit people to subscribe to an e-mail group in which all e-mail messages and replies are sent to everyone on the list, allowing a group discussion to develop. Some of these e-groups have more than a thousand members. Fourth, some sites facilitate real-time chat. People log on to the site and enter a virtual room where messages are typed on the screen and replies occur in real time. ICQ and IRC are programs, not Web sites, that also facilitate real-time typed conversations, typically between only two individuals. In the current lexicon young people describe speaking to others on the Internet when they participate in chat rooms, although technically they are writing to one another. With the exception of Witchvox, which is mentioned twenty-three times, and Children of Artemis, an English site developed by Witchcraft.org for children and adolescents, which is mentioned seven times by English Witches, most of the other sites are mentioned only once or twice, suggesting that a wide variety of sites are used.[3]

One of the most important roles played by the Web sites is their provision of a sense of a wider Witchcraft community for young Witches. This is illustrated by Water, who describes finding the Children of Artemis Web site: "I just really loved the Web site so I just got a full membership; . . . it helped me to expand my thoughts by talking to like-minded people—I was able to see different perspectives. I was seeing things from another point of view. That gave me the ability to go deeper into what I was thinking. . . . It was very comforting to know that there were other like-minded people about, it wasn't just me, because at that point . . . I hadn't any other contacts and nothing to go on." Several other Witches also express the sentiment that it is "comforting" to know that there are others who practice their spirituality. The listings on the Web sites provide contacts and, possibly more important, visible evidence that other people in the local area are also Witches.

Many people are afraid to talk about their Witchcraft beliefs because of the stigma still attached to the religion. Witchcraft organizations also tend to have low visibility. Melissa notes that without the Internet it would be very difficult to discover that there are other Witches: "I think Witchvox is the most amazing thing ever, because it is really difficult to meet other Pagans or Wiccans without being part of some type of networking. . . . People don't talk about [Witchcraft] much. If you tell people you're a Witch, they look at you like you have six heads. . . . Wiccans and Pagans don't have a church, so you can't look up in your phone book certain covens because they wouldn't be in there."

At least one-third of the young Witches we interviewed report that they have developed friendships with other Witches through Internet communities. About two-thirds of these friendships remain "virtual," without physical meetings, and the remaining one-third have mostly developed friendships with other Witches in their local area that they first contact through online Witchcraft communities. The significance of online friendships varied substantially. Some people describe their online friends as only casual acquaintances. Others say that most or all of their Witchcraft friends are online. A few say that their online friends are very important, and Laurel reports that her online friends are as important as her "real-life" friends. There are also a few romances that began online.

It is a truism of sociology that individuals develop their religious identities through interaction with other believers (see, for example, P. Berger 1967). Witchcraft is no different, although for many young Witches the medium of interaction is virtual community. Jodie recounts: "A lot of the time I was a lurker . . . just reading other people's posts and if I felt that I had something to contribute, I would. But I learned a lot by just watching or at least reading [giggles] what other people do. . . . I almost redefined my own beliefs. Before, I think, they were hazy—'Oh, I think I believe this' kind of thing. Whereas after I'd got different perspectives and different ways of wording things, it was, 'OK, I believe this. I don't agree with you on that point, but I believe this.'" Several other young Witches describe similar experiences of observing debates as a "lurker" that resulted in their developing more sophisticated understandings about their own beliefs and practices.

At some point young Witches become more active participants in communities as they begin to post, ask questions, and offer their own ideas and opinions. Discussion topics vary depending on the forum. Some online communities are more informal, and conversations can range widely, including boyfriends, schoolwork, and Witchcraft topics. Several people indicate that online book recommendations are important, along with discussions of rituals and ritual practice.

Interacting online with other Witches allows young people to develop confidence. One or two people recount giving advice and "teaching" others online. In his study of Wiccans on the Internet, Douglas Cowan (2005) maintains that the Internet permits young people particularly to "try on" the identity of Witch at no social cost. They can remain in the "broom closet" in real life while they develop and become comfortable with their Witchcraft identity online. Cowan conjectures that some may choose never to reveal their Witchcraft identity anyplace but online, although we found very few young people who remained Witches only on the Internet. As noted earlier, only seven do not know another Witch, and of those seven some are open with others who are not Witches about their spiritual path. But the Internet does permit them to develop and become more confident in their new identity. Marilyn, for example, suggests that the confidence she developed through interacting online led her to start a university Pagan society.

A few young Witches report that they are registered to participate in more formalized online training in Witchcraft, which they find valuable. For example, Laurel discloses: "I've just signed up for a Witch School, which is online. One of my friends lives in Perth that I know online and she's created her own sort of thing to educate you. It's basically like studying online. . . . You have to read pages they provide and also there's some extra reading and then you have quizzes that are multiple choice or there's even a thing where you send in an essay to her and she'll mark it and e-mail it back to you, so that's pretty good." Other of the young people report that they have seen this form of training advertised but were suspicious of its value. As in Laurel's case, these courses can be given by one young person to another. Cowan (2005) found that in some instances those giving online classes were ill prepared to teach others. Instead of preparing their classes, they cut and paste material from other Web sites and from books, often without appropriate citations. But the ability of the young to present themselves as teachers either in structured classes or in chat rooms does increase their sense of expertise and commitment to the religion (Berger and Ezzy 2004).

Online communities are not antithetical to face-to-face communities. To the contrary, the Internet often helps young Witches meet others in their vicinity. Wendy, an Englishwoman, provides a typical account of how people progress from online encounters to face-to-face meetings: "We'd chat on [AOL]. . . . We send what we call instant messages. So they do a search and find your profile on the Internet and then they'd send you a message saying hi and whatever. . . . You talk for ages. You really do talk for ages. You both phone and talk on the phone first usually, rather than just meeting after talking to them for [only] one day." A few people develop close friendships with those they met online. Charles, for example, met his girlfriend online. Others have met a person only once and the contact has not developed further.

Online communities often lead people to physical meetings with established groups. In England and Australia several young Witches indicate that online interactions gave them not only information about local pub moots, but also the confidence to attend. Several people have made contact with established working covens on the Internet and sought membership in these groups. Melissa reveals that she found her coven because the high priest was exploring some Web pages where she had posted her interest in Witchcraft. He contacted her, they began to discuss Witchcraft, and she was eventually invited to meet the coven and join. Some young Witches use the networking capabilities of the Internet to contact Witches in their local area and form local physical groups, as has Victoria, whom we met in the foregoing vignette.

Approximately twenty of the young Witches report chatting online. Their experiences ranged from positive contacts to negative exchanges with Christians who had entered the chat rooms to chastise and convert Witches. Others, like Charles, have met people online who made preposterous claims, such as that they were able to fly. A few people report that the motivation for a number of chat participants seemed to be dating and sex rather than spirituality. A few speak of being afraid of chatting because of a perception that it is dangerous and may lead to abductions, or that chat rooms are inhabited by psychopaths. Cherry provides an account of two different chat experiences: "When I was about seventeen, [I began using] the MSN chat rooms, which horrified me. There's so many kids who go in and say, 'I want a love spell. I need a love spell because I need to make him fall in love with me.' And you think . . . 'Yeah, goodbye.' Since then I steered clear of Internet chat rooms for about a year after I'd spent a few months using those. Hunting around, [I found] UK pagan, [which] really appealed to me because there's the hippies, which are love and light and heavy harmony ones, there's traditionalists, there's love pagans, beginners, a group of practicing peers, so it's a really good mixture."

Several of the young people are cautious about meeting someone in person from an Internet foray. Tim recounts meeting a young woman he chatted with on the Internet for a picnic in the park. "Her mum showed up a bit later to make sure I wasn't raping her [or] anything." Jodie provides an example of an Internet community that works to protect its members from predators: "Most of the communities, everyone's friendly and if people post messages like 'If you really wanna learn more about Wicca come and meet me at this place,' everyone else on the list would write back, 'What are you doing?' that kind of thing. . . . So it's like the whole community was looking out for each other 'cause they didn't want people to be sort of abused and stuff." Although on the whole young Witches did not have bad experiences on the Internet, two describe being belittled by older Witches in Internet forums; none report meeting predators.

Although only a minority of young Witches chat, the Internet nonetheless serves to create community. The information on the Web pages as well as the e-bulletin boards provide a sense for the young Witches of being part of a larger community—of a vast group of people who share their interests. Those not integrated into the larger Neopagan network in their local areas are introduced to the community of practitioners through the Internet and through books. Young people discover that Witchcraft describes not only their individual self-identity, but also a community of people who share common interests, goals, struggles, and aspirations.

Community is as much about the boundary definition of groups as it is about individual self-understanding. As Anthony Cohen (1993, 13) reminds us: "The consciousness of community is . . . encapsulated in perception of its boundaries, boundaries which are themselves largely constituted by people in interaction." Through their interaction in a variety of forums, including those on the Internet, young Witches change not only their self-identity, but also their consciousness of the boundaries of Witchcraft community in broader society. Witchcraft, in this broader sense, is not just an individual but a collective identity. Francesca Poletta and James Jasper (2001, 285) define a collective identity as "an individual's cognitive, moral, and emotional connection with a broader community, category, practice, or institution." Furthermore, they assert, collective identity does not have to be experienced in face-to-face interaction: "It is a perception of a shared status or relation, which may be imagined rather than experienced directly." Like the preceding generation of Witches, the young are participating in a community of choice that is somewhat amorphous and multilayered but nonetheless important to their sense of self, to their feeling of belonging, and to their spiritual development.

Privacy, Disclosure, and Discrimination

Many of the young Witches engage in "passing" (Goffman 1963), that is, they mask their Witchcraft identity. "Masking discreditable identities with more socially acceptable ones through passing offers individuals the potential to escape the expectations others impose on them because of their group membership and its related stigma" (Renfrow 2004, 488). Young Witches often present a non-Witch identity to friends, family, and the general public. This is particularly the case when parents or friends are hostile, or are anticipated to be hostile, to Witchcraft. Although passing has often been considered emotionally unproblematic (Goffman 1963), Renfrow (2004, 503) argues that it typically generates considerable fear that can have significant negative emotional consequences: "Inauthentic impersonations generate feelings of dissonance, and these responses are overwhelmingly negative across types of passing and identities transgressed." The formation of community and a sense of group solidarity provide important emotional support to young Witches that helps them deal with the fear of stigma and avoid the potentially damaging emotional consequences of hiding their Witchcraft beliefs and practices from friends and family.

The forms of Witchcraft community described to this point are typically supportive of young people as they explore the spirituality of Witchcraft. However, as we will see, responses from school friends and members of the general community varied from support, through disinterest, to persecution and hatred.

Most people find their close friends accepting and understanding of their Witchcraft. Some friends think Witchcraft is "cool." Others are simply uninterested and do not respond when told that a person is a Witch. Some of the young Witches are teased in a light-hearted way by their friends. A significant minority experience aggressive and negative reactions from some people they tell. Some of these reactions derived simply from the bad press that Witchcraft has received and the misunderstandings that still exist in the community. Debbie, an Australian, was spat on. Maggie, another Australian, was talking about Witchcraft to a friend when another friend overheard them and asked her, "Do you eat babies and stuff?" Maggie treated this question with humor and replied sarcastically, "Yeah, I totally do."

Other young Witches divulge that they believe they have to be particularly careful around Christians. Logan, a university student, said that posters advertising her Pagan society were ripped down, and Gemma and Louise, two British Witches, recount being insulted by Christians on campus. A Catholic priest told Vanessa's boyfriend that she was worshipping Satan and going to hell. Some people simply did not talk about Witchcraft with their Christian friends. Koehl describes people who, when they realized she is a Wiccan, "shoved a crucifix in my face and threatened that I'm going to hell." Susan no longer sees her Christian friends, as a consequence of their response to her Witchcraft. For them, "Witchcraft is evil. It's from Satan and they try preaching to me every time they see me and I say, 'Look, you have your religion. I have mine. Leave it at that,' and we just don't talk." Similarly, Tom, an American, reports that some people accept his Witchcraft and others don't: "I have lost a lot of good friends because they will not accept that aspect of me, and I can't call them friends because they can't accept you for who you are." Others are able to maintain their friendships with Christians whom they found respectful of their religion and with whom in some instances they regularly debate theology.

The extent of disclosure of one's belief in Witchcraft to friends who are not Witches varied significantly. Only five of the young Witches say that they have told none of their friends. These five are concerned about being persecuted, and their fear results in their keeping their beliefs private. Many others disclose their Witchcraft to friends in one circle but not in others. Some are open at university but kept quiet in high school. Others have not told their housemates, although other friends know. Marilyn confides that she is open at university but not at work:

> I am very careful about who I tell, because it has to be people who I get close to before I tell them because I don't want to be judged. And I would rather they got to know me first and then my religion. . . . I'm very careful because of my job, because I am a youth worker and therefore I am in a very responsible position and I work mainly with quite vulnerable and young people and therefore I don't want that to influence any decisions that, for example, my employers make. Or [have a] colleague thinking that I am not being responsible, . . . or [have] parents of the young people not understanding it and thinking that it is very scary that their son or daughter is involved with a Witch.

Approximately one-quarter of our interviewees have disclosed their Witchcraft to all or most or their friends. This is often the result of wearing Pagan jewelry. Asked about openly wearing a pentagram necklace, Melissa responds: "Yeah, oh, I don't mind at all. I tell people all the time. I would rather have people ask me. I have gotten comments like, 'Oh, that is the sign of the devil.' And then I will explain to them that it is not. . . . I think it is better to sort of get yourself out there and be proud of what you do and educate people rather than staying stuck in a closet and hiding."

About one in six people recount experiences of being mistreated at school because of their religious practice; at times the mistreatment was condoned or carried out by teachers. Leanne, for example, found that her classwork on negative attitudes toward Witchcraft became more personal than she expected:

> I was in a group with people I didn't know . . . and we had to do personal research study. I did mine on "Have attitudes to Witchcraft changed in five hundred years?" . . . I had people pushing me over. I had someone push me back over a table because they said I was lying, and I had a lot of trouble. . . . I said, "Well, actually, I'm a Pagan and this is quite interesting to me." And a lot of the girls were okay. It was the boys; . . . my teacher actually said to me it was my own fault and he didn't do anything to stop it. I had to move classes for the entire term.

Not all teachers were as cruel as Leanne's. Some seemed to express genuine concern. Jimmy, an English Witch, recalls that his French teacher spoke to him individually, saying: "I've heard you're dabbling in the occult, you know, I'm very worried about you." Jimmy played up to and generated these fears: "I used to wear black all the time. I'd have my pentagram. I'd get a lot accusations of Satanism. . . . To a certain extent I played up to it for a little while simply because some of the kids actually became scared of me." Jimmy's active encouragement of fear is the only such account in our interviews.[4] Others reveal that after they divulge their interest in Witchcraft, school friends expect them to have the powers of Sabrina and be able to hex others. These young Witches quickly dispelled such beliefs and assured their peers that that is not what Witchcraft is about.

Young Witches are often teased by their peers. Several have experienced social isolation and ostracism when they revealed their religious beliefs. A few report teasing about being Satanists, or being told that they would burn in hell. Two report that they have feigned interest in Christianity in order to avoid problems. For example, Freddy, an American who was raised as a Witch by her mother, confides: "I went to a high school, and elementary, in a Hispanic/Native American town. It was a very Catholic-based community. And it was very hard to be different. . . . I went through a small period in middle school where I would go to church with friends and I would wear crosses and try to be like everybody else, so I didn't have to hear the teasing anymore, [be] the outcast. And then when I went to high school, I pretty much told myself that it wasn't worth it. I just went back to wearing my pentacle and stuff like that."

At least fifteen young Witches report instances of abuse by people outside school because of their religion. For example, Freddy says that at the shop in which she works, a customer kept her children away from Freddy, saying she was scared Freddy would eat the children. Melissa offers the opinion that "Wicca is a minority religion and so you have to sort of stick up for yourself more."

Responses to disclosing their Witch identity run the gamut from, at one end, having friends who joined the young Witch in her or his practice, to the other end, being mistreated. In between are those who are supportive, others who are disinterested, and still others who are dismissive or teasing. A similar range of responses is evident among the parents and families of young Witches.

Parents and Family

Parental response is important to most of the young Witches. At least when they are not at school, most still live with their parents. Only one, Tim, whose father has disappeared and whose mother is homeless and an alcoholic, is completely disaffiliated from both his parents. Some young people are so worried about the responses of their parents that they are afraid to tell them about their interest in Witchcraft. At the other end of the spectrum, some have Pagan parents who have taken them to rituals since early childhood. A number of young Witches indicate that their mother and father have reacted differently to their Witchcraft, and hence the numbers we cite do not add up to ninety. Sometimes the response of only one parent is mentioned. In some instances the parents are separated and the young people do not know what one of their parents, most typically their father, would think.[5]

Most of the young Witches (seventy-seven) told at least one parent about their religious practice. Of the other thirteen, some confide that their parents are not really interested in what they do, or that they believe their parents would treat their beliefs as a joke and ridicule them. A few report that they are afraid of their parents' reactions, mostly because of the parents' religious beliefs. Koehl, whose mother and mother's family are Jehovah's Witnesses, decided not to reveal her religious affiliation after having a "bad reaction" when she jokingly mentioned Witchcraft once. She has twin three-year-old half brothers and is concerned about what her parents might do if she "came out" to them: "My stepfather is a Catholic and my mother is a Christian, a Jehovah's Witness, . . . and I didn't want them to disassociate me from my little brothers because of the faith that I practice. So that is another reason I didn't really feel comfortable telling them."

Six individuals report that their parents are extremely uncomfortable with their Witchcraft despite their attempts to explain their faith. A few young Witches describe similar negative responses from other relatives. Cailin relates: "I have very Christian grandparents and my grandmother still isn't quite convinced I'm not Satan, so I kind of strained that a little bit. But I think we are better on that after six years, but originally it was quite a circumstance."

Although some negative responses derive from the religious worldview of parents, others are a product of parents who habitually belittle and denigrate their children. A surprising number of the young Witches we interviewed have parents or other relatives who repeatedly disparage them. Laurel reports: "My mother happened to mention [to my aunt] that I was now Wicca . . . and my aunt, who's a real bitch anyway, is like, 'God, you're stupid, ah, ah, ah.' And I'm just like, 'Yeah, well.' So there's no one in my family [who] supports me. None of them think it's good. They think it's stupid and they think it's a cult or something. They're really misinformed about it. My family's always been putting me down about everything, so it doesn't really bother me much."

Sixteen Witches report that their parents, initially concerned, have become accepting after more discussion. Seamus says that when he told his Catholic parents about his Witchcraft, his father "freaked out . . . [and]

threatened to throw my altar out the window . . . and accused me of being Jewish—it was entirely amusing." The accusation of Jewishness suggests the level of misunderstanding that some parents have of Witchcraft. Similarly, Mish tells us that her mother was worried, thinking that Mish was going to sacrifice goats in the back garden. In nearly all these cases acceptance, or tolerance, by parents came as a product of a sustained attempt by the young people to explain their faith to their parents. Sometimes this did not take long, with parents quickly developing a more sophisticated understanding of Witchcraft. In other cases, such as that of the American, Brian, who was raised in the Church of Latter Day Saints, colloquially known as the Mormon Church, this was an extremely difficult process:

One day he [my father] found a chest that I had up in my closet and broke the lock and found my Book of Shadows and my tools, and a horn that I had, and from there it was completely out in the open. Me and my girlfriend at the time were out taking pictures for a class and we came home and all of my stuff was just laid out on the floor and my brother and my mother were there crying. My dad says, "So what is all of this?" And I was like, "OK, Madeleine, it's time for you to go home," and I put it all out on the table right there. I said, "Yes, I don't believe in Mormonism, and yes, I'm a Witch and yes, I'm gay." And, then it was the recovering process after that. A lot of healing. . . . It was pretty shocking for the whole family. But my mom tells me everyone knows ever since I was, like, three that I was gay, so that part wasn't much of a shock. It is the fact that I don't necessarily believe in Jesus of Nazareth as a Christ figure. I don't necessarily believe that you can be saved from anything. That is hard for them to accept because they very strongly believe that Jesus is what it is all about. . . .

I had to go through counseling and therapy. I was hospitalized for suicide attempts and put on medication. . . . I just recently weaned myself off of the medication. That was a goal of mine and I finally did it about a month ago, so I was excited about that. . . .

My dad, I finally think I have gotten him to the point where he is educated enough about Wiccan practices to realize that I am not worshiping Satan, but again the fact that I am not worshipping

Jesus, . . . I think that that is the biggest thing a person could ever do in the church, and worshipping anything other than that is just not OK, so he tolerates it, but he doesn't embrace it. . . . My mom still has a hard time because I think she has got the mindset that we are all going to be judged and Jesus is going to come down and there will be hell and brimstone for those who aren't accepting of his teachings. And I think that she fears for my mortal soul.

In contrast to the passionate response of Brian's parents, ten Witches report that their parents are not particularly interested in their religious beliefs or practice. Sometimes this was a product of a general disinterest in religion. Wendy, whose parents are atheists, is sure that her parents are aware of her Witchcraft, as she openly reads books on the topic, but she says that they are not really interested. Similarly, Tanya discloses that she has told her mother, but that her mother does not seem interested: "I remember we had a conversation once and I said, 'I consider myself a Pagan.' And she didn't pass comment."

Parents are variously described as open-minded, skeptical, wary, angry, respectful, and more or less accepting. Some young Witches receive ambivalent responses that fall between the passion of Brian's parents and the disinterested response of Tanya's mother. Sixteen report that their parents, although respectful of their choice, remain ambivalent about Witchcraft. Several of these young people convey that their parents think their Witchcraft is a phase they are going through. Cliff describes how he understands his mother's response: "Well, she didn't understand what it was about. So she wasn't keen on the idea, but . . . the attitude was: if you are going to do it, go ahead and do it, just be careful and let me know what you are doing, so that I am not in the dark about it. Mom cared and she would always offer her opinion, but she wasn't going to stop me from making my own mistakes. But she was going to be there to pick me up afterwards."

Seventeen young Witches report that their parents, while not Pagans themselves, are supportive of their religious belief and practice, encouraging them by buying books for them and affirming their choice. Some parents help their children find other Pagans, conduct research on the Internet, or discuss their religious beliefs with them. Tina tells us: "My dad's really cool with it. He's quite happy that I've found a path that I wanna do and that I've made my own mind up about it and that I seem quite sane and confident about it as well."

Eighteen Witches report that members of their family are also Witches; among these are some with one or both parents who are Pagan, and the others with Pagan siblings, cousins, grandmothers, and aunts. Australians are slightly less likely than U.S. and English Witches to have Pagan family members. This may reflect the more recent arrival of Paganism to Australia and the longer history of Paganism in the United States and Britain. As the difference is not large, it may also be a random product of sampling.

Freddy tells us that she has been taken to Pagan gatherings by her mother for as long as she can remember, and that her interest in Paganism developed out of those experiences. Other Witches had similar supportive relationships with family members. Parents, grandparents, siblings, or aunts have taught some young Witches to read tarot cards, use herbs medicinally, and meditate. A few women describe a first-menstruation ritual with their mothers and Jen with her father's CUUPS group as well as her mother's Dianic group.[6] Monica, who since childhood has attended group rituals with her parents, describes a first-menstruation ritual with her mother that led to the development of her own practice: "'I think the first ritual that I did, . . . I was about nine and me and mom had one ritual together. It was just a bonding between two [of us] I think because I started menstruating too, I think, as well and it was just a really powerful moment, and from then on I realized you didn't have to have a whole group of friends around or associates, you could do it on your own and benefit from it just as much. So from then I started doing just little things to make me feel a lot clearer and focus on certain things and try and get understanding."

A number of other young Witches describe Pagan tendencies in their families. These include a mother who is a Christian who also reads tarot, a grandmother who is a Japanese Buddhist Shinto, a Freemason father, a mother who attends psychic fairs, and mothers who use tarot, herbs, crystals, and incense. While none of these family members are explicitly Pagan, the young Witches view their relatives' ideas and practices as supportive of, or sympathetic to, Paganism. Tina, whose mother is Malaysian, relates: "I went to Malaysia for the Chinese New Year a couple of years ago. It was so similar. It's like Paganism in a way. . . . My mom's friend said, 'Oh, you'll have to come and see my mom.' So I said OK and I went round to her house, this friend of my mom's. And in her house she had a big ancestor shrine and a little picture of her mom and food [as an offering]; . . . it's just so similar in many ways [to Neopaganism].[7]

Young people whose parents are part of the New Age or another alternative spirituality on the whole find their parents supportive of their spiritual journey. Those who have a good long-term relationship with their parents are most likely to find that their parents come to accept if not support their choice of religion once it is explained to them. Parents who are themselves traditionally religious sometimes have difficulty with their child choosing an alternative religion, particularly such a nontraditional one. But for a subset of young people whose parents have been abusive, dismissive, or disinterested throughout their lives, the child's Witchcraft identity is just one more area of conflict.

Conclusion

The most striking aspects of the Witchcraft community are its dispersed nature and its fluidity. It does not have the centralized authority structures and organization of other new religious movements such as Bahai, Soka Gakkai, or the Children of God. As Daschke and Ashcraft (2005, 4) note, the religious groups traditionally referred to as new religious movements are "organizations more often than they are movements." In contrast, contemporary Witchcraft is not an organization but a social movement. New social movements, Nelson Pichardo (1997, 416) advises, tend to have organizational structures that are "open, decentralized and nonhierarchical." As Helen Berger (1999) observes, the networking and community formation of Witchcraft bear a similarity to secular social movements such as the environmental movement or the gay and lesbian community, and diasporic ethnic groups such as the Hmong (Julian 2004) or Maori (Harvey 2001). Similar to social movements, Witchcraft has umbrella organizations that arrange festivals, maintain Web sites, and offer classes. But young people can pick and choose among which, if any, of these organizations' services to use.[8] As Charles observes at the beginning of the book, there is no organization one needs to join to become a Witch. Witchcraft differs further from new social movements such as the environmental or feminist movement in that it lacks an explicit political orientation, although aspects of these social movements are reflected within the religion (see Chapter 5).

Community, used sociologically, is a complex concept. Local community, virtual community, community of relationships, symbolic community, community boundaries—all form part of this concept. Sociologists have argued that traditional local community has declined as a consequence of modernity (Tonnies 1957). Beck (1992, 128), for example, describes the process of "individualization" as the disembedding of relationships from historical social forms and commitments. But in place of traditional local face-to-face community, other forms of community are developing, such as communities of interest—that is, groups of people who interact around an area of mutual concern. These communities may be local, national, or international. They are based on what Giddens (1992) refers to as pure relationships—relationships based on shared interest and affection, not on economics or tradition. Among Witches, communities of mutual interest develop through journals, in face-to face interactions, and on the Internet (H. Berger 1999). In our study, the virtual communities formed on the Internet also serve to recreate new forms of local face-to-face interaction and community, as people move from virtual space to meeting in person and to seeking out local Witchcraft events such as classes, gatherings, and open rituals.

Meeting other Witches, developing friendships, and finding Pagan community present a substantial challenge for young Witches, most of whom come to the religion through books and secondarily through the Internet. Because of legal concerns, many covens will not permit underage individuals to join (H. Berger 1999; K 1998; Harrow 1994). A minority of teens belong to groups or covens that they joined after reaching the age of majority or to which they were introduced by their parents. Most young Witches we interviewed are not part of a coven, but only seven are isolated from others in the religion. Although most define their practice as solitary, they tend to join others at open rituals, in their university clubs, at pub moots, and at festivals. They also form small groups to explore Witchcraft, often reading the same books and sharing information from Web sites. A virtual community also exists online. In contrast to the geographically based communities of mainstream religions or of a variety of other new religious movements, face-to-face Witchcraft community, particularly among young Witches, typically occurs among groups of fewer then twenty people, and often of no more than three.

For young people, finding community is a way to affirm and develop their identity as Witches. It also gives them the confidence to present themselves to their parents, extended kin, friends, and neighbors as part of a minority religion and to combat prejudice when they experience it. In many ways the forms of community described in this chapter are an extension of the processes of identity construction described in Chapter 3. However, community has a larger significance beyond self-definition, as Witchcraft is not just an individual but a collective identity.

Parents, extended kin, friends, and schoolmates are all important parts of young people's daily lives. Some of the young Witches come from supportive families who are themselves Neopagans or part of the broader New Age movements. Other parents, like Beverly's father, support their child's spiritual quest. But some parents are not supportive, either because they are affronted by their child's choosing a religion other than the family one or because they rarely support their children in any way. Some young people we spoke to describe families in which they were physically or emotionally abused since early childhood. Their parents' lack of support for these young people's religious decision is consistent with their previous behavior toward the young people. Young Witches who have good relationships with their parents are able to speak to them and, through sharing literature and information, make their parents more accepting of, if not happy with, their choice of religion. Those young people who believe that their family and others around them are not going to be supportive are the most likely to keep their Witchcraft identity hidden. Group participation, whether in face-to-face groups or on the Internet, is particularly important for these young people, as it provides a safe venue to explore their identity. Parental support or lack of it, however, does not appear to influence a young person's commitment to Witchcraft.

Vignette

Nika—The Goddess as Role Model, Healer, and Mother Earth

Nika asserts that in calling herself a Witch she is reclaiming . . . [the] word, reclaiming it from its negative connotations . . . in the sense of supernatural powers used for murdering people, orgies in the woods with devils, green-faced hag, lower class, that type of thing. . . . I think I like the way it is described in [books on Wicca as] "Wic: to bend or to shape." Another way of describing it that I have heard is "Wic: off a willow," and willow is used a lot in Witchcraft because it is pliable—the wood itself—and it is used for making wands because of its pliability. And it is also associated with the Goddess so it is very much feminine in its aspect. *Asked which goddess the willow is associated with, Nika says it doesn't really matter to her and that the willow is associated with the feminine and provides an alternative image of womanhood from that provided by the mass media. The Goddess or goddesses as manifestations of alternative images of the feminine and womanhood are a central aspect of Nika's narrative of becoming and remaining a Witch.*

Nika is also concerned about the environment. She does not participate in protests; however, she does recycle, discuss the issues with her contemporaries, and write articles about environmental issues. Although she has begun to think about the broader social and political issues of environmentalism, as for most young Witches, concern for nature is not central to Nika's life. Her main focus in on self-development. The Goddess as manifestation of womanhood and nature is central to her project of the self.

As Nika recalls, her interest in Witchcraft began with an attraction to Greek goddesses. In the fourth or fifth grade in a well-to-do town in Connecticut, her elementary-school class studied Greek mythology. We started studying Zeus and Hera and all that, but I think the goddess that got my attention was Artemis, . . . Artemis because of her wild aspects. Wildness not as in going out partying and get drunk kind of thing, but the fact that she is not in the house, not cooking, not cleaning, not bowing down to any man type of thing. She is out in the wild [with] wild animals. I know wolves have been associated with her. I have a thing for wolves. And the moon in its maiden aspect—or waxing. [She is] just kind of like nighttime goddess. I think her Roman aspect would be Diana. Those two [Artemis and Diana] were the ones that got my attention.

For Nika, Artemis or Diana offered an alternative image of woman. It wasn't the type of womanhood where you were bowing down to any man. . . . It seemed like what in American society [are the] masculine aspects would be associated with her. . . . It was nice to see a goddess represented in that light. Instead of the meek and mild behind-the-counter type of work, and if anyone wants to do that [clerical work], it is fine with me, but it just didn't feel right for me. [The goddesses provide] very much an alternative image; . . . the way Artemis is depicted or Diana is depicted, that is the feminine way of being. The same with early Celtic or even the pre-Celtic people, [among whom women] were on an equal footing with men; . . . you could be part of nature, be in the wild, and it was a good thing, not seen as a bad thing.[1]

Nika's interest in the Goddess continued long after she stopped studying Greek mythology in school. One day at her local library she was doing a word search on "goddess," "goddess figures," and I think what caught my attention was "goddess worship." I put that in and the woman behind me said, "Well, if you're interested in that, I can recommend a book." It didn't show up on the search engine because the library didn't carry those type of books because of, at the time, the negative connotation of Witchcraft, Druidism, and stuff like that; . . . and she recommended *Drawing Down the Moon* by Margot Adler, and then I was recommended other books by other people. It was through the Internet that *Nika came in contact with these other people who suggested further readings.*

The Internet remains part of Nika's spiritual world, but it is not the most central part. When she began her Internet search, she had mixed experiences on some Witchcraft Web sites. I have gotten some really weird people who were like, "OK, what do you look like, what is your breast size?"—stuff like that. So I am kind of turned off by that. Another girl kept hounding me because . . . [she was] trying to push her opinion on me type of thing and judging me because I wasn't going with what her idea of Witchcraft is, [which was] structured, very Gardnerian, you had to be initiated, you have to go through a prescribed education starting with first all the way up to third degree. You had to be part of a coven that had its lineage from Gardner himself, yadadadada. I was like, "OK, I won't go there." But when I did do a search engine, I came up with Starhawk's *The Spiral Dance.* I think that was published around the same time that *Drawing Down the Moon* was first published, which was, I think, mid to late 1970s. So I read that book and I was very much inspired because it [Starhawk's form of Witchcraft] wasn't structured. It was one of those situations where you find your own way, and what is your way is your way, and what is somebody else's way is somebody else's way. You find your own connection to the divine, not someone to be a mediator between you and the divine. And that direct connection and the nonstructured way of going about it is putting yourself into your ritual and making it something for yourself is what caught my attention. That is why I became very interested in Reclaiming. However, I studied and read other books, like Scott Cunningham's *Wicca for the Solitary Practitioner.* And his other book is *Wicca, the Further Guide for the Solitary Practitioner.*

Nika's initial negative experiences on the Internet have not completely turned her off to using the Internet spiritually. She is on a listserv for Reclaiming Witches and regularly visits Witchvox.com. The things she objected to on the Internet are also the things she objects to in person-to-person interchanges—the attempt by others to dominate her. Not surprisingly, it was Starhawk who caught Nika's attention. Starhawk's Witchcraft is politically active, nonhierarchal, and feminist, and this spoke to Nika and her spiritual needs and has helped inform her spiritual practices and views.

Nika, who was in college in Vermont at the time of the interview, describes her journey to becoming a Reclaiming Witch. She was thirteen when she began reading and within a year was doing small spells to increase her allowance and for self-love. When I was down in Connecticut and dabbling in it and doing my own thing down here, I was very much a solitary, and very much, even at school, I was looked down at even though they didn't know what I was doing, and I kind of started rebelling in my own way, and I felt bad that I was keeping things secret, and I think what happened was I started running away from myself and who I was and I wanted to try being more normal and like the cliquey normal that was at high school.

It was very hard for me during high school and there are times when I am still very bitter about it. When I was fourteen, I was sexually assaulted; . . . the ironic thing about it was the person—I did not see because he had his face covered. However, there is this one particular time when I was at my locker [in school and] . . . a kid kept coming up and he knew a lot about what happened during the incident [that] I never told anybody. So I had my suspicions, but I didn't actually see who it was, really. I remember how it was in high school with that [the rape]. No one really wanted to come near me after it. And I was trying to make myself more normal; as I was doing that, I felt like I was living two lives, to be honest with you. And I finally—I think the stress of it all kind of just broke down in me. I just had to get away. I know it is not healthy to run away from your problems, but sometimes that's what you did, [but] you realize that your problems follow you.

After the incident when I was fourteen, I did a lot of self-love type of spells to help build up my self-esteem. [I was] finding myself. Yeah, trying to reconnect with the spirit, the spirit that I had lost. I would have to say more like soul-piece retrieval would be the best way of putting it, because part of my soul or spirit kind of like died, would be the best way to report doing it. It was trying to find the pieces again and put it back together. I knew I wasn't going to find the same person that—or the same piece in me that had died again, I mean died, but I [could] at least put back those pieces—I could be reborn and something.

And it was in my sophomore year [of college] that I met Suzanne [her spiritual mentor]. What it was that started it off was I started becoming stressed again; I started feeling the same overwhelming sensations. Initially [I was] running away from [it], and for some reason I felt attuned to go speak to Suzanne. She just lived down the hall. I knew her through classes and various acquaintances on campus. And I asked her, "I don't know what to say, but I am having trouble." I mean, it got to the point where my stress was literally in my dreams. I remember a big T. rex, of all things, chasing me, so my stress was the *Tyrannosaurus rex* getting too much and tiny little me. And there were times when my roommates would wake up to me squirming around in bed and literally living out really weird things that they couldn't even understand. And there were times when they thought I was speaking another language, but I never really knew about all of this because I was asleep. And they would try to wake me up, and there were times when I would sleepwalk.

Nika reports that after hearing her story, Suzanne looked at me and she was like, "Well, there is something I can do for you, but that path you have to choose for yourself." . . . Her message was very much schematic, in a sense. Schematic being—you understand what she is trying to say, but it goes way over your head. You don't get it until later. . . . She basically didn't tell me what I needed to do. I needed to find it myself.

I was in the [university] library and they don't have many books [on Witchcraft] there, but on the shelf that I saw one day when I just looked up—and there was a copy of *Drawing Down the Moon*. And my whole memory of study that I had done through high school came back to me. And Starhawk's *The Spiral Dance* came back to me. And I reread *The Spiral Dance* because I did happen to bring my copy up with me, and I went to Suzanne's room with a copy of *The Spiral Dance* and said, "OK, I think I know what it is. . . ." And when I brought that book and myself to her room and she is like, "Ah, it seems like you caught on to what I was thinking." And I said, "Yes, I'm a Witch." She was like, "You had to say that because I couldn't, because that is something you have to say." And she basically started, I guess, in her own way training me and showing me different ways that she did, that was helpful for her, and it was more like learning at the same time, so I guess you would say—mentor might be the wrong way— . . . I think she was more like somebody who was . . . learning from me and I was learning from her. That type of thing. So it is not a hierarchical type of thing, type of relationship, it was more like a friend, and . . . I wanted her to initiate me and after about a year and a day of study and doing that I was initiated.

Nika, although not calling it feminist, has incorporated many feminist con-

cerns into her discussion of her spiritual path. Like Starhawk, who has clearly been an important influence in her spiritual path, she is concerned with issues of domination, power, and force. Her spirituality, while multivocal, involving her love for nature and her strong spiritual connection to the environment, is also helping her to heal the wounds of the rape, to regain her own sense of self and her own power. Throughout her interview she speaks of her distaste for hierarchical relationships, whether with the woman she met on the Internet who attempted to get her involved with traditional British Wicca or with the woman who initiated her into Witchcraft and has served as her guide.

Because of a faulty tape recorder, Nika's interview was recorded in two parts. During her initial interview she insisted she was not a feminist, but when she was interviewed the second time she changed her mind. As she stated it: Now that I have seen the answer to your question [about] a goddess aspect in my life, I think, yeah, I would [say I was a feminist], in association with my practice, yes. *She was, at least initially, uncomfortable taking the label "feminist," even though she is a Reclaiming Witch. However, in both the first and second interviews Nika sounds like a feminist, in part because of her experience with rape, in part because of her readings and her academic studies. For example, she confides:* I would never handfast with anyone who is of that type of nature where I have to be the [subordinate] type of woman in the kitchen—that is not me. I like to be out in the middle of doing everything, fighting my own fight and not having someone fight it for me. I am very opinionated and aggressive in a sense when I feel like someone is trying to invade my space, my space being my physical space as in boundaries, energy boundaries. *Her concern with power and maintaining and regaining power and her sense of self and personal space after the rape are all feminist issues, which she at times acknowledges and at times does not.*

Nika is also concerned about the environment and sees this concern as linked to her Witchcraft practice. Nika recalls a conversation with her mother: When I was eight, I said: "I think God is actually the universal consciousness of all living beings on earth . . . [consciousness] could be the rocks and the trees." And she kind of looked at me and like OK. And I remember saying that, because I remember the look on her face, but I was very intuitive as a child—very, trying to pull away questions from my original religious background.

Nika's orientation to magic reflects an intimacy with nature that derives from a Pagan worldview: I do self-affirmation [spells]. However, simple magic for me right now is going for a walk in the woods and just enjoying the cycles of nature. I mean, nature right out there. That is magic happening out there every single day. It is just natural, it is just cycles that happen each and every day that I like attuning with. Just watching animals go about their daily patterns. It is fun watching.

Nika's nature-oriented spiritual practice has transformed her understanding of her self and her life in perhaps small but potentially significant ways: I mean, doing a meditation and trying to become a part of the consciousness of a wild animal or tree, it is very different because their idea of time is, there is no such thing as time for them. Time is a human thing . . . in the sense of, you have to go to school, you have to do this, and it is twenty-four hours, and stuff like that. That is a human concept. Because you are always stressing about that. Time can be a millennium or something. I mean, it seems like the consciousness for some of the beings out there are slower and that is not a bad thing. I wouldn't mind just idling and having my roots in the ground every day.

It is important to note that while Nika's understanding of Witchcraft is individualistic, this does not lead to selfishness. Rather, it leads her to begin respectful and critical discussions with others, in particular about environmental issues. This is clearest in her thoughts about the essence of Witchcraft: The essence of Witchcraft . . . is, yes, a nature spirituality. However, it is defined by the person who chooses it as a life path. Because each person brings their own thing to it by way of their heart, their spirit, whatever you want to call it. Each one of us has our own connection to the divine and we do not need to have anyone interpret something for us. However, getting into discussions about different things and respecting people and we can learn from listening to other people, yes.

Asked if Witchcraft has changed her politics, Nika replies: [Witchcraft] affected my politics in realizing that, yes, it is very individual . . . and it does effect me type of thing, and that we are all interconnected and whatever we do to the earth or do to other people is going to come back to us and stuff, well, not punishment but return in some shape or form. . . . I am very much interested in the environment. . . . Besides the simple taking care of what I need to do as recycling stuff, I do a lot of writing about it. . . . I don't go to those protests that involve like the WTO and FTAA . . . because a lot of that stuff is scary, like what is going on, that they can make laws that are above other country's laws. Because that in a way effects the environment.

I do a lot of raising awareness about it around here, talking to people about it. Even if one person knows, it is a lot better than having to keep it to yourself because it is almost like a ripple in the pond. The ripples keep going and going and going because other people keep talking about it. And I have done a few articles on the environment for . . . [her] college newspaper *and an online journal.*

Nika, a political science major, has come to an interest in all forms of politics. The interesting thing was, when I went [to college], I hated politics. . . . I took a course with a man by the name of Peter Stevenson.[2] He was also very influenced by Starhawk. And finding his own way that way. And he . . . is an aspiring Witch and has no problem announcing it to anybody. And he used a lot of her [Starhawk's] work and work that was based in her material. . . . I took a course called Politics to Drama and Fiction with him. We did *The Fifth Sacred Thing* in there.[3] There is another book that is also very good, Linda Hogan's *Solar Storms,* [and] Alice Walker, *The Color Purple,* [and] John Steinbeck's *The Grapes of Wrath.* Where they [the rich and powerful] own the land and nature and when society and progress went in there, it was basically like raping the earth. You know, stuff like that. It was his Intro to Politics class that got me interested in political science. I originally started with a minor in politics and then I just basically switched my major in journalism back to my minor and politics to my major. Basically why I hated politics was because I thought it was a waste of time. I realized [after taking Stevenson's course] that politics was more than just what was going on [in the political system], and it concerned me. My own politics was dealing with the stuff that happened to me when I was fourteen, and women's rights and stuff like that. And "power over" is the term that Starhawk likes using, I felt like a "power over" type of situation [in the rape] that he was using on me because it was dominion over and trying to suppress something.

Nika believes her spiritual and magical practices are helping her deal with her rape and her sense of disempowerment as a woman in the United States of the twenty-first century. But she notes: I am still very, very critical of myself. I will admit that. I still have my moments. A large part of that is looking into a mirror that is created by society where I have to be a certain size or I have to look a certain way. But I have to look into the mirror that nature provided and realize that everyone comes in all shapes and sizes, but the one thing that is most important about us is our spirit. *Witchcraft gives Nika that alternative mirror—one she is still working on consistently using, but one that affords her a more powerful image of herself and of womanhood.*

Nika, like many of the young people we met, is concerned about the environment and issues of gender equity, particularly as they apply to her own life, but is at best hesitant to take the label "feminist." Most of the young people are not politically active but are interested in acting responsibly toward the environment, which they view as part of the divine, and in what would traditionally be considered feminist issues: questions of power, the media-generated images of the perfect body, and equity between men and women. For many, part of what drew them to the religion was its incorporation of environmental and gender issues into the fabric of its rituals. In turn, much of the literature they read emphasizes these values, reinforcing their beliefs.

CHAPTER FIVE

The Goddess Is Alive:
Feminism *and* Environmentalism

Among the generation of Witches that joined the movement before 1990, many saw their spirituality as conforming to and enriching their political views. Speaking of this earlier generation in "The Resurgence of Romanticism: Contemporary Neopaganism, Feminist Spirituality and the Divinity of Nature," Tanya Luhrmann (1993) reports they first and foremost joined a religious, not a political, movement and were drawn primarily by their desire for ecstatic spiritual experiences without the strictures of more traditional religions. Nonetheless, the image of the Goddess spoke to both their ecological and feminist concerns.

Within Witchcraft, the Goddess in her three aspects—maid, mother, crone—serves as a symbol both of Mother Earth and of empowered women. As Mother Earth she is often portrayed decked in flowers and leaves in the spring, and bringing forth fruit, vegetables, and grains, and birthing both humans and animals in the summer and fall. In the winter she is viewed as embracing the dead, promising new life in the spring. For most Neopagans the notion of protecting Mother Earth is part of their religious ethic. Young Witches, like their elders in the religion, often see themselves as ecologically concerned and environmentally conscious in their lifestyle choices, even if not politically active. They view protecting the environment as consistent with their religious, moral, and ethical views. The Goddess is visualized as alive and in nature, or nature is viewed as the Goddess's body—sacred and deserving care and protection.

The Goddess has also been a symbol of women's empowerment. Some groups and individuals have turned to worship of the Goddess as a way of balancing the power inequity they see as stemming from the exclusive worship of the male godhead. Others see the Goddess or the goddesses as providing prototypes for alternative roles for women—as warriors like the Hindu goddess Durga, or independent women like the Roman goddess Diana, as well as mothers, lovers, and the bringers of life and death. Some groups, most notably Dianics, venerate the Goddess to the exclusion of the God, but more commonly, particularly in Wicca, there is a belief that the male and female elements of the divine must be balanced. In practice, however, the Goddess is often treated with more import than the God.

Luhrmann, among other scholars (see, for example, Jacobs 1989, 1991; Goldenberg 1993), argues that for the baby-boomer generation the image of the Goddess served as a therapeutic tool for healing what some have referred to as the wounds of patriarchy, much as Nika uses Goddess worship to "rebirth" herself after the rape. In particular, Luhrmann views the embrace of the dark goddess—the goddess of death and destruction—as part of women's attempt to reclaim those things that have been viewed negatively in a male-dominated society, such as menstruation or women's aging bodies. She argues that the veneration of the dark goddess provides a venue for women to come to terms with losses they have suffered as women within a society that devalues the feminine.

In her landmark essay "Why Women Need the Goddess," Carol Christ (1982) goes further than Luhrmann, arguing that religious symbolism is a central element in either maintaining the status quo or helping to transform society. The Goddess, according to Christ, is not merely a tool for healing but an important element of changing social and political consciousness and, through that, political action. Quoting Clifford Geertz (1973, 90), she tell us that religion is "a system of symbols which act to produce powerful, pervasive and long lasting moods and motivations in people of a given culture." She argues that symbols "have both psychological and political effect because they create the inner conditions (deep seated attitudes and feelings) that lead people to feel comfortable with or accept the social and political arrangement that corresponds to the symbolic system" (Christ 1982, 72). God the father, Christ contends, provides a justification for male dominance: as God rules in the heavens, men rule on the earth. The image of the Goddess, according to Christ, provides a different set of "moods and attitudes" that are politically and socially empowering to women.

Regina Oboler (2004), also referring to Geertz's definition of religion, raises the question of whether Paganism, as an earth-based religion, results in practitioners becoming more ecologically active. Both Christ and Oboler lead us to question if the image of the Goddess provides different "moods and motivations" that influence political activity among young Witches. As we will see, there is variation among our respondents—not all are either feminists or environmentalists, but most are sensitive to the issues that surround both these political movements. In some cases there appears to be an elective affinity, with those who are concerned about gender equity and environmentalism being drawn to Witchcraft. In turn, their participation in the religion and at times interaction with other practitioners help strengthen their resolve. In other instances participation in Witchcraft appears to have influenced their thinking about these issues. Although only a very few are activist or willing to take the label "feminist," almost all support gender equity and none are antienvironmentalists.

Witchcraft, of course, is not unique among religions in both influencing individuals' political views and appealing to one group or another because of the religion's views on political or social issues. Some Catholic bishops attempted to influence the 2004 election in the United States by condemning Senator John Kerry's pro-choice stand. Much has been written about the Evangelical influence on both the 2000 and 2004 U.S. elections (see, for example, Wallis 2005; M. Taylor 2005). Radical Islam has served to transform the Middle East. Some members of pro-life groups have become Catholics because of the Church's stand on that issue. The Unitarian Universalists, to the contrary, are noted for drawing liberals to their churches. As a result, they are active in primarily liberal causes both in the United States and in other nations where the religion has spread.

The Christian theology used to justify the Religious Right's politics has also been used to justify liberal and even radical politics. African American churches, for example, were instrumental in the civil rights movement in the United States. Many continue to work for political and social change in their communities (Kostarelos 1995). In Latin America some Catholic priests and lay people participate in the "option for the poor," which emphasizes a theology of joining fights to aid the poor (Adriance 1995; Cousineau 1998). Some U.S. Evangelicals ordinarily noted for their support of conservative candidates are now raising concerns, based on their theology, about global warming and the death penalty.

Drawing on a wide variety of studies of the influence of religion on public political life, Casanova (1994) argues that religion is not being marginalized, as secularization theory would suggest, but is being "deprivatized" and playing a more central role in public life. By the "deprivatization" of religion, Casanova means the ways in which members of various religions, such as the Religious Right, are becoming politically active and are significantly influencing public discourse and policy. However, as Wald, Silverman, and Fridy (2005) argue, not all religious concerns that might have political implications are translated into political action.

This is precisely the case with teenage Witchcraft. Although Witchcraft has potential for political activism, it in many ways remains privatized, at least in part as a product of its organizational structure. Witchraft's religious principles are sometimes translated into political activity but more commonly remain a matter of lifestyle choice and attitude.

One difference between mainstream religions and Witchcraft is the latter's lack of central authority or even a pulpit from which to call for particular political activity or to vote as a block, as happens in the Religious Right (Wald et al. 2005). Instead, it is the rituals and writings within Witchcraft that both draw people who have certain political attitudes and encourage those attitudes and behaviors. Although most Pagans are liberal, some are quite conservative. Some forms of Paganism, such as the Ásatrú, tend to draw more conservative members (Berger et al. 2003). Mainstream churches are not monolithic either, but the minister in weekly sermons, or the leader of a tightly organized new religion, can encourage particular political activities or remind congregants of the church's stand on particular social or political issues, such as abortion or the environment, scenarios absent from the dispersed and individualistic movement of contemporary Witchcraft. Nonetheless, the focus on self-transformation characteristic of Witchcraft can result in change-oriented politics if the self-transformation challenges the power of contemporary social structures. Some scholars (see, for example, Finley 1991; Starrett 1982; Greenwood 2000b) argue that this is particularly a possibility within the feminist-oriented traditions of Witchcraft.

Gender Equity

Feminism and gender equality, although concerns for some young Witches, are not the central issues they were for their mothers' generation. Although many young Witches would not claim to be feminist, the Goddess and her relationship to the empowered and divine feminine remains a central element of Witchcraft for the new generation, as for the previous one. Four major types of response to the image of the Goddess and feminism are present in the interviews with young Witches. First, many claim to be "equalists" but not feminists. Second, some self-define as feminists. Third, some describe ideas consistent with essentialism and its first cousin, chivalry. Fourth, most treat the Goddess as an archetype that provides alternative and more feminist images of men and women than exist in the general culture. These four categories, while not mutually exclusive, capture the variety of the responses of the young Witches to images of the Goddess and to gender roles.

Feminism and Gender Equality

Jennifer Baumgardner and Amy Richard (2000) assert that feminism is the new "f word" in the United States, as it is in England and Australia. Many young women disclaim being feminists, believing that all the battles have been won. In all three countries some of the young speak of our now living in a postfeminist era. Koehl, who describes herself as being part of three minorities—women, Latinas, and bisexuals—tells us: "I have never been really, really big on feminist issues . . . but I do find it terrible what they did to women before—I mean, we weren't allowed to vote, we weren't allowed to hold jobs." Maggie similarly suggests: "I believe that the feminist movement in the sixties and seventies was integral to our Australian society now and without it we would still be in a patriarchal [society] . . . and everything would be down the toilet hole. But I think it might have gone a little bit too far in, I guess, maybe disenfranchising the male as a sex." Several of the young women from each country who believe women in the West have gotten equal rights express concern that women in other countries, particularly Muslim countries, have not.

A number of the young people claim that they are not feminists but that they do believe in gender equity. The Australian Witch Denise tells us:

I wouldn't say I was feminist. I'm an equalist, I suppose. I'm a big fan of equality. For example, at work my [male] colleague is not allowed to wear earrings, and I'm going, "Hey, that's crap"—like I can get away with it, like I can get away with dressing up as a Goth to work. I can get away with wearing eyeliner, but he can't because he's a guy and we [in society] have certain restrictions on guys, apparently. Things like that for guys that aren't fair. Like hiring women just because they're women—that's stupid. I'm a fan of equality. Like, OK, there are some things you can't make equal. Men can't have kids at the moment, but it's not here yet, so there are some things that women just need. Like the whole issue with—Oh, what is it?— women being worried about their jobs because if they have a kid they might lose it [their jobs] because their bosses are an idiot—very short-sighted, and that's valid [as a feminist issue], but even that's for society. We need to keep going. At the moment the Australian population is reducing and it's like, Let's have a look at our businesses, shall we? How are they treating their women employees who want to have kids?

Denise feels strongly about issues of equality. She is as troubled by what she perceives as discrimination against men as that against women. She is quick to tell us that the reason one should be concerned about discrimination against pregnant women in the workplace is that there is a population shortage in her country. Her argument appears to be that since the society needs more children, there is a need to make it easier, not harder, for women to both work and mother. She seems to be less worried about individual rights for women than about societal need. Denise does not describe herself as a feminist, although she supports equal rights. Like Denise, many of the young Witches state that they support gender equity.

Zoë, an Englishwoman majoring in American studies at a prestigious English university, is ambivalent about taking the label "feminist." When asked if she is a feminist, she says yes and no. Some of her concerns reflect Denise's. "I'm actually watching a documentary as part of my course on feminism, and there are a lot of them saying, 'Well, women should be more . . . in society and in the workplace, and they should be more important, not less important.' And I thought, 'Well, yes, they shouldn't be less important, but I don't think they should be more important either.' I think that everyone has to work together. And then you got the whole abortion issue; . . . I agree with the feminists that people should have the right to choose if they have one or not, but as a person I don't believe [in abortion for myself]." Like Denise, Zoë indicates that she supports equal rights but opposes anything that might result in women being viewed as superior to men. Zoë also expresses support for women's right to choose whether to continue or end a pregnancy, despite feeling that she would not herself have an abortion. The issue of abortion rights may be particularly thorny for Zoë, who was born to an unwed mother. But it also suggests a distinction between her views of personal choice and public policy. Like Denise, Zoë speaks about the importance of equity, although she is less focused on what she believes are the truncations of men's rights than Denise is. She is clear that she would not support women's rights at the cost of a limitation of men's rights.

Many of the young U.S. Witches also speak about the importance of social equity. Fritz, for example, tells us: "Women's rights. . . . Well, I really view that this should have never been a problem in the first place. I really view that all rights should be equal; . . . it's easier said than done, but as far as women's rights, they [women] should be as good as men. I think they are; . . . I just feel that a lot of people for some reason still view that tradition dictates policy, and that is a real issue." Like Denise and Zoë, Fritz is an advocate of equality, but there is a difference between his response and that of either of the women. He seems more aware and concerned about women's inequality in contemporary society. A recurring theme in most of our interviews is a strong belief in equity, balance, and fair treatment for all people. However, the Americans report a stronger commitment to gender equity than do their English or Australian counterparts.

More U.S. Witches (sixteen) state that they are feminist than do either the English (ten) or Australians (nine). Some of this difference may be the effect of Helen's conducting all the U.S. interviews and Douglas conducting all those in Australia, but the British interviews, which both conducted, do not show a sharp difference. Of the ten English Witches who are feminists, Helen interviewed six and Douglas interviewed four. There may be an international difference in how the question was interpreted. In Australia, the word "feminist" is commonly associated with a person who is an activist working for women's rights. In the United States, one can claim to be a feminist because one believes that women should, but do not, have social equity. However, more striking than the numbers is the language the young people use to speak about feminism, women's rights, and women's lives.

Although there is variation among the young people in each country, the U.S. Witches appear to be more sympathetic toward women's issues, even if they are not feminists; Australia's are more concerned that men's rights not be truncated (although this may in part reflect the influence of a male interviewer); and the British Witches, regardless of who interviewed them, fall somewhere in the middle. Leslie, who majors in religious studies and has just completed her undergraduate thesis on contemporary Witchcraft in the United Kingdom, offers the opinion that "I'm not really feminist. I have never thought of myself as feminist at all. That is something I tend to associate more with Americans, and I don't know why." Possibly because she was being interviewed by Helen, Leslie adds: "I apologize if I am stereotyping all American females to be feminists."

The feminist movement may have made more inroads in the United States than in the other two countries, making it more acceptable for the U.S. youth to state greater concern for women's equity. The influence of Starhawk and the Reclaiming Tradition, which is feminist, is significantly stronger in the United States. Although Starhawk is read worldwide and the influence of the Reclaiming Tradition has spread to Europe and Australia, it is much more a peripheral movement outside the United States.

Although our sample is too small for any firm conclusions, country of origin seems to have some effect on whether the young Witches self-define as feminists or not, and the degree to which they are sympathetic to women's issues; however, as noted, there is a good deal of variance among young Witches in each country. We have heard from young Witches in all three who support feminism, as well as some who feel it is unimportant, has gone too far, or is not consistent with their spirituality.

Feminist Witches

Although the women's spirituality movement grew out of the feminist movement, not all feminists are comfortable with Goddess Spirituality (Griffin 2005). Ann-Marie Gallagher (2000) suggests that the tensions between the feminist and Neopagan communities in England are stronger there than in the United States, where she believes the Goddess movement has been comfortably ensconced within the women's movement. But in the United States as in England and Australia, there remains opposition within some parts of the women's movement to the Goddess movement, of which Witchcraft is one form. Cynthia Eller (2000) is a recent example of those in the United States who believe that the Goddess movement removes women from important political work. Gallagher, furthermore, notes that some elements of the Neopagan community are not friendly toward feminism. It is therefore not surprising that among those who state that they are feminists, some do not credit Witchcraft with having influenced their political views. For example, Bonnie explains: "I was a feminist before [I became a Witch]. I just happened to find a feminist religion. Yeah, . . . they fit together quite nicely actually—one had nothing to really do with the other. It just happened to work out that way."

Beverly, whom we met at the beginning of the book, bemoans the fact that there is not a stronger link between young Witchcraft practitioners and feminism. But she is not alone in seeing a connection between feminism, or a concern for women's rights, and Witchcraft. Brianna reveals: "I have always been fairly liberal, but I think maybe I have become more feminist. . . . Before, when I was younger, I didn't really care about issues like equality and stuff. I got [that] through the Witchcraft books—they always mention women's spirituality and how women have different spiritual needs than men. . . . And I guess that has pushed me into reading other completely feminist books having nothing to do with Witchcraft, and just wanting to fight for more rights, not even just women's rights, like rights in general."

For some, like Logan and Simon, contact with others within the Pagan community stimulated their political concerns. Logan suggests that it "is more of a contact issue, I think, because a number of the Pagans that I worked with were strongly feminist." Simon contends that his interest in social justice, which includes a concern about gender issues, grew because "a lot of the Pagan pages I would view [on the Internet] had links to places like Oxfam" and other sites concerned with social equity.

For others, participation in Witchcraft rituals, practices, and celebrations influences their thinking on gender roles. Wendy Griffin (2000) describes all forms of Goddess worship as embodied spiritualities—the divine is not outside but within, not in another realm but in this world. Griffin tells us that it is in and through ritual that women come to "rewrite the body," that is, on a deep internal level come to rethink being a woman—menstruation, the ability to birth, and the body at all ages and in all shapes. Dane suggests that this is true not only for women but also for men: "The idea that we may be male and female physically, but in Wicca we just do stuff using masculine or feminine energy within us. There should be a balance of that. And I saw myself at the outset of going into women's studies and even before, like in high school, trying to think about masculinity and almost deconstructing it on my own and reconstructing it."

Griffin's research focuses on rituals performed by groups, not by solitary practitioners. She specifically mentions rituals of first blood that celebrate girls' reaching menarche. Most of the young Witches practice alone and only a few have parents who are involved in any form of women's spirituality. Jen, however, had two first-blood rituals, one with her father's Wiccan group, the other with her mother's Dianic coven:

Wicca helped me out a lot with my own self-worth. . . . I was in a Dianic coven for a while—that was mostly because my mom was Dianic and she brought me all through the women-type things especially; I was twelve or thirteen, I was coming into womanhood. So, of course, there is [a] push that womanhood is good on the kid so that she knows and she is OK. I think that definitely formed my life a lot. It has made me stronger and it has made me a little bit better as far as boys go. . . . Because I see a lot of my friends, and it is like, you are better than them. Even though I know we're not better than them, but it is like you have to have that in order to be OK with everything and get through guys dumping you and doing this and doing that, and whatever.

As we have seen, most of the young people believe Witchcraft helps them in their growing sense of self. For many of the young women, one part of that growth is an alternative or better image of womanhood than they have seen in the media. But it is not only the young women who believe that Witchcraft provides them with an alternative view of gender roles; as Dane illustrates, it also provides an alternative gender role for some young men. For some gay men this is consistent with their sexual orientation, which they view as challenging traditional gender roles. For example, Brian tells us:

As a gay male, I have always had a—if you will—kinship with feminism and its teachings because I didn't identify with a normal male image. So in that respect I always identified with females and I have always seen the inequalities between males and females in our society. Wicca has opened me up to understanding the female side of divinity better. When I was growing up, I think it was just because of my training in the Mormon Church, I always believed that there was a God, the father, the almighty creator. And then there was a Mother Earth spiritual aspect that wasn't necessarily the Goddess. And over time that has evolved and changed into the Goddess because I realized, "Well, crap, why is there a male god and not a female goddess?"

For Brian, as for many of the young Witches we spoke to, the Goddess is an important aspect of spiritual life. She provides one part of Brian's questioning of gender roles, although his commitment to feminism comes, he feels, first and foremost from living as a gay man, particularly one whose family is part of the Church of Latter Day Saints.

Like many in their generation, most of the young Witches eschew the label "feminist." However, most are interested in issues of gender equity, although rarely do they fight for it. The Goddess is a central image within Witchcraft, and she is seen, among other things, as providing alternative gender roles for both straight and gay women and men.

Essentialism and Chivalry

In her book on the Reclaiming tradition in the San Francisco Bay Area, Jone Salomonsen (2002) claims that although the group is known for its feminist theology—or "thealogy," as many of it members prefer to call it—within the group there are elements of essentialism, that is, the notion that men and women have different innate tendencies. Salomonsen argues that this essentialism runs in contradiction to the group's professed feminism, which she contends advocates the view that gender is socially constructed and hence can be socially deconstructed. Some of the young people we interviewed, particularly those in England and Australia, consider the belief system of Witchcraft antithetical to feminism. For example, Jackie offers the opinion:

I suppose it's a bit hard to be a feminist and hold traditional Pagan roles for the female—the idea of a female, the maiden, and then growing up and being the mother and producing [children]. The male is like hunter/protector. These seem to be [in contradiction to feminism]. . . . A modern feminist view says: "Oh, no, the females can do it all themselves and we don't need male protectors and stuff like that," but on the other hand I think it's very healthy to say—for a female to say—"Well, yes, I can protect myself, but I've got a male here to protect me." Similarly for a male to say: "Well, even though I'm strong and I can do it all myself, I still need female company." So it becomes very much the two halves making a whole, and then, of course, the lines become blurred between which one is which. So that's definitely how I view male/female roles is the two halves.

Susan offers a similar insight: "I don't think feminism is as important to me now as it was a couple of years ago. I think I've evolved. [I am] more sure now that the dual aspect of Goddess and God—you need both. So now I see mainly the feminism thing is just a bit overboard, . . . just too much."

Although a minority, it is clear that some in our sample believe that Witchcraft or Neopaganism is contradictory to feminism because the images of the gods and goddesses are imbued with traditional gender images. For what has been called "difference feminism"—the belief that men and women are different but equal, or women's way of doing or being is better—this essentialism would not be a problem. Nonetheless, for these young people the engendered images of gods and goddesses pose a problem for their embracing both Witchcraft and feminism.

Although some of the men, like some of the women, claim to be feminists, some to be neutral, and some to advocate equality, a few suggest that they are chivalrous toward women. Zack, a dynamic young American whose mother became a Witch in his childhood, exemplifies this view. Zack considers himself a second-generation Witch; he is very proud of his mother for both her spiritual openness and her success in a small business. Zack began a Wiccan club at his university with the help of two women who are first-generation Witches and feminists. He is also a member of ROTC and of a fraternity.[1] When asked if being raised as a Wiccan, venerating both a God and a Goddess, influenced his notion of gender roles, he discloses:

I presume that worshiping a God and Goddess—I believe it is the same as anyone who worships, as long as I still [have] respect for people—people as the whole, everything as a whole. Of course, I treat women nice because that was how I was brought up. I try to look at things from all angles. I see women in the army, I just don't know, because I'm a guy—I don't see putting women on a front line is something I respect, type of thing. I guess I am a little bit the Old World and chivalry or something like that. But, yeah, I do have respect for women getting a job or all sorts of different things. I don't want to see them just as housewives, and just being like slaves to men. I'm against that sort of thing.

Ollie, holds similar sentiments: "My view of the God and the Goddess is of them as very equal, but I think there are things that—and I'm not just talking about children and whatever—but there are things that women can do that men obviously can't do, and there are things that men can do that women can't do and I don't think [should do]." Like Zack, Ollie specifically mentions the army, although he is ambivalent about this issue. He feels that if a woman really wants to join the service, then it is a matter of personal freedom, a notion that is important within Wicca. But on the whole he sees combat as a man's world.

The notion of being "Old World" is not inconsistent with either Wicca or Witchcraft. Practitioners often call Witchcraft the old religion, suggesting that it preceded Christianity. This view has come into question, as noted earlier, but the notion that practitioners are returning to a historic practice that reflects earlier sensibilities is common. Zack's chivalry is consistent with one thread of Witchcraft, but neither he nor the others who speak of women being treated chivalrously want to turn the clock back to 1950s gender stereotypes.

Goddesses (and Gods) as Archetypes

The notion of ancient and culturally diverse deities serving as archetypes or role models for contemporary women and men permeates the early and contemporary Witchcraft literature (see, for example, Starhawk 1979; Budapest 1986) and has entered into the larger culture (see, for example, Bolen 1984, 1989). For most of the young Witches, the deities are more than just archetypes, but they do believe that they are useful in that role. Bianca, a nineteen-year-old university student in London, has a dual major in "history of science and philosophy of science," which she says "completely fits in with Paganism for me 'cause I have quite a scientific skeptical approach—basically I think that maths is God, but that kind of translates into Paganism for me. So it's a bit unorthodox Paganism." Nonetheless, when discussing a ritual she did to help with her A-levels, Bianca notes that she invoked the goddess Athena. Bianca tells us: "Athena is one of my favorite Goddesses. Definitely, she is like in a man's world doing academic and war stuff, but she's a woman." Athena, or by her

5.1 Australian Witch visiting a goddess temple in Glastonbury, UK. Photo by Brooke of Brooke.

Roman name, Diana, is also mentioned as a favorite goddess by Nika, who is featured in the vignette preceding this chapter. She is the most often mentioned of the goddesses among the young people we spoke to. Within Witchcraft circles Athena is typically associated with the maiden aspect of the triple goddess and with the hunt and war—an active goddess who is able to take care of herself.

Bianca believes the Goddess is important for men as well as for women: "But the really big thing is developing a philosophy, thinking about comparative religion as well, thinking about why it's useful to personify Gods. . . . A lot of Pagans would disagree with me, but I think the Gods exist in us and in the earth and in the universe, but not in any other way. . . . I can communicate with this idea of sort of intelligence and all the qualities of Athena—that's like an aspect of women that is in me and in my mum and in all other women in the world, because that's just an aspect. It's in the men as well probably. In the whatever it's called—the Anima." As Bianca suggests, not all Neopagans conceive the divine in the same way. For some, the deities are supernatural beings that exist in another realm; for others, they are thought forms, archetypes, and/or within each of us. The notion that Athena, another goddess, god, or the generic God and Goddess are within each of us, is, however, a common Neopagan image of the divine.

The notion of a female divine is important for Bianca as a woman. She reflects: "Reading about Paganism has definitely made me realize how powerful women are and how it's sacred and important, and every child should be taught this when they're little. You can grow up thinking you're the bad one [if you are a girl] because you tempted Adam or something. . . . It makes you feel a lot more special if you know that the divine is in your form as well as your boyfriend's form or every man's form."

Bianca reports that she believes that in contemporary Western society the Goddess is wrapped up with feminism: "Goddesses today are really

5.2 Young Witch with chalice, USA. Photo by Brad Kinne.

with the feminine movement and stuff, but I'm sure people were practicing natural magic and things in the Renaissance, although that's kind of been incorporated into Paganism now, they didn't have the same attitude to women then at all." Although Bianca is correct that natural magic was practiced during the Renaissance, Goddess worship was not part of it. But her larger point is well taken: historically there have been societies that worship the Goddess but do not treat women well. She would not agree with Carol Christ, who suggests that worship of goddesses necessarily translates into women's being treated better or becoming empowered. Bianca's belief is rather that within the contemporary context, goddesses provide women with positive role models: "There's all these go-getting new roles for women. They've got loads of role models in the Goddesses and stuff, like Athena."

Bianca is, however, concerned about the lack of an equivalent for men. "There's a magazine called *Sacred Spiral* and it's new and it's for Pagan families and I love that, and there was an article in there about this chivalry and about boys playing with swords and how it's all right and that was actually what got me thinking about this." With a laugh she continues: "I wanna invent a new god for men; . . . I'm really concerned about men . . . because the God has been underemphasized because people want to redress the balance—of course, that's totally understandable, but it's made me think about the role of [the] man." With a male friend with whom she works at her part-time job at a metaphysical bookstore, she "had this plan—we wanted to invent a new God, the househusband god. But for the men I think there's too much emphasis on the Goddess or not enough emphasis on the God, rather, and men, I think, are having a bit of a hard time and so they need a new god. . . . Even if there wasn't [a god like this] in the Greek times, we're different to the ancient Greeks, so we should be allowed to invent a new god." The new god Bianca is suggesting would reflect new gender roles and serve as an archetype for men, as Bianca believes Athena and other goddesses do for women.

Brian would agree with Bianca that the gods are not given enough emphasis in contemporary Witchcraft: "A lot of people—and mainly Dianic Wiccans—try to get people to believe that [it is] the Goddess from which all things came from, that we are all of the Goddess, and the God doesn't have a role in that. Because I think they are getting caught on the gender thing, and I personally believe that the God and the Goddess, they are beings, and they are male and female." Even though Brian conceives of the God and Goddess as actual beings—differing from Bianca's concept—he too sees them as archetypes.

Although not all our respondents spoke about specific goddesses or gods, most consider their relationship with the divine important. Possibly in part because we interviewed more women than men, the goddesses are more often spoken of than are specific gods, or even the more generic "the God." For a number of the women, as for Bianca, the goddesses are important role models. The Goddess is often cited as important for the men as well, as a balance to the Judeo-Christian notion of a male godhead or as a nurturing figure. For some like Melissa, who is being trained in a Wiccan coven, the Goddess is part of her notion of feminism:

My high priest yells at me because I tend to be a little bit more Goddess oriented and he is like, "You have to have the balance," because I do believe that you have to have the sort of male/female unity and balance. But I tend to be more on the goddess side, but I think it is because I'm a woman. . . . Wicca has this female who sort of is the nurturer and the mother and the caregiver and the one who is—she is not . . . like the Virgin Mary, who is sort of supposed to be this pious virgin. But rather the Goddess is a strong woman—female—who just is in charge and is in control and who is respected and honored, and that was why it resonated with me. . . . For a long time society was matriarchal, and then Christianity sort of made it into a patriarchal society, and the Goddess got pushed under the table, and so I think now, you know, she is starting to make a revival and has gotten a lot of feminists excited to say a woman is more than supposed to be barefoot and pregnant in the kitchen—like a woman is a woman and she is in charge, and she is strong and she is powerful.

Melissa's belief in an ancient matriarchy is common within feminist spirituality, although it has not been substantiated by research (see, for example, Eller 2000; Hutton 1999). Not all within feminist spirituality or all

Witches adhere to this mythology. Michael, an Englishman, notes that he was drawn to Witchcraft after hearing about the myth of the ancient matriarchy and stayed even after he learned that it was just that—a myth.

Worship of the Goddess is part of Melissa's commitment to feminism; Nika, whom we met in the vignette preceding this chapter, is ambivalent about the link between feminism and the Goddess; Bianca does not see the focus on the Goddess as linked to feminism. However, all three women agree, along with many other young Witches, that the Goddess or specific goddesses offer role models for women that help them go beyond traditional gender expectations. Many also see the Goddess as aiding men to get in touch with their feminine aspect. The God is spoken of less often and is at times seen as an archetype for both men and women to connect with what Witches often refer to as their "male energy."

Witchcraft as a Nature Religion

More than half the Witches refer to the worship of nature or a connection with the earth as either central to, or part of, the essence of Witchcraft. Jacqueline explains that, "instead of God [in heaven], our god is actually the earth." Similarly, Leslie describes the essence of Witchcraft as "probably nature." Asked to explain this, she continues: "I think nature, the connection between nature and deities, that's . . . the core part of Wicca. Without that it would just be casting spells and stuff. You need the natural world. You need the nature basis for it."

Many of the young Witches perform magical spells for self-esteem and health, among other things, as we saw in Chapter 3. However, Witchcraft is not simply the instrumental practice of magic but a religious worldview that makes the natural world sacred, as Bonnie explains:

The essence of Wicca is an earth-loving religion. Your main goal is to only do what is right for the earth and what is right for yourself and what is right for the good of others. . . . There are a great deal of people who believe in the earth and the powers of the earth and respect and preserve what is around us that don't necessarily go in and cast spells. I happen to do both. The essence really is, you have to believe that everything is equal—the tree outside is no better or no further beneath; you are equal with it. You're equal with the grass. You're equal with all of that. And you respect it as such. [In contrast,] when you are talking about spellcraft and things like that, that is a little bit different. The essence of that is energy and the manipulation thereof.

A number of the young Witches identify the celebration of the sabbats as a way of connecting with the energies and seasons of the earth. The seasonal cycles lead them to a deeper sense both of their relationship with the earth and of their own lives. Stella describes how Witchcraft has changed the way she sees things around her: "Finding innate beauty in just simple things. . . . Sometimes it'll be pouring down rain and, you go, "Shit, rain." Then you sort of see that in a different way and how that's helping the rebirth come along for the springtime. . . . I always thought that nature was important, but not to the extent that I do now. I just never really took no-

5.3 Young Witch with laurel wreath, UK. Photo by T. K. Morris.

tice of seasonal cycles. They were just there and, you know, winter was cold; summer was hot. Somehow they didn't mean anything to me personally—that [seasonal change] just happened—but now they do."

Many of the young Witches similarly report that seeing nature as sacred helps them come to terms with the cycles of their own lives. The interrelationship between the changes in nature and those in people's lives is discussed in many books about Witchcraft. For example, in her influential book *Wicca: The Old Religion in the New Millennium,* Vivianne Crowley (1996) develops an analogy between the wheel of the year and an individual's self-understanding. Bianca reports that after reading Crowley's book she realized "that the divine should be manifested in feminine form, that nature was sacred, that we should live life and not be obsessed with having to die afterwards, and death was . . . sacred as well. Not to be afraid of [death], but [it is] just the other side of the wonderful coin that's being alive."

Because Witchcraft is understood as a nature religion by most young Witches, nature is an integral part of their religious symbolism, mythology, and practice. Like Stella, most believe the celebration of the sabbats changes their understanding of themselves, the world around them, and difficult issues such as death and dying. Their beliefs about nature are not separate and compartmentalized. Rather, new understandings and experiences of nature derived from the religious symbolism of Witchcraft significantly influence and shape the way these young people understand other aspects of their own lives and relationships. As Bruce phrases it: "It helped me understand the beauty of how things work in a sense that everyone has a dark side, but they also have a good side as well. Like in nature there's destruction and there's beauty. It's part of the natural cycle." Not all Witches describe the earth as sacred or the worship of nature as essential to Witchcraft. As we will see, a minority are uninterested in nature or the environment.

Environmentalism and Witchcraft: Which Comes First?

Does the nature symbolism central to Witchcraft transform the "moods and motivations" of Pagans to the environment and to environmental activism (Oboler 2004)? The evidence of changed attitudes toward the environment among Witches is mixed. Some academic commentators such as Andy Letcher (2000) argue that much contemporary Witchcraft and Paganism are nature religions in name only and do not typically result in any form of environmental activism. To the contrary, say practitioners such as Starhawk (1979), environmental activism is integral to Witchcraft.

Based on a survey among a small number of U.S. Pagans, Oboler (2004) reports that Pagans are more likely than the general U.S. population to be members of environmentalist groups and participate in environmental political action. However, Oboler is not convinced that it is Paganism as a religious culture that causes this difference. Rather, drawing on qualitative interviews with her respondents, she reports that the higher level of environmentalism among Pagans is the result of environmentalists being attracted to Paganism: "Follow-up interviews have led me to the conclusion that, for many if not most informants, environmental concerns preceded involvement in their religious path" (98).

Our research leads us to different conclusions. Although there are a few young people in our study whose environmental activism drew them to the religion, for the majority of young Witches greater environmental activism is a product of practicing Witchcraft. Of those who report that they are concerned about environmental issues, approximately 20 percent said that they had been environmentalists prior to practicing Witchcraft, or that they are uncertain about which came first and that their environmental concerns might have developed regardless of their Witchcraft practice. Cherry's comments are typical of several responses: "I recycle as much as I can. I use public transport. I won't knowingly buy from a company who use battery hens or slaughter animals in a way I don't like, but I was like that before I was really thinking of myself as Pagan. So that hasn't really changed much."

Similarly, a few people mentioned that they grew up on a farm or in the country and that they had a strong sense of a relationship with the natural world before they found Witchcraft. Marcia, an Australian, tells us: "I'm originally from the country, which I suppose is why I've got a lot of ties to the natural world. I grew up with grass and trees, running around and playing with things, growing flowers and stuff. Talking to the animals [laughs]. There were not a lot of people around to talk to, so I'm just quite interactive that way with nature, which is probably why it [Witchcraft] appeals to me in a lot of ways. . . . I don't know if that's my natural inclination to do that [be concerned about the environment] anyway."

However, the vast majority of young Witches say that Witchcraft has led them to a greater awareness of nature, and some add that it has led to various forms of environmental activism. Cailin provides one of the strongest responses when asked if Witchcraft has changed her views on environmentalism: "Completely. I am Miss Environmentalist, vegan freak." And Bianca observes: "If you worship the earth, you've gotta look after her."

Many Witches identify changes in personal behavior when asked whether Witchcraft had influenced their attitude toward the environment. At least fifteen mention that they have begun recycling, with a further five expressing the desire to recycle but finding it difficult because it is not supported where they live. Five mention that they have stopped littering. Six say they have become vegetarian. Another eight mention spending more time outdoors in parks, hiking, in the woods, and "dancing in the rain" (Carolyn). Three say they have become more active gardeners.

For some, Witchcraft has simply led to a heightened awareness of nature. For example, asked about her concept of deity, Clarissa replies: "The duality of deity [is] for me a balanced system that I hadn't really identified with elsewhere. And I also . . . started noting the cycles of the moon and getting more in touch with making a note of the times of the moon rising and setting and just watching the cycles and watching nature as well. So it was just more of a passive observance–type thing." For others, Witchcraft led to active changes in lifestyle. For example, when asked whether Witchcraft had changed her recreation activities, Maggie replies: "Ah, it does a bit, yeah. I'm more inclined to go outdoors and find untouched nature. Like me and some friends took a hike to South Cape [in Australia]." Many other Witches report similar recreational activities that provide the opportunity to spend time "in nature."

Although for some of the Witches there is an elective affinity between their environmentalism and their religion, for the majority it is the practice of the religion that has made them environmentally aware and active.

While the extent of the change varies considerably, the nature-oriented symbols that are central to Witchcraft practice produce "powerful, pervasive, and long-lasting moods and motivations" that influence their attitudes and, in some cases, their behavior (Geertz 1993, 90).

Animism

Some young Witches develop their concern for respectful relationships with the environment into a worldview that has many of the characteristics of an animist worldview, although none of the young Witches use that label. According to Harvey (2005, vii) contemporary animism describes a way of living in the world that respects the variety of living beings, only some of whom are human. Animists respect these other beings, such as plants, animals, or geography, because they are understood to be "animate"—sharing in the same life force or spirit that animates humans. As an animist, he believes that "a better world would be possible if all people would act towards one another respectfully, and that the 'good life' is by definition a respectful life."

Many of the young Witches draw a similar link between acting respectfully toward nature and understanding flora and fauna as imbued with spirit. For example, Jason says: "Before I was a Witch I always cared about nature . . . [but] I sort of care more and on different levels because it [Witchcraft] has taught me that a tree is not just a tree, it is not just a thing that is out there. It has a spirit."

The most common term used to describe the shared life force is "energy." Many of the young Witches describe the essence of Witchcraft as working with energy and see themselves as part of an integrated energetic network. As Mish phrases it: "My mode of thought is to see things in terms of energy. I see things as very holistically, sort of very interconnected. Because the Great Goddess is actually the universe. . . . Every tree, stone, person, gods and goddesses [are] parts of the larger whole, because we are all interconnected—we can influence the way that energy flows throughout the whole."

Animist understandings of the world have a profound impact both on the way young Witches understand the natural world and on the way young Witches understand their own responses to nature. They begin to treat nature with more respect, and an animist worldview also encourages a less fearful response to the dangers of nature, such as snakes or "bugs." Koehl provides an account of how Witchcraft facilitated the development of an animist worldview that subsequently changed the way she relates to nature:

When I was in high school, . . . I used to take walks in the woods because they were pretty close by. I would just sit there and socialize with my friends, talk about everyday life, and, it was . . . something to get away from the city. Then, once I got into this faith, I realized how everything has a symbolic value, like the tree or the grass, the sun or the moon—everything has a symbolic value. I started taking much more notice of it. I realized I was constantly afraid of every single bug in the world, but after being a part of this faith a few months then I started realizing, "Oh, a bug, someone reincarnated in that tiny little body of an ant." And I thought they had the right to live. It's like a snake may have just jumped out of the woods suddenly giving me a snake bite, but I realized it was a person who was awfully scared, so I'll just walk away and leave that creature be.

In speaking of the natural world, many of the young people used animist imagery. This is more striking because we did not ask them about beliefs associated with animism. The notion that nature is alive and that divinity is not in another world but in this one encourages this type of thinking.

Environmental Activism

The attitudes of young Witches to environmental activism and politics fall into three major categories. First, some believe that politics is separate from their religious beliefs; second, others see environmentalism as related to Paganism but they are not politically active; or third, they are activists because of their religious commitment. The group who sees no link between politics and Witchcraft is the smallest, making up approximately one-tenth of our sample. Asked whether Witchcraft has changed her attitude toward politics, Doreen replies: "I don't think so. I never cared about politics before and I still don't [laughs]."

Some people in this category are concerned about the environment, but they do not see it as an important part of Witchcraft. For example, Leanne contends: "I think it's important, but it's wholly detachable from Witchcraft or any religion. . . . [Environmentalism is] not a big thing in my life and it probably should be. I mean, if I see litter on the floor I pick it up and if I can get a bus, normally I would, but other than that not really. I don't recycle or anything like that [laughs]."

The second group, those who believe Witchcraft has led them to be concerned about the environment but do very little about it, includes approximately half our young Witches. Reasons for inaction include fear of politics, avoidance of politics, being too young to vote, and lack of interest in environmental activism. A number in this group indicate that aspects of their personal situation make environmentalism difficult. Some say that they are not sure what to do, and others indicate that the pressures of work and study leave little time for environmental action. A few say they are lazy. For example, the British Witch Sophie says she is an environmentalist "to a point. I actually feel kind of bad that I don't do more than I do. Unfortunately I am chronically lazy and totally do as little as I can possibly get away with." Sophie further reports that recycling is quite difficult in her residence hall. Similarly, Water asserts that Witchcraft has made him more aware of environmental issues but that the pressures of working, studying, and caring for a sick parent leave him little time for such activities.

To some extent, the resistance to activism among this second group of contemporary young Witches reflects a more general individualism that permeates contemporary Witchcraft and Western culture more universally. Alexis de Tocqueville in 1835 defined individualism as "a calm and considered feeling which disposes each citizen to isolate himself from the mass of his fellows and withdraw into the circle of family and friends; with this little society formed to his taste, he gladly leaves the greater society to look out after itself" (1969, 506). More recently, Zygmunt Bauman (2001) argues that contemporary Western societies are undergoing a relentless individualization.

Individualism works, as Tocqueville suggests, by focusing attention on the concerns and issues of the individual to a degree that other concerns are simply ignored. Aspen, an Englishwoman, makes this point in our context: "Witchcraft is linked with nature, but I just don't seem to have many environmental issues." John, an American, specifically draws attention to the individualistic nature of his relationship with the environment: "What really struck me was the passion for an individualistic relationship with one's faith and particularly with nature. I am a very, very outdoorsy person. I love to be outside. Very active in Boy Scouts, and the fact that you have a culture, an entire religious culture, that is based on trying to harmonize with nature more so than just utilize it for our own purposes struck me as something that I liked a lot."

Individualism is an element of Witchcraft, as we have seen, in that each person may develop his or own form of spirituality and can practice alone, and because most of the young Witches learn about and practice Witchcraft outside the coven system, this individualism is more developed among them than in the earlier generation of practitioners. For most of the young Witches, individualism influences their relationship both to the divine and to environmentalism. Although they may think that the environment is important and even develop some sophisticated ideas about respect for nature, as John has, this does not translate into political activism because of their individualistic approach to life.

Members of the third group, approximately two-fifths of interviewees, are involved in environmental activism of various types: writing letters to politicians and newspapers; voting for environmentally oriented political parties; participating in environmental marches, petitions, or protests; donating money to environmental causes such as the World Wildlife Fund or People for the Ethical Treatment of Animals; and participating in environmental organizations such as Friends of the Earth and local environmental groups.

About politics, Debbie says: "I do tend to go for parties that deal with the environment." However, she was not sure whether this is a product of her Witchcraft or something she would do anyway. A few in this group make similar suggestions when describing their intentions to vote green—they might have voted green independent of Witchcraft. However, the majority say that their support of the Greens is clearly a product of their Witchcraft, as does Carolyn: "I realize that nature is sacred."

At least ten report that they have supported an environmental group or cause financially through memberships or donations. For example, Vanessa declares: "My sister and I are involved with endangered species; we send money and we get things from them." Bianca has been more activist: "When I was in [a particular town], I was in Friends of the Earth and we had this food action and we had like a big campaign to stop GM [genetically modified] planting because it was going on quite a lot, but on the sly; . . . it was quite an interesting thing to be involved [in]."

At the more dedicated end of the spectrum of environmental activism, Cailin describes how concern for the environment has become "the number one thing in my life." She is volunteering fifteen hours a week with a bird rehabilitation association and an animal shelter. Although she was previously concerned about the environment, she notes, Witchcraft has led her to a much stronger and deeper sense of its importance. Cailin's is not the most common response in our interviews, although it is not an isolated one, with at least five people reporting involvement in environmental groups and actions that involve more than an hour a week of their time.

Antienvironmentalism

One of the clearest indications of the proenvironmentalist stance of young Witches is the absence of any strong antienvironmentalist views. Even those who did not see a link between environmentalism and Witchcraft were still likely to report proenvironmentalist attitudes, such as thinking that recycling was important or that there were significant environmental issues that should be addressed.

Jodie thinks that global warming is still a long way off and nothing to be worried about, and Susan suggests that some environmentalist groups are "a bit extreme. I mean some of them just go a tad overboard—like some of the big protests of Greenpeace." In a similar vein, Kevin thinks that some environmentalists are not concerned enough about the needs of humans: "I am generally for the environment. I recognize that there has to be a balance between business and environment, or using the environment and preserving the environment. So I don't think that all land should be allowed to grow over with vegetation and allow animals to live there, because humans need urban settings."

These are some of the strongest antienvironmentalist statements we heard. In other words, almost all the young Witches are positively oriented toward environmentalism, although the extent of their concern and activism varies considerably. However, none dismiss the concerns of environmentalists and none indicate that they are strongly opposed to environmentalists.

Conclusion

Young Witches, on the whole, are not politically active, although most support gender equity and environmentalism. As Geertz's definition of religion suggests, the images and symbols of Witchcraft—particularly the symbol of the Goddess both as a reflection of the divine and powerful feminine and as embodied nature—influences the "moods and motivations" of the participants. But symbols are always multivocal and can be interpreted in various ways. As Bianca, Jackie, and Zack, among others, illustrate, one can worship the Goddess without embracing the basic tenets of feminism or environmentalism. Alternative images exist within Witchcraft, as Melissa's high priest's comments suggest. However, through reading some of the classic and major books on Witchcraft and interacting with other Witches on the Internet or in person, most of these young people have made the ecological and gender equity imagery of the Goddess, even in a somewhat watered down version, part of their thinking, as can be seen by the lack of strong antienvironmental or antigender equity sentiment. Even the two men who argue against women being in the military modify their claims, one stating that if women really want to participate they should, the other saying that women should have equal opportunity in other areas of the labor force.

A small number of the young Witches are activists for either gender issues or the environment. For some, there is an elective affinity between their religion and their politics. Others became activists after finding

Witchcraft. In some instances books they have read or people they have met encourage this activism.

However, there is a countervailing trend in the religion. The individualism that is part of the larger society and embedded in Witchcraft discourages traditional political activity as people look inward. Giddens (1991) argues that in late modernity a new form of politics has developed, which he refers to as life-politics. It is a politics in which, through self-transformation and actualization, people's life choices become political acts. The example he uses is the second wave of the women's movement, which took as its motto "The personal is political." An equally good example would be the environmental movement, in which the demand for recycled paper has encouraged in some communities curbside pickups of used paper for recycling. Even those young Witches not active in traditional politics are participating in life politics—in their daily lives, they are rethinking gender issues and expressing concern about the natural world.

Vignette

Annie—The Moral World of Teenage Witches

The first book I read was *How to Turn Your Boyfriend into a Toad.* I had a boyfriend I wanted to turn into a toad so bad, at fourteen. It didn't work— I was really upset. *Annie tells this story of her first exploration into Witchcraft with a glint in her eye and a small smile on her face. She delights in the memory and enjoys thinking about both her naïveté and her attempted wickedness at age fourteen.*

Annie is a lithe young woman with sandy light-brown hair. She has the look of a pixie, with somewhat short legs, a lean body, and bright blue eyes. She is a quiet thoughtful woman, more likely to listen than to speak. She is now twenty and studying at a U.S. state university to become a high school English teacher. Her minor is philosophy, specifically theology, which she is studying for the pleasure of learning more about religious theory. She has always loved to read and now is as likely to read about religion, whether Witchcraft or another religion, as to read novels. Although her first foray into Witchcraft was driven by a desire for revenge, her path began with questioning the religion in which she was raised.

I had so many questions about Catholicism and Christianity in general, so I went to bookstores and would look in the Christianity section. They never covered anything like this [the type of issues discussed in Witchcraft books]. So then I would go to the philosophy section. When I went to the philosophy section, the New Age section was right there and I was like, OK. So I kind of ended up drifting over to the New Age section and I started reading all these different books. At first, Witchcraft was, like, I get to turn my ex-boyfriend into a toad, you know, things like that. But then as I started reading it I realized this is an entirely different thing than how it was portrayed in . . . the media and so I started reading and research[ing]. I started reading things about God and spirituality and a lot of stuff by Starhawk and other things that were really just pertaining to a philosophy behind Witchcraft and not necessarily the religion. And I started learning about all the different rituals and the magic. I started getting into Buddhism and all the East Asian stuff too, and so I found that that was really incorporated into Witchcraft. So I was so excited. So then I started balancing the two. It really helped me realize that Christianity just wasn't for me.

Annie was sixteen when she first began to seriously study Witchcraft and eighteen when she converted, which for her entailed telling her parents and her priest of her decision. She told her parents: "I am not going to church anymore, I don't believe in it." They're fine—I was so surprised. They were like just, "Don't tell your brother," because he is thirteen. But he is having a lot of questions now too. So he is coming to me with questions, and he doesn't know. So he is starting to ask me, "Who was Jesus?" and "Who's God?" and "If God's all good, why is there a hell?" and things like that. So maybe it runs in the family [laughs].

Annie did not want to simply run away from the Catholic Church. She felt it was important to speak to her priest, explain her decision, and say good-bye. She told him: I didn't believe that the Bible was divinely inspired. I didn't believe that Jesus resurrected. I didn't believe that he was the son of God. I don't believe in the idea of sin. I don't believe that we need to be saved from anything. I don't believe that there is a hell. I believe that we all go to one place and have rebirth. *Initially he did not understand and could not give her his blessing, but ultimately he told her that he saw that she had her reasons and did not try to dissuade her from leaving the Church.*

Although quiet, almost shy, Annie began a weekly column on spirituality in the student newspaper at her conservative university. Not surprisingly, her focus is on alternative spiritual expression. She said everyone on the staff is excited about the column, but not all the readers feel the same. I get flack from the readers, who are usually . . . fundamentalists, like fundamental Christians or Muslims. But otherwise everyone seems to love it. I am amazed at people who can go through life just thinking that this [their religion] is the only way. I want to change that. I want to say, "Look, you can learn so much from other people if you would just stop thinking you are right." You know. So I don't think I'm right either, but I really don't know, but . . . for me, this [Witchcraft] is where I'm comfortable. *The notion that all spiritual paths are valid is an idea that permeates Witchcraft and much of Eastern spiritual thought. For Annie, intellectual and spiritual openness is central, as is a notion of accepting diversity in lifestyle and behavior.*

Annie defines herself as a feminist. Although she believes that Wicca is not about feminism, she sees her own commitment to gender equality as part of what made Wicca particularly exciting for her. I think being a feminist I am much more conscious of women's issues as well, and I think that the female plays such an important role in Witchcraft and I don't think she plays a very important role in other monotheistic traditions. I think that for a female, it [Witchcraft] is much more open, but not just for females, I think it is for homosexuals as well. I think for males who don't want to live up to the male stereotype of a macho guy all the time. I mean, I definitely think that coming into Witchcraft, it is just open, it is for anyone who really wants to. They can just come in, sit down, and feel accepted right away. Like you don't have to work for that acceptance. You are already accepted just for being who you are, and I don't see that in any other religion.

Part of the ethics of openness that Annie sees in Wicca is an acceptance of alternative gender roles and of homosexuality. But it also includes the notion of people accepting themselves, particularly of women learning to love the bodies they have. I think coming into Wicca I realized a lot of the media is portraying how girls should be a certain way, how we should look a certain way, and how we have all these magazines telling us what to do and how to get a guy and how to impress someone. That is really not necessary. But it took . . . my spiritual belief and feminism for me to realize I don't have to look like that. . . . but it is so unconscious, especially because now I am going to be a teacher and I go to high schools and I do observations and these girls there are starving themselves. It is just that I see that because it is not necessary. They are beautiful just the way they are and I don't think many women realize that today.

Like many in Witchcraft, Annie sees women and their bodies as a reflection of the Goddess and therefore beautiful. Annie fits the physical ideal of contemporary

U.S. society, but she refrains from wearing makeup or a complicated hairstyle that would require blow-drying or too much fussing. Although slim, Annie feels that without feminism and Witchcraft she would seek to be even thinner, as one cannot be too thin in U.S. youth culture—if one wears a size four it would be better to wear a two, and even better to fit into a zero at the Gap. She contends that the ethic of acceptance she sees in Witchcraft must include a notion of self-acceptance. Witchcraft and feminism both help her fight against what she views as the societal pressure to be constantly weight conscious, and to focus on what are defined as her bodily imperfections.

Openness and respect for other people's points of view and acceptance of diversity are important parts of Annie's moral universe. In describing what attracted her to Witchcraft, she tells us: I think the Wiccan Rede at first, when you read the last line [If it harm none, do as thou will], it is like the golden rule, but it is so much more poignant and said . . . so much better than the golden rule because as long as you don't harm anyone; . . . you can't completely not harm anyone because you are always going to do it indirectly, but I think there is something about just living by that one tenet that it is so much more difficult than just "Love your neighbor." . . . So it just helped me relate to it better and for me it helped.

It is a very open and accepting religion and I was—when I was a Christian, I was very homophobic, I was very anti, you know, no sex before marriage and all that. But it [Witchcraft] helped me realize now that that is all OK. Like you can accept that. And even though for me personally that doesn't work for me, it works for somebody else. That helped me become conscious of other people too, and I realized that [other] people have their own world, I have my own world, and we can come together and I can learn so much from other people, where in Christianity I really couldn't.

So it really helped me—if I could say one thing—it helped me open up and I was just thinking, conscious of everything that surrounds me. I am a much more conscious individual than I was at thirteen or fourteen. I am more conscious of everything that is going on around me. I love to listen to people and what they . . . have to say, what they believe. And when I was Christian, I was so worried about going around and converting everyone because I wanted to save everyone's soul. You know, I was trying to help. But now I can just listen and I can understand. You know, these people aren't doomed in the afterlife; . . . this is something that I can relate to these people, I can learn something from these people, I don't have to be afraid for these people. These are elders or these are other people that I can relate to and learn from and then I can incorporate their spiritual beliefs into my system too. I am not in a bubble anymore. I can reach out and talk to different people.

In addition to her growing acceptance of difference, Annie has also become more environmentally conscious. I love how we have a holiday with both the equinoxes. Everything is set around nature and I have become so much more conscious of nature itself. I am much more careful—when I was maybe thirteen, I would throw trash on the ground, and I wasn't respectful of what was around me and now I realize, this isn't my property. I can't just do what I want with it. So, I am much more clean, I am much more careful about what I say to other people, but I am also much more careful about what I do to the earth. I always recycle now, and I'm just much more conscious of ecology and just the earth in general.

Annie's moral world is a complex one. She tries to incorporate a sense of openness to other people, to their sexual orientation, their views, and their religious perspective with a sense of caring. The notion of care is important for her. She would include in this a sense of caring for others, caring that all individuals are treated fairly, and caring for the earth. She also has a strong ethic of individual responsibility and individual autonomy. The Wiccan Rede for her is a license not to act irresponsibly but to act as one thinks is right for oneself, within the context of taking responsibility for the impact of one's actions on others. Annie sees the Wiccan worldview influencing her life choices and how she interacts with others and the earth. She maintains something of a desire to proselytize. As a Christian she wanted to save souls; as a Wiccan she desires again to share her joy in her new worldview—trying to get others to see that whatever path they choose, they can honor others' diversity, whether of religious expression, sexual orientation, race, ethnicity, or gender.

Annie believes that she was drawn to Witchcraft not only because of its openness but also because the religion fits her sense of what is right. As soon as I started researching Wicca, it really all came together and I started postulating and theorizing more, and then I realized that on my own I would theorize and think about my own innate belief system, like what do I really believe happens after death, and the more I researched Witchcraft, the more I realized that is what I believe. It wasn't battling to try to live up to that standard like in Christianity where you have to believe, you have to accept, you have to believe something—it was something that I already believed.

For Annie, Witchcraft has both helped to provide a framework for her beliefs and moral standards and helped her further develop them. She would be the first to say that she is not a perfect person, that she does not always live up to her moral standards, but she remains concerned about how her actions and beliefs influence the world around her. In becoming an English teacher she wants not only to earn a living but also to make a difference in others' lives. Her religion, she believes, reinforces her desire to change the world around her, to be more accepting of diversity and more open to alternatives.

CHAPTER SIX

If It Harm None,
Do As Thou Will

Annie's description of her moral universe in the foregoing vignette involves many of the themes repeated in our interviews. Almost all the
young people we spoke to say that they are drawn to the openness and acceptance of diversity—of belief, of race, of sexual orientation—that they
find in Witchcraft. Many describe becoming better people as they become
more aware of the effects of their actions on others and themselves. Self-
acceptance and self-love are part of this moral universe. Instead of seeing
self-acceptance as selfishness, it is part of their larger notion of acceptance
and understanding of the world, of both self and others. Just as they see
their own bodies as beautiful whatever its shape, so they see others' as
beautiful. Almost all we interviewed saw Witchcraft as providing them
with not a set of prescriptions but an ethical system that influences how
they act in the world. (These testimonies were spontaneous, as we did not
include a question on morals or ethics in our interview schedule.)

Vanessa, who attends the same university as Annie and belongs to the
same Wiccan Society, found that Catholicism, the religion she was raised
in, "just wasn't working for me at all." She was drawn to Witchcraft because it "wasn't full of damnation and punishment. It was just everything,
like the gods are loving and cruel at the same time because nature is. It is
not just good versus evil all the time. It is a complete balance of everything. That is just how I saw it. It just brought harmony and balance to
my life." Vanessa's understanding of ethics and morality in this statement

reflects the immanent theology of Witchcraft, which defines good and evil relationally with respect to ongoing individual and community struggles. Rather than seeking ultimate and transcendental explanations for good and evil, Witchcraft, like other forms of Goddess worship and some indigenous religions, understands human life, nature, and the Goddess as ambiguous entities in which good and evil, or pleasant and unpleasant events, are interwoven. It is a different sense of morality than that presented in Christianity, Judaism, or Islam, in which good and evil are defined with reference to a transcendent male deity who provides a set of rules or laws.

Some commentators have found the relational understanding of ethics in Witchcraft problematic. For example, religious studies scholar Melissa Raphael (1996) argues that the "thealogy" of Goddess Spirituality does not provide a good explanation of suffering and pain, particularly of the innocent, such as children dying of hunger, noncombatants dying during wars, or even illnesses for which there is no cure. She suggests that the image of the divine or Mother Nature as neither good nor bad but merely as seeking a balance results in the acceptance of arbitrary unhappiness for some. This, she believes, ultimately cannot provide transcendence, which she tells us is necessary to accomplish two important functions of religion: first, to "do some of the most important work of a popular religious theory, namely, to reconcile people to existential pain and to construct meaning in the face of it" (210); second, to provide criteria to enable individuals to fight against evil and work for an alternative future. (The first of Raphael's issues we discussed in Chapter 3; we turn now to the second.)

Other commentators disagree with Raphael, arguing that to abandon the transcendental ethics of the monotheistic traditions does not lead to the problems she identifies. Michael York, who would agree with Vanessa's comments, asserts that all forms of paganism, including contemporary Paganism and Witchcraft, view the cosmos as neither moral nor immoral but as amoral. It is humans who infuse the universe with "an aesthetic telos that is to become the foundation of ethical action and aspiration" (2004, 8). For York the Pagan notion of morals stands in stark contrast to the abstract universal laws that permeate Western moral thought. York, like Barbara McGraw (2004), who conducted a study of a Dianic coven in the San

Francisco Bay Area, argues that it is the influence of Kant's ideas on contemporary Western moral philosophy that leads individuals to seek out
transcendental moral laws. Both York and McGraw contend that Kant's
ethical system originates from the monotheistic tradition in which an omnipotent God provides his followers with a set of abstract laws that must
be followed. Like York, McGraw suggests that contemporary Witchcraft
provides an ethical system in sharp contrast to Kant's: instead of abstract
principles, McGraw tells us, Witchcraft relies on a radical form of empathy—similar to the ethical system of girls suggested by Gilligan (1982).
Gilligan argues that girls' moral system is not based on an adherence to
universal laws, which Lawrence Kohlberg (1969) believes are the highest
level of moral development. Instead, Gilligan argues, girls make moral
choices from within a set of social relations, attempting to empathetically
find a way to meet everyone's needs. McGraw asserts that Witches similarly make moral decisions through empathy, not through universal laws.

In one sense empathetic concern for others leads to an individualized
form of transcendence that provides the moral imperative to fight against
"evil" and work for alternative futures, which Raphael is concerned will be
lost. Drawing on the work of Charles Taylor (1989, 1992), we have argued
earlier that young Witches' turn toward reflexive self-awareness does not
lead to selfishness but to authenticity and to a broader appreciation of, and
consideration for, other people and concerns beyond the self.

Although most of the young people we spoke to are not philosophy
majors and do not frame their ethical system as an alternative to Kant's, they
clearly demonstrate an ethical system based on a radical form of empathy.
They report over and over that Witchcraft makes them more accepting
people. Although most do not see themselves as crusaders for social or
political change, many do see themselves as living lives that would provide
a more ecologically balanced, just, and kind world.

In part the difference between Raphael's concerns about Goddess Spirituality and our respondents' sense of their religion may lie in the teenagers' not being theologians. They are not haunted by an extensive education
in the theology of transcendental ethics and may not notice the contra-
dictions that bother Raphael. In much the same way, Christians find solace
in their religion, even though philosophers question the apparent contra-

diction between an all-loving, omnipotent God and the suffering in the world. The ethics of teenage Witches are formed in relationships as they struggle to make moral and ethical choices about how they live in the world.

The Wiccan Rede, Self Interest, and the Other

Laurel suggests that she likes being a Witch because, among other things: "You know it's not like you have to go to church every week on a Sunday—and there's no actual set concrete rules as well. The basic rule of it is: 'If it harm none, do as I will,' which is, you know, as long as you don't hurt anyone else you can pretty much do whatever you like, which offers a lot of freedom in itself." The notion of having freedom and not being constrained by a series of what appear to be arbitrary rules is important to young Witches. Denise, who was raised in Reformed Judaism, notes: "I wasn't really into sacrificing being who I am, so I couldn't be a good Jew or a good Christian." But most acknowledge that the Wiccan Rede does not give them carte blanche. For example, Charles tells us of the Rede: "Long as it doesn't hurt anybody, then go ahead. So I take that quite literally to mean, don't hurt people with it [your actions]."

Not hurting anyone is not always easy, as Charlotte, an Englishwoman, acknowledges: "It seems very simple, but . . . sometimes there are only a limited number of options I have, and any one of them is going to cause hurt to someone, and sometimes you just have to take the one that is going to cause the least hurt. Sometimes even the most hurt, because that is what you feel is the right thing that has to be done." Many of the young people we spoke to are quite concerned that their behavior, particularly their spell work, not hurt other people. Rachel speaks for many when she discusses why she would not do a love spell: "It interferes with another's will. I mean, you can't really make anybody do anything that they are not going to do anyway. But even that little bit is just an infringement, you know, and I think that if I did actually cast a spell like that, then fell in love with somebody, I would always kind of wonder. People have stories like they cast spells for finding love, and then they meet somebody they just can't get rid of. And I [would] always wonder is this because I tried to bring this person to me and get lasting love, and it is not worth it. It is not worth having to wonder that." Love magic is the most often discussed as something that young people avoid, as they are concerned about binding others' wills, something they see as in contradiction to the Wiccan Rede. Some young Witches are so concerned that they might inadvertently harm someone through any of their spells that they infrequently do them. As Pete tells us:

> Unless all the physical options are out, and even then I will look ten times more harder, then I will do the spell. If it is an instance, [for example,] I lost something, and I need to get that back, and I have done everything that I could and I just [say to myself] let's light a candle and say a little prayer almost as a spell, you know, I will do that. And it is very hard to define doing the spell work, and because even lighting the candle and saying a prayer is spell work. Even wishing is pretty much spell work, because you are putting out the idea, you are putting out your will and your goal and hoping it manifests into something real. So I am very, very cautious in even what I say. If someone says, "Oh, I wish you would fall over," I don't even say that. I'm going, "No, I don't, because that could happen to me ten times worse, or that could come back to me." So I don't.

Li similarly notes the Law of Return affecting his behavior. "I look out for other people more. Just try to be nice, because the whole thing of what you do comes back to you times three."

The Law of Return, which is a corollary to the Wiccan Rede, states that whatever someone does, either good or bad, will return to them either three- or tenfold. Karen notes the similarity of this to Christian notions of sin: "I guess you could say with the Christian religion they have the threat of Satan there all the time saying, "If you do this, Satan will come and get you and you'll go to hell" and all that. It's kind of the same in Wicca. If you do this, it's going to come back times three, you know, so don't do this. It's kind of the same." But others suggest that there is a difference. For example, Percy tells us: "I've always felt that the idea of the

devil is all very well and good except for it seems to be missing the problem in that sense that humans do the misdeeds themselves and they're the
people responsible for their actions. If you do something evil—undeniably
evil—it wasn't put into you by some divine entity. It was your choice and
you should take responsibility for it yourself. So I don't even believe in the
devil at all. I mean, why should I believe in something as a scapegoat when
if I do a misdeed I should own up to it and say, 'Look, you know, I did this.'"

In her ethnography of contemporary Witchcraft, *Magic, Witchcraft, and
the Otherworld,* Greenwood (2000b, 203) argues that the "Wiccan Rede is
a problematic basis for the creation of morality in everyday life: it is difficult to interpret practically." Quoting from an article in *Circle Network
News,* she suggests that there are three problems with the Wiccan Rede as
a basis for ethics. First, for fear of creating dogma, practitioners have not
sufficiently questioned the Rede. Second, the notion of "harm none" has
not been adequately debated. Third, the Rede is too broad and open to
personal interpretation to provide an ethical base for a community. It is
true that the Rede, like the golden rule, is not questioned. However, as illustrated by Annie and Pete, young Witches do question and think about
what it means to "harm none." But it is the last of Greenwood's criticisms
that is possibly the most important, as it raises an issue not unique to
Witchcraft or Neopaganism, but to ethics under the conditions of late or
postmodernity.

Traditional morality is based on a series of rules—or a set of "oughts"
and "ought nots." Acting morally in the past "was not a matter of choice:
it meant, on the contrary, avoiding choice—following the customary way
of life. All this changed, however, with the gradual loosening of the grip
of tradition. . . . and the growing plurality of mutually autonomous con-
texts in which the life of a rising number of men and women came to be
conducted" (Bauman 1993, 4). With the growth of individualism and the
demise of the grand narratives upon which traditional ethics were based,
there is now a marketplace of alternative ethical programs from which
each person must choose. Bauman warns us that this freedom often feels
oppressive, as we are confronted daily with ethical questions and issues
that we must engage without a fixed roadmap for action. This does not,
for Bauman, result in complete moral relativism. Quoting Steven Connor

(1993), he suggests that "the lack of absolute values no more makes all values interchangeable than the absence of an agreed upon gold standard makes all world currencies worth the same" (Bauman 1995, 6).

Traditionally, according to Bauman, religions have provided individuals with an ethical scheme. These schemes never anticipated that people would be sinless but provided them the means to find redemption. This, he argues, has disintegrated with the advent of globalization, in which there is no single moral standard. Instead the state has developed laws, which supercede morals, take responsibility from the individual, and at the same time create greater uncertainty, as we must face moral decisions without knowing for certain what is right (Bauman 1995). Manuel Castells (1997) contends that one response to this uncertainty is the growth of fundamentalism, which he views as a retreat into certainty in the face of the "unbearable" levels of choice and freedom that contemporary globalized and mass-mediated society offer. In contrast to fundamentalism, contemporary Witchcraft celebrates choice, individualism, and freedom. It is within this context that Witches seek an ethical framework.

McGraw (2004) argues that the Rede and its corollary, the Law of Return, provide an ethical framework, which she calls "radical partiality," consistent with a focus on the self, a sense of freedom, and a belief in individual choice. The Law of Return requires that each person empathetically treats, wishes for, and does for another as she or he would be willing to have return to her or him three- or tenfold. Self-interest is viewed not as selfishness but as the basis of the creation of connection with others and with the natural world. Each person must think of receiving what she or he "sends out." This is illustrated by Mish, who tells us what it means to her to live as a Witch:

Following the natural cycles of things, worshipping the Goddess, and . . . not harming anything that lives, basically. Discovering yourself. Though that sounds very selfish. Well, it doesn't sound selfish, but it sounds very self-orientated. And Witchcraft isn't, because Witchcraft is about when people are in trouble, not charging in there and saying, "I'm a Witch," and then help[ing], because that is bad. But just gently interfering, trying to make things better. [When asked if she felt this was noble, she responds:] No, not noble. Noble . . . is what Amnesty International does. Being a hedge Witch is sort of a scaled-down version.

The young Witches in our study see the Wiccan Rede as creating a context in which they attempt to become responsible for their actions and for their treatment of other people, animals, and Mother Nature. This does not mean that none in our study act in ways they regret. Brian confides: "When I got upset at my mom, I asked for vengeance on her and unfortunately she broke her foot, and she chooses to not believe that that was of my causing, but I do. It was just too coincidental for it to not be. I worked through my guilt and eventually came to a place where I realize why I did it, and I have forgiven myself, and I think I have wiped it clean from my karma plate, if you will. It definitely came back to me. I felt very bad for a long time." Whether or not Brian is actually responsible for his mother's broken foot, what is important is his ability to think through his anger at his mother, take responsibility for it, and come to a resolution about it. Self-reflection is an important element of his sense of morality. He must reflect on his actions, magical and mundane, to determine his future behavior in the world. Brian understands that his actions returned to him. His mother broke some bones, but he felt guilty and unhappy with himself.

The Wiccan Rede as an ethic can be seen as legitimating selfishness. The individual's self-expression is limited only to the degree that his or her behavior does not cause another being harm, a tenet reinforced by the Rule of Return. Of course this is not always simple—as both Annie and Charlotte point out, any magical or mundane act can have unanticipated repercussions, and one's options are often limited. This concern has resulted, some young Witches report, in a choice rarely to do spells any longer, focusing instead on the celebration of the seasons or the veneration of the gods and goddesses. But, more importantly, we did not hear from these young people that they interpret the Wiccan Rede as permitting them to withdraw from the world. Instead they view it as a way to explore their own needs, desires, and development while remaining connected to others. In fact, they tell us that through exploring the self they are able to more fully engage with others, and to take responsibility for their interactions with others.

Caring for Others

Vivianne Crowley (2000) observes that healing spells are the most common spells novice Witches perform, as these spells display the Witches' magical prowess and indicate that they are using magic for kindly, not harmful, acts.[1] Like the earlier generation of Witches discussed by Crowley, young Witches are quick to note that they use magic for positive, not negative, goals. Young Witches in our sample describe spells to do better on exams, help partners get work or have success at job interviews, help ill relatives or pets, and help improve financial situations (see Chapter 3).

Seamus, an energetic young Irish American who serves as president of his university club, described in detail his efforts to save a suicidal friend. The young woman, he said, was raised in the mountains of New Hampshire and had a stressful childhood. Because her parents' financial situation is so precarious, she is on a full scholarship to the private U.S. university they both attend. Seamus describes a young woman who has suicidal tendencies exacerbated by alcohol consumption. He states that at the time of the incident, he was the young woman's best friend but, as he is gay, not her lover. One night after she had been drinking, she phoned Seamus crying and asked him to come to her room. When he got there, she told him how much he meant to her and said she wanted to give him her most prized possession, a stuffed toy carrot that had been with her since childhood. He said that the combination of her past history, her emotional state, her giving away her childhood toy, and her failure to refer to the future (such as by saying, "I'll see you tomorrow") made him realize she was suicidal. Although she kept saying she just wanted to go to sleep and he should leave, he stayed in her room until 4:30 in the morning. At that point he thought her sober enough to be safe alone.

When he returned to his own room he decided to do a ritual. As he describes this:

> If you absolutely, direly need something in order for you to be OK, or in order for someone else to be OK, like that comes through the hardest and I was extremely distraught and so I don't recall exactly what I did, but I took a whole bunch of herbs that had healing properties and kind of like mixed them together and I was pretty much

very fervent when this was going on. . . . I just went straight in and I had my need and I was very much, very pumped. . . . I was crying, actually, because I was so afraid and I was calling for my gods to please save her and to help her and to protect her, and she can't die like this and please don't let her take her life and I did a spell with some candles and with some herbals and I made a herbal sachet for her. I was like, "You can't have her, she is not going anywhere," and when—I don't know—when I tend to know that something is true and when I know that something is going to happen like it does, so I knew right then and there that I was asking for her life and they were going to give it to me and she was going to survive.

When he called her the next morning, he was pleased to hear her voice and learn that she had survived the night, but by the time he returned from classes in the afternoon she had been rushed to the hospital after being found unconscious by her roommate. She had taken a large number of pills and was close to death. When he and the roommate arrived at the hospital, the doctor spoke to them. As Seamus describes:

He explained to us that there was no reason why she should still be alive right now. The amount of stuff she took should have killed her and he doesn't understand how she made it this far. She should have been dead some hours ago, but she was still there, and all I could think was this vision of my God stuck in my head and I was holding on to that. And I knew that since I was there with her that night keeping her awake for however many more hours, keeping her from eating those pills. . . . Yeah, I knew that I had saved her life, but I gave her the sachet afterwards and told her that I did something to keep her around and I was glad that she was still here. And she took her . . . carrot back. . . . You know, I think that was the first life that I had saved with Witchcraft. And on that day I went to my altar and I said, "A life for a life"; I was like, "You gave me her, now I'm giving you mine," so I have been serving them [the Pagan deities] willingly ever since.

6.1 Teenager's altar in her room, UK. Photo by Emma Stanton.

Seamus's story is more dramatic than many. He has no doubt that his ritual is what saved his friend's life, although he acknowledges that his willingness to sit up with her the night before also helped. With the suicide rate among youth at such a high level, it is probably not unusual for young people to try to help one another through suicidal feelings or attempts. If one substituted Christian prayer for Pagan ritual, Seamus's behavior would seem quite consistent with being a Good Samaritan— helping a neighbor in need. Seamus's description of what happened does suggest that he felt more in control of the process than he would if he had used prayer, but nonetheless there is a similarity.

The ethics of teenage Witches are not completely different from those of their neighbors. Five of the young people in our sample note continuity between their present ethical system and that which they previously held as Christians. For example, Louise describes her discussion with a fellow student at her university:

One of my—I wouldn't call him my best friend, but—acquaintances, called Kevin, who is a highly intelligent person and a devout Catholic and was quite interested to sit down and talk to me one day about his beliefs as a Catholic and my beliefs as a Wiccan, and I realized they were virtually identical. Virtually all his views about what makes a good person and my views of what makes a good person and how you should live your life were the same. The only points that we disagreed on was what happens when you die. We [Witches] believe you get reincarnated and he believes you go to heaven. Or contraception—he doesn't believe in contraception, and he definitely [thinks] you shouldn't have sex [outside of marriage]. Wiccans think it is OK to have sex outside of marriage. The only thing you have to remember is don't bring children into the world if you don't want them. And protect your own well-being and other people's. Safe sex and don't hurt people, basically. And that was about all we disagreed on.

Percy reports: "I've always identified with Jesus' teachings in a very basic sense in saying, 'Yeah, I agree with 'Love thy neighbor.' It just makes sense." Tanya sees some of her ethical beliefs as a continuation of her upbringing:

I was brought up a Catholic and in a way I've kept some of those views from Catholicism. I'm not as strict as the Catholics but I've kept some of those views and somebody has actually said to me on-line that I have very Catholic views—very Christian views. . . . We [a person in a chat room and she] were talking about killing people in self-defense, if you killed someone, and I said, "Well, yeah, if you killed someone in self-defense, that would be you were defending yourself, so fair enough, but it would still be bad that you'd killed a person." And they said: "No, if this person was attacking you or your family, it's fair enough." [I said:] "Yes, but you'd still be bad because you'd killed that person—because you've taken a life." And they said, "Well, it is a Christian view." And I thought, "Well, it is part of my upbringing and I'm never going to get rid of that, probably."

So I suppose really that's a sort of homage to that. It's like I've got a statue that was my Nan's [grandmother's] of Mary, which is on my—sort of altar, I suppose you could call it. Because I've been brought up with it, I don't have a problem with it and I'm not particularly threatened by it, really.

The eclectic nature of Witchcraft, which allows individuals to incorporate elements of other religions that they see "working," makes it possible to incorporate the Virgin Mary or Jesus Christ as elements of Witches' practice. Salomonsen (2002) describes members of the Reclaiming Witchcraft collective in San Francisco attending church and incorporating elements of Christianity into their practice. Not all Witches, however, would view combining Christianity and Witchcraft as acceptable. For example, Zack tells us: "I met one person back in high school who claimed to be a Catholic Witch. It took a good deal of explaining to him, to explain that you are either a Witch or a Catholic. It is a belief system. It is not, basically, that you can just take from it what you want, although most people seem to do that." Nonetheless, Zack later in the interview contends: "So I believe that anyone who follows—well, actually all religions [that] work towards good are righteous. I have had discussions with Jehovah's Witnesses about that. But basically as long as you're headed toward the right path, I think it's all good." Ken, an American, similarly notes: "Most religions have the same basic rules, moral structure."

The sense that at least a few of these young people have of continuity with Christian ethics is not surprising—the vast majority of those in our sample were raised as Christians, and all were raised in societies in which the majority of people are Christians. Ethics, like other aspects of culture, must be understood as developing within a cultural milieu. However, despite the similarities, there is a significant difference between the two moral systems. In the Christian religion there is a clear set of precepts or rules that the individual is to follow. These are created from tradition, interpretation of the Bible, and, in the case of Catholics, Vatican decrees. This is very different from the focus on the individual and on individual determination of correct behavior found in Witchcraft. For Witches, each person, to use Bauman's (1993, 74) words, must "take responsibility for the other."

In Witchcraft, one who does something bad has to deal with the unpleasant consequences but is encouraged to take personal responsibility for one's actions. Both Christians and Witches try to avoid doing things that will have bad consequences, as Karen notes. However, as Vanessa contended earlier in this chapter (and as we discussed in Chapter 3), Witches understand unpleasant events, such as the death of a loved one, as a "normal" part of the balance of nature, whereas Christians see unpleasant events as a product of evil, or of God's will, that is to be transcended in either heaven or after the Second Coming of Christ. Witches' ethical system is based primarily not on their connection to God or gods but on their sense of the interconnectedness of life. As Mary describes: "I keep coming back to its [Witchcraft's] connection in the sense of a connection with the energy and forces that move through everything. And that sort of takes in the earth, the earth power, the universal paradigm, the spiritual, and particularly the spiritual energies within other people. It's the sense of connection and the ability to be personally responsible and to personally direct your path through that." For Witches, the earth and this life as lived now on earth are sacred. Although most believe in reincarnation, the arbitrator of action in the world is not one's next life, but one's connection now to all of life in this world.

Caring for the Earth

Part of being connected to others and the world for young Witches is a sense of being morally responsible for, or caring for, the earth and all living matter. Morgan informs us she is not a good Witch because she does not recycle, reuse, and reduce her consumption of nonrenewable resources sufficiently. Most, as we have seen, state that their religion makes them more aware of the environment and their moral responsibility to protect Mother Nature. Most are not activists or part of green political parties, but they do feel that their religious beliefs change their personal behavior. They are more mindful of picking up litter, recycling, and, in some cases, voting with environmental policies in mind. They see their treatment of fauna, flora, the landscape, and other people as influenced by their religious practices and beliefs. They speak repeatedly of Witchcraft's making them more caring people, as they see all life as a manifestation of the Goddess. They frequently note the ways they fall short of their ideal, but nonetheless they see Witchcraft as providing them with not precepts but a more general sense of how they should treat other people, animals, and the environment. As Annie illustrates in the vignette that precedes this chapter, her increased consciousness of others underscores that, although the Wiccan Rede is an important moral precept, morality within Witchcraft is derived to a large extent from an increased sensitivity to and respect for others.

A number of Witches described their increased concern for the environment in the context of a discussion about how Witchcraft has led them to have greater sensitivity to the concerns of others and greater respect for other people and the environment around them. Many say that Witchcraft has led them to be more tolerant and compassionate. For example, when asked how Witchcraft has shaped her day-to-day life, Tina states: "I've become more aware of environmental stuff and being considerate to others." Seamus, asked whether Witchcraft has changed his friends and relationships, replies: "I seem to be more compassionate. Because now I feel connected to everyone and I know my place in the universe and I know that we are all connected and it has kind of given me a better sense of duty and responsibility as far as how I am acting in regards to other people. It gives me a lot more reverence for the earth."

In his study of ethics and human relationships, *I and Thou*, the Jewish philosopher Martin Buber argues that I-it relationships treat another person as a detached "thing." In contrast, approaching another in the spirit of I-thou "establishes the world of relation" (1958, 6). Viewing other persons as "thou" involves understanding them as entangled in mutual relationships. Buber's understanding and that of another Jewish philosopher, Emmanuel Levinas (1969), who presents a similar relational ethic, are framed within the context of a transcendental relationship with deity as "other." However, Pagan scholars contend that this relational ethics can also be applied to the development of an interpersonal environmental ethics (Davy 2005). In a similar way, many of the young Witches discuss their changed attitudes toward the environment within the context of generally new ways of relating and living that include both humans and the environment. Harvey (2005, xi) describes animists as "people who recognize that the world is full of persons, only some of whom are human, and that life is always lived in relationship with others." While none of the young Witches describe themselves as animists, it is clear that the ethics of how they relate to "nature" is bound up with an ethics of how they relate to people.

Annie mentions her general attitude to relationships with other people when discussing whether Witchcraft had changed the way she relates to nature. Similarly, Chloe responds to a general question about whether Witchcraft had changed her in any way: "I think it has made me more aware of my own self—my own personal development as well as religious development. It has also made me feel a lot more in tune with the environment and surroundings, and that in turn makes you more concerned about your environment and your surroundings." These quotes suggest a link between deeper self-understanding and concern about acting in ways that demonstrate respect for both humans and the environment. For these young Witches, the growing concern with the environment does not develop out of moral injunctions but out of a worldview and ritual practices that frame the other-than-human world as important. Concern for the environment relies on a deeper self-understanding that allows these young people to transcend, to some degree at least, a self-centered gaze. The gaze moves out of the self toward others, both humans and other-than-humans. To use Buber's (1958) terms, relationships move from "I-it" to "I-thou."

The Pagan worldview emphasizes that humans are one part of the broader cycles of nature. The wheel of the year, the ethical maxim that Witches should "harm none," and the emphasis on the interconnection of all things as expressed in the law of threefold return—all encourage young Witches to think of themselves not just as individuals but as embedded in a network of relationships. The emphasis on relationship, respect, and orientation to nature as a valued "other" is clear in Jacqueline's passionate criticism of big business: "Well, we're destroying ourselves. Businesses care about money—they don't care about what trees they cut down, what animals they kill, they just want more money."

Diversity and Respect for the Other

Kevin suggests that the essence of Witchcraft is "acceptance, diversity, and variety." He emphasizes that, while something may work for him, he does not presume that his way of doing things should necessarily apply to others. Erica reports that "Witchcraft has probably made me a lot more understanding and more tolerant of other people." Zoë says she has become more tolerant of other religions: "I have friends who are very Christian and they usually have more problems with me [being a Witch] than I do with them." She discusses an interfaith debate at her university in which several members of her university Pagan group participated. She was taken aback by the Christians in the debate feeling that "they should talk to others and not try to convert them." She suggests that she and her [Witchcraft] friends "agreed [it] is much better if you don't force anything on anyone, especially religion, when it is such an important issue. Someone's religion is their religion; you don't go, 'No, no, if you don't believe what I believe you will go to hell.' No!"

This acceptance of religious diversity resonates in other aspects of these young people's lives. Although many hold strong opinions, particularly about environmentalism, they speak of being willing to listen to others respectfully. There are limits to this acceptance of diversity, as many of them, similar to their elders in Witchcraft, have negative views of what they call fundamentalists, or "fundies," in the United States. Greenwood (2000a) contends that Witchcraft was infused with an anti-Christian bias by one of the founders, Leland, who viewed Christianity as the religion of the rich and Witchcraft as a religion of those who were concerned with social justice and liberation. However, the lack of a "live and let live" attitude among some of the young may in part be the result of conflicts with students in Christian organizations. At West Chester University in the United States, where Helen Berger served as faculty advisor for the Wiccan Society, a group of Christian students disrupted one of the early meetings of the club. One of them called members of the Pagan group Satanists and informed them that they were damned. University policy requires that clubs be open to all students. The West Chester University club feared, without cause, that students from the Campus Crusade for

Christ would join their club in large numbers, vote each other into office, and change the focus of the club from Witchcraft to Christianity. The students claim that the Campus Crusade has done this on other campuses.

Although the student adherence to a notion of diversity may not be flawless, it is an important aspect of their self-definition and their behavior, as is clear in Annie's statement that she has become less homophobic since leaving Christianity and becoming a Witch. A number of the young men in our sample are gay and some of the women, lesbians. They claim that one of the things that drew them to Witchcraft was the condemnation of their sexuality in their families' religions and the acceptance they found within Witchcraft.

Morgan, speaking for many of the teen Witches, suggests that Witchcraft led to her coming to understand that "there are so many more ways of living a life, even in America. Just by being in the [Pagan] community, I have known more polyamorous people than anywhere else. I have known more adult gay men. I have known young gay men [laughs], the story of my life, and bisexual men, but older men living that life, I have met a lot more." Morgan is more part of the Neopagan community than some of the other teens in our sample; she is a member of her university Pagan society and is taking classes in town from an older Witch during her school year. The president of her university Pagan society is openly gay. Some in our sample are more isolated, mostly interacting with others only on the Internet or sometimes with the owners of local occult bookstores. But most of the young people have some contact with other Witches, even if it is only with the friends with whom they first explored Witchcraft. Nonetheless, most observe that either they have become more accepting of gays and lesbians, or that the tolerance for various lifestyles that they find in Witchcraft is consistent with their own beliefs. For example, Cailin tells us: "I'm a very, very liberal type of person. I am a very generalized hippy type of person. At my school, at my college, it is not really like that, . . . not a lot of people like me, and the people that generally gravitate toward me—my group of friends includes all the kind of out-there musician types, and the homosexuals, and the Wiccans, and just all the kind of "other" category-type people."

Jen informs us that, although involved with the Women's Center at her university, she is more interested in working for issues around sexual identity because her mother, now deceased, was a lesbian. She is aware of the discrimination that her mother suffered. Jen somewhat wryly notes that she did benefit from this discrimination, as her mother's romantic partner's income could not be counted toward Jen's financial aid package. But the acceptance of homosexuality she feels within Paganism is important, as it makes her feel more comfortable as the child of a lesbian, and she believes that others that she associates with support her own sense of social justice.

Sex, Drugs, and Self-Love

Bauman, in distinguishing the topic of his book *Postmodern Ethics* from a discussion of postmodern morals, notes that contemporary Western society is confronted by a number of moral dilemmas—some a continuation of those of previous eras and others that arise under current conditions. "The plight of pair relations, sexuality, and family companionship" (1993, 1) are three that he explicitly mentions. Given the ages of our respondents, few are in settled relationships and only one is married with a child. Most, however, are concerned with forming bonded relationships and with the issue of sexuality. Sexuality among teenagers is a controversial issue. Although not mentioned by Bauman, drug use is also a contemporary moral issue. We did not explicitly ask those we interviewed about either sex or drugs. However, a number of them discussed these issues with us.

Clarissa, echoing Morgan's comments, reports: "I've met [Pagans who are] a lot more relaxed and comfortable with their sexuality and don't necessarily define themselves as necessarily straight or gay or bi—some would say they're equiv, which maybe doesn't necessarily fall into any category [laughs], or a bit fairylike, which—they're all a bit strange, I think, sometimes in their sexual relations. It's all a bit colorful. But, yeah, I think Pagans are definitely more open to differences. Definitely more open." The sexual openness of Witches has been noted by several scholars of the movement (see, for example, H. Berger 1999; Pike 2001; Salomonsen 2002). Most young people in our sample claim to be solitaries but nonetheless have contacts with others in the Pagan community—if nowhere else then online and through books. They therefore, in most instances, have learned about this sexual openness.

The young Witches' responses must be understood in the context not only of their participation within the Neopagan community but also of their membership in the larger society. Pundits in the last two decades have expressed increasing concern about teenage sexuality, the spread of sexually transmitted diseases (STDs), and teenage pregnancy. This concern remains, although recent data in the United States suggest that there is a small increase in the age of first coitus and a corresponding decrease in the number of teenage births and the spread of STDs. Barbara Reisman and Pepper Schwartz (2002) review the literature on teenage sexuality in the United States, which indicates that the decrease in sexual activity noted by other scholars is most prevalent among white and Hispanic males. The rate of sexual activity among females has remained more or less constant, resulting, particularly among white youth, in a similar level of sexual activity for males and females. Reisman and Schwartz argue that although the double standard has not been eradicated, the data suggest that girls are gaining increased control over sexuality and demanding some level of commitment with sexual activity. Lillian Rubin (1990) a decade earlier argued that teenage sexuality is not random but related to a sense of commitment, even if this commitment is for only a few weeks. Benoit Denizet-Lewis (2004), however, contends that there is a growing trend, particularly in U.S. suburbs, of hooking up on the Internet, where teens get together explicitly and only for sexual activity. Many of the youth he interviewed said that they were too young to make a commitment and didn't want any of the problems they associate with a relationship. Most hoped to form a long-term relationship in their late twenties but in the interim wanted to have fun, which included having sex without commitment. He equates today's youth's interest in playing the field with that of their grandparents or great-grandparents in the 1930s, although noting that members of this earlier generation were not so often or so openly involved in sexual relationships. Denizet-Lewis argues that although both boys and girls participate in "hooking up" and many of the girls say it is equal, there seems an inherent inequality, as the boys' sexual pleasure is more often the issue than the girls'.

Clearly there is disagreement about whether sexuality among youth today involves greater or less commitment. In part, this may be a matter of semantics. What is clear is that most teenagers in the United States, England, and Australia are sexually active. Teenage sexuality raises thorny problems. The second wave of the women's movement defined sexual liberation as part of women's larger liberation. Early in the movement, concerns were raised that sexual liberation could be a form of exploitation of women (see Firestone 1970). Linda Jencson (1998) has raised a similar concern about the sexual openness among Witches.

Witchcraft as a religion celebrates sexuality; it also celebrates the self. Our respondents almost universally state that the religion has been self-empowering for them. In some cases they clearly make a link between their views on sexuality and their growing sense of self-worth. For example, Bianca describes how she believes Witchcraft has helped to create a different attitude toward sex than the one she learned in Catholic school:

I think it's [sex is] sacred. It really is the most sacred thing, but at the same time it's made me think. . . . It's not just what would I be like without Paganism in a way, just 'cause having read so much about sex and stuff it means that you're quite liberal. . . . You're not ashamed of your body or anything because, like, you're the Goddess and you don't need to worry and because of the power of women as well in Witchcraft and Paganism. . . . Like inhibitions and shame and all that kind of thing that I learned about in school assembly have gone. . . . The best person in the world in Christianity came without sex, so that seems to mean to me that sex is bad. . . . [Witchcraft] made me feel really free, and like it [sex] just really should be enjoyed and it's not something in itself to be ashamed of and it's the most sacred thing in the world as well. But it's also kind of made me think that . . . one-night stands are really awful because it's a sacred thing. It's not a sin. . . . But it's [Witchcraft] made me feel powerful, but it's made me have a lot of respect for sex as well. It's not made me feel powerful, but made me feel strong and free and beautiful.

Stella makes a similar observation: "With sexuality and things in our culture it's either one extreme or another, or you either suppress it or you're out there. But . . . I think Witchcraft is really helpful in that way to teach you that these things are natural and that there's nothing wrong with them."

The notion that Witchcraft gives at least some of these young people a sense of balance and makes them feel that their bodies are, as Erica phrased it, "temple[s]" influences their sense of taking control of sexuality and their bodies. For some, this same sense of seeing their bodies as temples makes them resist drugs—even legal ones such as tobacco. Zack, for example, tells us: "I don't do drugs unless like medication; I don't smoke. If I drink it is only moderately. This is just again to keep—just my value system because with [my] religion, I don't want to bring personal harm to my body." Several others tell us that they believe "harm none" includes themselves and that they have a responsibility to take care of their bodies. Susan believes Witchcraft "helped me go off the drugs as well. . . . I think I'm more aware of what's going into my body now. I mean, I still smoke cigarettes, but I'm trying to give them up. I'm more aware of what I put in [my body], and it makes me a better person. And losing a lot of friends as well through drugs, I sort of thought, 'No, I don't want to go down that path.' The more I read, the more it was like, drugs are bad for you and they don't help you spiritually. I think getting in touch with the Goddess helped as well."

Our study does not permit us to determine if young Witches are more or less likely to smoke, drink heavily, take drugs, or have extramarital relations than are other teenagers. As is noted by both the teenagers in our study and scholars of the religion, Witchcraft celebrates sexuality in all its forms. Neopagan parents, like other liberal parents, are often ambivalent about teenage sexuality (H. Berger 1999). Nonetheless, the current reality is that most teenagers are choosing to be sexually active. Some of the young Witches believe that their relationship with the Goddess makes them better able to gain control of their bodies and their sexuality. Similarly, with drug use there are countervailing tendencies within the Witchcraft community; some adult Witches advocate the use of drugs to put them in an altered state of being. But, as some of the young people in our sample report, their adherence to the concept of harming none includes themselves.

Part of not harming the self is getting off, or not using, harmful drugs and having a comfortable relationship with their bodies and their sexuality.

Conclusion

"In contrast to Kant who considers freedom the obligation incumbent on individuals to act in accordance with the transcendental and universal moral law, freedom for the pagan is the this-worldly ability for humans to develop and evolve an ethic in the face of an amoral world of nature," argues York (2004, 8). For Pagans, York reminds us, the divine is not separate from humans—beyond or above the everyday world—but in the world; it permeates all aspects of it. For young Witches, like their elders, the world is not to be shunned or avoided. Although most believe in reincarnation, the focus of their spirituality is on this world, not the next. It is within this context that they create an ethical system not based on a priori categories but negotiated through active engagement of the other.

Several of the young Witches in our study advocate moral relativism. For example, Brianna, who is an anthropology and criminal justice major tells us: "I don't really believe in a concept of good versus evil because everything can be evil, like something can be evil to some people but good to other people. Like materialism, it is good in this society, but in tribes in South Africa or anywhere else, it is really an evil. So it's kind of relative." Brianna's focus on relativism appears, at least in part, to be an outgrowth of her anthropology studies, but an advocacy of relativism is common within the liberal segment of the larger culture. This belief in relativism is consistent with late modern ethics. As Bauman (1993, 1995) informs us, in late modernity there is no single set of precepts around which moral life can be formed. Late modernity or postmodernity pushes us each into freedom—not the freedom, as Kant would suggest, of choosing to follow universal laws but the freedom of having to choose correct action without the help of guidelines.

The moral precepts in Witchcraft are few and, as Greenwood (2000b) notes, open to individual interpretation. But this has not resulted in an ethical wasteland for the teenagers we interviewed. Instead, like all people in late modernity, young Witches must become responsible for making daily choices about their interactions with others and with the environment. Young Witches tell us that they take this responsibility seriously, even if they often feel they could do more. They also take seriously the notion that they themselves are Goddess and God—that the divine resides in them as it does in all of nature. For Witches, we are each the embodiment of the divine. The young people report that this sense of themselves as part of the divine combines with including themselves as among those that should not be harmed by their own actions to help them resist drugs and feel in control of their sexuality.

The young Witches we spoke to repeatedly describe how Witchcraft has significantly influenced the ethical choices they make. Witchcraft encourages them to reflect on the consequences of their actions as they see themselves in a web of relations with other humans and with nature more generally. Through this process they have developed what McGraw (2004) calls "radical partiality"—the notion of empathetically engaging the other to determine moral behavior. These young people live in a world in which they no longer seek transcendentally guaranteed moral certitude. This has not resulted in selfishness or unbridled hedonism. Rather, through their engagement with the Wiccan Rede, the Law of Return, and the images of the Goddess as bearer of life and death, they attempt to participate in what Bauman (1993, 74) speaks of as "taking responsibility for the other."

It is worth once again stressing that the individualism of Witchcraft does not necessarily lead to selfishness. Rather, Witchcraft can lead young people to develop a strong sense of self. Similarly, relativism does not lead to an "anything goes" attitude. Rather, respect for the self and an empathetic ethics of responsibility for the other can lead young Witches to act in moral ways that transcend self-centered individualism. This result is consistent with Taylor's (1989, 1992) argument that individualism can lead to authenticity through locating the individual in a community of relationships.

CHAPTER SEVEN

Teenage Witchcraft:
Why, What, *and* Where To?

Why are young people turning to Witchcraft? The answer is not simple. A complex set of factors makes Witchcraft particularly attractive to teenagers in Western societies.

First, the growth of Witchcraft is a product of a cultural orientation that makes Witchcraft accessible (see Chapter 2). The *cultural orientation* to Witchcraft refers to the positive, even if trivializing, images of Witchcraft in the mass media, including movies such as *The Craft* and television shows such as *Buffy the Vampire Slayer* and *Charmed*. Positive information about Witchcraft is also widely available on the shelves of mainstream bookstores, in the magazines on mainstream newsstands, and on the Internet. Although other new religious movements have Internet sites, few have been so widely and positively represented in mainstream culture as has Witchcraft.

Second, Witchcraft is attractive because numerous people already share many of its central ideas and values. The feminist and environmental movements have spread the understanding that men and women are equal and that nature is something to be valued. Witches worship both the God and Goddess and see nature as sacred (see Chapter 5). Popular culture has also encouraged the acceptance of magical realism through movies such as *The Lord of the Rings* and, somewhat ironically, through the influence of some forms of Christianity (Clark 2003). In this context, a belief in magic and in the performance of ritual seems acceptable. In a sense, the presence of positive images of Witchcraft in the mass media legitimates Witchcraft for young people, as there is a perception that many of the beliefs of Witchcraft are socially accepted (Lewis 2003).

While this cultural orientation to Witchcraft does not make people become Witches, it makes exploring the idea of becoming a Witch easier. Many more people explore Witchcraft and decide not to become Witches than actually identify as Witches. Although we are somewhat tentative about predicting which young people become Witches (see Chapter 2), they appear to share two characteristics: they had an interest in the occult or New Age before exploring Witchcraft, that is, they are intrigued by alternative realities and court direct mystical experiences; and they view themselves as different from their peers and enjoy that status. The widespread availability of Witchcraft books and literature and the positive mass-media representations of Witchcraft must, to a large extent, be seen as the product of these young people and others looking for and purchasing Witchcraft-related commodities.

A third factor that draws teenagers to Witchcraft, as many commentators have observed, is that individualistic self-discovery or self-reflexivity is central to contemporary culture (Giddens 1991; Taylor 1992). Witchcraft is nondogmatic, lacks a central hierarchy, and in its main rituals and practices encourages self-reflexivity (see Chapter 3). Its rituals promote exploration and empowerment of the self (but do not necessarily result in selfishness).

Fourth, social analysts have observed that community based around place and family is in decline, replaced by geographically scattered communities based around identity and consumption (Giddens 1991; Bauman 1995). Witchcraft community is often geographically dispersed and facilitated by the Internet (see Chapter 4). Some young Witches know other Witches only virtually, and for most the Internet facilitates an important part of their community activities. Witchcraft is attractive, at least in part, because the dispersed and flexible nature of community it provides is consistent with the demands of contemporary postmodern society (Krueger 2004).

A final key factor in the growth of Witchcraft is the rootlessness of contemporary society. With the decline of traditional religions centered in churches, synagogues, and other institutions, which is one part of this rootlessness, individuals are more open to exploring alternative religious traditions (Roof 1999; Heelas et al. 2005). Furthermore, a set of broader social processes, including postmodernization, globalization, and detraditionalization, lead to a sense of rootlessness or a homeless mind. In this social context many young people are searching for a personal myth or worldview that provides them with an orientation to, and a guide for, how to act in the world (see Chapter 6).

The Consequences of Becoming a Witch

What are the consequences for young people of becoming Witches? First, involvement in Witchcraft as a religious tradition poses similar dangers, risks, and benefits to involvement in most mainstream religious traditions. There are dangerous and malicious people in all walks of life, and some of them are Witches. However, our interviews do not indicate that Witches are any more dangerous than members of any other religious group. Furthermore, our research suggests that participation in Witchcraft offers positive benefits similar to those gained by participation in mainstream religious traditions.

Based on a large national survey of U.S. twelfth graders, Christian Smith and Robert Faris (2002, 7) conclude: "Religion among U.S. adolescents is positively related to participation in constructive youth activities. In addition, those who participate in religious activities seem to be less likely to participate in many delinquent and risk behaviors." Smith and Faris studied factors such as substance abuse, crime and violence, school problems, and participation in constructive activities. Although we did not ask specific questions about all these factors in all our interviews, the overall impression from our research is that a similar survey of adolescent Witches would reach similar conclusions. Of course, adolescent Witches do adopt some values and practices that challenge mainstream culture. However, the overall effect of practicing Witchcraft on factors listed by Smith and Faris is likely to be similar to other forms of adolescent religious participation.

Is there any evidence that Witchcraft might lead teenagers into activities that could be harmful or dangerous to themselves or others? First, it
is important to distinguish, on the one hand, Witchcraft that is primarily
countercultural and not likely to result in harm to self or others, from, on
the other hand, forms that may be harmful to self and others, such as the
delinquent activities listed by Smith and Faris. Although Witchcraft can
be seen to share values and beliefs with one strand of contemporary society, it challenges many traditional norms and taken-for-granted beliefs in
mainstream Western culture. Witches have an attitude toward death different from a traditional Christian one—death is an accepted part of the
cycle of life. Witches accept sexual diversity, including homosexuality and
bisexuality. Witches value intuition and the emotions, celebrating them in
rituals and working to integrate them into their lives. Witches have a
strong sense of magic as a part of life, whether through dreams, intuitions,
or tarot readings. Witches typically worship the Goddess as well as the
God. Witches see nature as sacred. Of course, many of these understandings are not particularly deviant in some sections of contemporary society,

7.1 Oh my gods, USA. Photo by Helen A. Berger.

notably among a section of the urban educated middle classes. However, many of the beliefs and practices of Witches are not mainstream, and in this sense potentially deviant.

While there is no evidence that becoming a Witch makes young people more promiscuous, there is some suggestion in our data that Witchcraft has brought young people into contact with alternative sexual practices. One such practice that is occasionally discussed is polyamory, which can take a variety of forms but typically involves both partners in a relationship agreeing to have other sexual partners on a casual or regular basis. For example, Morgan says: "Just by being in the community, I have known more polyamorous people than anywhere else." Chris talks about reading a Pagan novel that included a discussion of "polyamory and multiple relationships" that he found fascinating. Brian similarly notes: "I have met polyamorous people, I have met drug addicts, I have met all kinds of people, because Pagans are very accepting of pretty much anyone."

Has this exposure to polyamory encouraged sexual promiscuity among young Witches? We do not think it has changed the sexual practices of most of the young Witches; if anything, the improved self-esteem that seems to be associated with Witchcraft may lead to a more responsible attitude toward sex. However, at least one young person has considered adopting a polyamorous lifestyle. When asked if Witchcraft has changed her attitude toward relationships, Jackie describes an attitude that sounds as if she is willing to consider polyamory: "Umm [pause of six seconds], I don't know. I think it's clarified a lot of abstract concepts for me. Things like love and truth and things like that. The more I learn, the more it clarifies what these things mean to me. As far as relationships go, the more I think about it, love becomes more important than fidelity, and being honest with each other becomes more important than having lots of things in common." However, Jackie then suggests that Witchcraft has made her more comfortable with committing to one partner: "I believe in reincarnation . . . [so] you're not so reluctant to commit. It's like, what am I committing to, really? One life." The uncharacteristic six-second pause at the beginning of Jackie's response suggests that she is still somewhat uncertain about these things. Whether polyamory is a dangerous activity is debatable, but research suggests that although it is often spoken of among

Neopagans, it is rarely practiced—most are monogamous (Ezzy 2003b; H. Berger et al. 2003).

Some conservative Christians portray Witchcraft as the link between Harry Potter and Satanism (Helm 2005). They contend that people get interested by reading the *Harry Potter* series, explore Witchcraft, and then move on to Satanism. To the contrary, our research suggests that although a small minority of teenage Witches explore Satanism, Witchcraft may lead young people away from Satanism, rather than toward it. More research, particularly on teenagers who are Satanist, is needed before anything definitive can be said. As noted in the introduction, Satanism is a different religion from Witchcraft (Lewis 2001). None of the young Witches we interviewed worship the devil, nor are any involved in Satanism. However, three have explored it, among them, Jacqueline, who informs us that she has read Anton LeVey, a well-known Satanist and founder of the Church of Satan in California (Wright 2005). She "did a report on that for school; . . . it was sort of like a way to express the dark side, I felt—it is not necessarily a very good path and I wouldn't recommend it. But again, it wasn't totally evil; it is not quite what everyone thinks. It is really about yourself. It is really about getting things for you and screwing everyone else. Well, it is good sometimes to think of yourself instead of just constantly self-sacrificing. But it is, like, to the extreme; it is not really a religion—there is no really worship, no spirituality in it, compared to Wicca, which does have that." Jacqueline, like the other two young people who explored Satanism, finds it selfish and not sufficiently spiritual but notes that what they found was not the Hollywood image of Satanism. All three young Witches who explored Satanism moved away from it.

Ellis (2000, 2) argues: "We must be careful to distinguish folklore *of* witchcraft and Satanism (i.e., what witches and Satanist *do* believe) from folklore *about* witches and Satanists (what anti-occult crusaders *think* witches and Satanists believe)." As is evidenced by the Satanism scares of the 1980s, it is quite possible for considerable social panic to be generated about Satanism despite there being little evidence of malicious Satanic practitioners (Richardson et al. 1991; Wright 2005). Ellis (2000, 5) argues that the anti-Satanist movement really reflects not evidence of an increase in the dangers of Satanism, but "the emerging needs of certain [Pentecostal] movements to legitimate themselves by launching a crusade."

Some of the young Witches themselves sometimes report playing up fears about Witchcraft and Satanism. Jimmy encouraged other students at his school to think of him as a Satanist engaging in practices that might be dangerous and fearful; he seemed to enjoy the attention (see Chapter 4). Similarly Ruth, whom we met in one of the opening vignettes, enjoyed telling her school friends about the "spells" she had performed over the weekend. However, Jimmy's Satanism, at least as he reported it to us, involved little more than using dowsing rods in the schoolyard, and Ruth's "spells" consisted of dancing around a backyard fire under parental supervision.

Witchcraft is often misunderstood, particularly by Christian groups, who presume that Witchcraft is necessarily evil and damaging to the individuals involved. These fears tell us more about the beliefs and practices of these Christian groups than about the practices of Witches. As Wright (2005), James Lewis (2003) and Ellis (2000) suggest, Christians' fears about the evils of Witchcraft are mainly oriented toward legitimating their own religion. Interestingly, some Christian apologists are now arguing that Christians should try to engage in dialogue with Witches to find out what they actually do and believe, rather than presume to know about Witches a priori (Lausanne Committee for World Evangelization 2004).

However, there are occasional indications in the interviews of some aspects of Witchcraft that should perhaps elicit concern. For example, similar to all religions, a small minority of Witches are malicious individuals. Victoria's vignette includes a story that appears to be mainly about the politics of Pagan community but that may have problematic dimensions. She describes an older couple who were trying to take over a Pagan discussion group and turn it into a ritual circle focused on their leadership. As Greenwood (2000a) has documented, some self-centered individuals in positions of power in Witchcraft covens engage in damaging psychological games with coven members. There is no evidence that this is what happened in Victoria's case, and very few young people are involved in covens, but the possibility is there.

Another potentially problematic aspect of Witchcraft is that some young people may be using Witchcraft as a defense or escape mechanism to avoid dealing with mental health issues. John Swinton (2001) notes that statistical studies demonstrate that religious beliefs are associated with both improved mental health and decreased mental health. He suggests that decreased mental health is the result of forms of religious adherence that are used as a defense or escape mechanism associated with instrumental concerns, exclusionary orientations, and security seeking. We did not ask the young Witches systematic questions that might allow an assessment of their mental health, and we are not trained to assess mental health. We do not want to suggest that beliefs or practices that involve spiritual experiences or supernatural encounters are linked to mental health problems, nor do we think that Witchcraft causes mental health problems. To the contrary, it typically appears to have positive consequences (see Chapter 3). However, we do note that some Witches may have mental health issues that might require professional assistance. Further, two or three of the young people we interviewed may have unresolved mental health issues and are using Witchcraft to avoid dealing with them. The avoidance of mental health issues is probably reasonably common among all teenagers, and in this case young Witches are probably no different from their non-Witch peers.

Joining a minority religion opens the young people to ostracism, prejudice, and misunderstanding. Even with the relatively positive images of Witches in the media, many people in mainstream society have significant misunderstandings about what Witches actually do. Many Witches report tensions with family or friends, persecution from fellow students at school, or negative responses at work. Many others are afraid of such persecution, even if they have not experienced it. Witchcraft remains countercultural and it may continue to be perceived as "dangerous," despite evidence to the contrary, at least among some segments of society.

The practice of Witchcraft by teenagers typically involves simple rituals and practices such as meditation, burning candles, and saying prayers to Pagan gods and goddesses (see Chapter 3). The aims of these rituals are primarily religious. Through them, the young people give their lives meaning and experience a religious sense of connection with the world around them. The rituals are also about the concerns of teenagers. The young Witches may construct a spell to improve low self-esteem, to improve their love life, or to heal themselves or a friend. Fears about the dangers of Witchcraft are largely misplaced. Witchcraft, as practiced by teenagers, primarily involves young people struggling to make sense of their place in an often confusing and disorienting world and finding ethics to guide their choices and actions.

Witchcraft Ethics and Authenticity

What are Witchcraft ethics as practiced by teenage Witches? To understand the ethics of teenage Witches, it is important first to understand how the self has changed in contemporary society. Some people celebrate the increased individual freedom and choice supposedly available in postmodern consumerist society (Giddens 1991; Bauman 2001). They argue that the self in contemporary society is no longer a fixed thing, but rather is reflexively created, a transitory expression of aesthetic style. In religious terms, an extreme example would be an individual who moves among various religious traditions, searching not for truth but for a religious expression that "feels right" at that particular time. According to the postmodernist thinkers, there is no "true" or "core" self. Rather, as Kenneth Gergen (1991, xiii) notes, although there are moments of lament, "our best option . . . is to play out the positive potentials of this postmodern erasure of the self." However, not all commentators are so enthusiastic about the postmodern freedom and individualism provided by the consumerist mass market.

Critics such as Ann Swidler (2002) and Peter Berger and Hansfried Kellner (1973) argue that the transitory postmodern self is empty. The result is a sense of rootlessness and homelessness. The pleasure of continually trying on new identities is no substitute for a strong sense of self-rootedness in stable institutions. Swidler argues that the institutions that support community, collective interests, education, and health have all been hollowed out, leaving individuals to rely on themselves. The pressure to strengthen the self, to be independent and autonomous, is a product of the cutting away of the traditional institutional structures that supported the self: "The irony is that it is hard to develop strong, more integrated, more genuinely autonomous selves in an institutionally depleted social world" (Swidler 2002, 54). Similarly, Berger and Kellner (1973, 166) trace the way the pluralization, migration, and uncertainty of contemporary society have led not only to a physical "homelessness" for many people, but also to a "homeless mind." According to them the traditional function of religion to provide meaning and a "home" in the world has been undermined. Questions of meaning and mortality no longer have clear answers for many people. In other words, they argue that the individualism of contemporary society inevitably leads to narcissism, a self-centered ethics, and anomie.

We think Swidler, as well as Berger and Kellner, are in part correct. Current social changes are reducing the social and institutional infrastructure that supported the older style of self. We share some of Swidler's concerns about the "depletion" of economic, political, and social infrastructure. However, we disagree that a "strong, resilient self" is necessarily associated with a selfish individualism (Swidler 2002, 53). Nor do we think that pluralism and uncertainty necessarily lead to a lack of meaning or of morality (see chapter 6).

Following Taylor (1989, 1992), we argue that the individualism of contemporary culture can develop in two quite different ways. The first way is toward an individualistic self-centered narcissism. However, there is a second possibility that Taylor (1992, 82) refers to as "authenticity." The person who seeks an "authentic" self is individualistic in the sense that she or he is seeking her or his own truth or way of living in the world. However, the aims or ethical orientation of the authentic self are beyond or outside the self and often involve a concern for others: "I can find fulfillment in God, or a political cause, or tending the earth."

Another way of saying this is to observe that the twentieth century saw the disintegration of "grand narratives" and shared myths and symbols that used to be sources of identity integration and values. Rollo May argues that psychotherapy offers an alternative. Through therapy, "the person can then cultivate his own awareness of his personal myth, which will yield his values and identity as well as give him some shared basis for interpersonal relationships" (May 1975, 706). Although Witchcraft is not psychotherapy, it is one of a variety of religions that James Beckford (1984) refers to as new religious and healing movements. These religions incorporate alternative healing methods, including those oriented to psychological health. Among other things Witchcraft provides is a personal myth through which individuals develop a sense of self-identity and values. It also provides the basis for shared interpersonal relations. Giddens (1991, 215) contends that "self-identity today is a reflexive achievement." May and Taylor add the notion that rituals and myths play a central role in the ethical or value orientations of the identity that is reflexively created. In particular, it is possible to have an individualized reflexive sense of self as part of a sophisticated understanding of ethical obligations.

Analysts such as Swidler and Berger and Kellner argue that, although there is increased individual freedom and choice in contemporary society, there is a concomitant loss of a sense of place in the order of things. The disenchanted world we live in leads to a loss of sense of purpose, less concern with others, and greater selfishness and narcissism. Taylor unhinges the link between these two aspects, arguing that it is possible to find a sense of purpose and greater concern for others through "authenticity" as part of the individualism of contemporary culture. Taylor is not arguing that the individualistic nature of contemporary society is always good, as do analysts like Gergen, but that there is an underlying tension in the contemporary turn to the self: "We face a continuing struggle to realize higher and fuller modes of authenticity against the resistance of the flatter and shallower forms" (1992, 93). This is precisely what we observe among many young Witches. It is not simply the Wicca Rede or the Law of Return that inform their ethics. Rather, as they begin to understand themselves and the world in which they live in terms of the worldview of Witchcraft, they develop values that lead them to develop a greater concern for others. Values for young Witches do not derive primarily from moral injunctions, but from understanding themselves as living in a world of relationships with others. For instance, young Witches choose to recycle or to not litter because they care about the earth (see Chapter 6). Their sense of being in relationship with all living beings makes them think about how they treat each other, their families, and schoolmates.

There are ambiguities and tensions in the ethics of teenage Witches.

Our sampling methods are not representative, biased toward selecting educated people with access to the Internet, so we cannot say anything with certainty about the class and ethnic distribution of young Witches. Our sample includes people from varied class and ethnic backgrounds, but most are well educated, white, and middle class. Studies of the older generation of Witches show that this is the typical background of those who practice Witchcraft (Adler 1986; H. Berger et al. 2003). The high educational attainment and middle-class status of the majority of contemporary Western Witches have brought into question the long-held notion that it is the poor and uneducated who turn to magic as a way of gaining powers they lack in their daily lives. However, this class distribution has resulted in some, like Susan Hopkins (2002, 153), contending that, for girls at least, "Witchcraft is another mainstream metaphor for channelling ambition and energy to get what you really want, to discover your hidden girl powers." Hopkins's criticism may be justified with respect to some of the witches on television shows such as *Charmed* or *Buffy*. However, although Witchcraft is a way of discovering oneself and there is some evidence of instrumental spellwork, most of the young people are not using Witchcraft to channel ambition or as a self-centered aid to material success.

Another potential tension for teenage Witchcraft is that the commodification of Witchcraft and with it of self-actualization may ultimately undermine its spiritual aspects. With respect to New Age spiritualities Jennifer Rindfleish (2005, 358) argues that, "once appropriated and commodified, the initial purpose of such New Age discourse and practice is lost and new ways of discussing and practicing self-care must emerge." Rindfleish's argument relies too heavily on published New Age texts rather than on interviews with New Age practitioners. Although Witchcraft is distinct from the New Age, it shares with it rituals and practices of self-help or actualization. Our research demonstrates that the practices and purposes of young Witches are quite different from the practices outlined in the commercial books on Witchcraft designed for teenagers. Teenage Witchcraft practitioners take the spiritual and religious dimensions of their practice more seriously than some of the books do. While the books tend to emphasize instrumental magic (Ezzy 2003a), teenagers' practices tend more toward religious ritual and spiritual experience.

The reflexivity central to contemporary identity described by Giddens is also central to contemporary spirituality (Roof 1999). Kelly Besecke (2001, 366) takes this a step further, arguing that reflexive spirituality is a *cultural resource:* "Specifically I argue that when individuals come together to practice reflexive spirituality in groups, this form of individual religiosity becomes a shared language people use to talk to each other about meaning." Besecke notes that the dichotomy between institutional religion and individual spirituality ignores important contemporary shared cultural resources: "What gets lost in this dichotomy is religion's non-institutional, public, cultural dimension" (379).

Teenage Witchcraft is just such a form of reflexive spirituality as a cultural resource. Books, movies, and Internet Web pages provide a shared cultural resource and language that facilitates reflexivity and provides young people with access to a spirituality that provides meaning, or a home for the mind, and an embodied ritual practice to support this understanding. As we observed earlier, Witchcraft has similar benefits to other types of religious participation, and part of the reason for this is that Witchcraft, similar to many other religious and therapeutic practices, facilitates self-actualization. The vignettes of Beverly, who searches for a way to make sense of her mother's death, and of Karen and Ruth, who both struggle with depression and low self-esteem, underline the role of Witchcraft as providing an integrative myth. The understanding of themselves and the world that these young people derive from Witchcraft enables them to respond constructively to these difficult emotions and experiences. Furthermore, Witchcraft "works" for young people not simply because of changed understandings (in the mind), but also because the rituals of Witchcraft engage with embodied emotions (see Chapter 3). Varja Ma (2000, 205) observes about Goddess spirituality: "For women's empowerment to be full it must activate and integrate all aspects of self: physical, emotional, mental, and spiritual." Similarly, for many of the young Witches, the rituals of Witchcraft go beyond ideas and thoughts to engage them ritually in the symbolism and mythology of the religion.

Witchcraft provides young people with a worldview and an ethical orientation that assists them to make moral choices. This does not mean that they always act in ways that are consistent with this ethical orientation.

Several young Witches thought they should recycle but did not do it. Others were quite intolerant of Christians. However, Witches do have an ethical framework and this framework is very different from that of the monotheistic religions. As York (2004) and McGraw (2004) note, Pagan ethics do not derive from adherence to transcendental laws, but from individuals finding themselves embedded in a network of relationships for which they begin to take responsibility, however inadequately and imperfectly. The ethics of teenage Witches are consistent with, and derive from, the individualism and search for authenticity that are central to contemporary culture.

We have drawn on various theories and studies to make sense of the world of teenage Witches. However, our greatest concern is that the voices of young Witches are heard and respected. Our overriding reaction, gained after listening to more than a hundred hours of interviews and reading thousands of pages of transcript several times, is a sense of respect. Teenage Witches are often misunderstood by older Witches, who look down on them, forgetting that the world of teenagers is a different one from their own. Teenage Witches are also misunderstood by conservative Christians, friends, parents, priests, and other public figures. Some of this lack of respect by both older Witches and those outside the religion may derive from the mass-media presentation of teenage Witches. Although positive, it often depicts the practices of teenage Witches as lacking in spirituality and geared completely toward instrumental spells, particularly love spells. The media presentation is a two-edged sword, one edge providing a sense of familiarity to some aspects of the religious practice, such as spellwork and circle casting, as well as presenting a friendly face to those practices, the other edge trivializing the mystical and spiritual aspects of the religion, making it seem foolish or less "real" than other religions. This trivializing of the Witches' practices and beliefs may in the long run have more serious consequences for Witchcraft than the Religious Right's portrayal of it as Satanism and something to be feared. Although not satanic and rarely harmful or dangerous, Witchcraft does challenge the values of contemporary society. This challenge is one aspect of Witchcraft's appeal to the young, but of equal importance is their sense of the religion as authentic, empowering, and ethical.

APPEПDÎX A

Interview Questions

How did you first learn about Witchcraft?

What did you first learn? Has your practice changed over time? If so, how?

Do you now study to learn more? If so, how?

When did you first become interested in Witchcraft?

When did you actually start doing something? What was it that you did?

What do you do now?

Which TV shows if any about Witchcraft do you watch? Are there any that you used to watch but no longer do?

What do you think about the characters in those TV shows who are Witches?

Do you read any books and/or magazines about Witchcraft? If so, which are your favorites? What do you particularly like about these?

Do you use the Internet? If so, for what purposes? Do you go to chat rooms? Visit web pages?

How many of your friends know that you are a Witch?

Do you do rituals or magic with friends?

What do you hope to achieve?

Do you believe in reincarnation? In ESP? In communicating with spirits? In an after-life? In astrology? In premonitions? In having direct inspiration or direction from the spirit world or from the Goddess or a God?

243

Do you think magic works? If so, how?

Has practicing Witchcraft changed other aspects of your life? (Friends, relationships, study goals, recreation, political view?)

Do you have any contact with Witches in their late 20s, 30s, or older?

Have you ever attended a festival? If so, what did you think of the experience?

Have you ever attended an open ritual? If so, what did you think of the experience? Did you go alone or with others?

Do you know or have contact with initiated Witches?

How would you define the essence of Witchcraft?

What are your views on environmentalism? How important is it to you?

What are your views on feminism? On women's rights?

Have you met many other people who are Witches? Where?

Do you practice with others? Who?

Were you raised in a religion? If so, which one? How involved in that religion were you? How involved was your family? Do you still practice that religion?

Are your parents religious?

Does your family know about your interest in Witchcraft? If so, how do they feel about it? If not, what do you think would be their response if they did know?

Does anyone else in your family know that you are a Witch?

If you are dating anyone now, is s/he also a Witch? How about your previous girl/boyfriends?

What do your parents do for a living?

APPEnDİX B

Information on Interviewees

NAME	COUNTRY	AGE	AGE BEGAN	PARENTS' RELIGION MOTHER	FATHER
Aguina	USA	20	14	Baptist[a]	Baptist
Amber	AUS	22	13	Nom. Anglican[b]	No religion
Annie	USA	20	13	Catholic	Catholic
Aspen	UK	18	15	No religion	No religion
Beverly	USA	23	12	Presbyterian	Presbyterian
Bianca	UK	19	13	No religion	No religion
Bonnie	USA	21	18	No religion	No religion
Brian	USA	19	12/13	Nom. Mormon	Mormon
Brianna	USA	20	16	Catholic	Nom. Catholic
Bruce	AUS	17	12	Nom. Catholic	Nom. Catholic
Cailin	USA	19	13	Occult Christian	Not stated
Carolyn	AUS	17	14	Nom. Catholic	Nom. Catholic
Charles	UK	18	16	Nom. Anglican	Nom. Anglican
Charlotte	UK	19	18	Anglican	Psychical Research
Cherry	UK	23	15	No religion	Nom. Methodist
Cheryl	AUS	19	14	Catholic	Catholic
Chloe	UK	20	12	No religion	No religion
Chris	UK	23	15	Nom. Catholic	Nom. Catholic
Clarissa	AUS	23	14/16	Pagan	No religion
Cliff	USA	23	17/18	Nom. Methodist	No religion
Dan	UK	19	12	Hippy spiritual	No religion
Dane	USA	23	13	Catholic	Not stated
Debbie	AUS	21	—	Nom. Catholic	No religion
Denise	AUS	21	17	Jewish	Jewish
Doreen	AUS	21	14/15	No religion	No religion
Eleanor	USA	18	15	Episcopalian	Episcopalian
Erica	AUS	20	15	Atheist	Atheist

NAME	COUNTRY	AGE	AGE BEGAN	PARENTS' RELIGION MOTHER	FATHER
Freddy (F)	USA	19	—	Pagan	Not stated
Fritz	USA	19	17	United Methodist	United Methodist
Gemma	UK	19	15	Nom. Catholic	Nom. Catholic
Haley	UK	23	13	Methodist	Agnostic
Heather	AUS	18	14	Agnostic	Spiritual
Iris	AUS	20	15	Agnostic	Christian
Jackie	AUS	20	13/14	No religion	No religion
Jacqueline	USA	19	16	Nom. Methodist	Methodist
Jane	AUS	18	15	Uniting Church	Uniting Church
Jason	USA	19	15	Baptist	Baptist
Jen	USA	20	10	Women's Spirituality	Pagan
Jimmy	UK	22	15/16	Nom. Catholic	Atheist
Jodie	AUS	19	15	Catholic	Catholic
John	USA	19	14	Catholic	Catholic
June	AUS	19	15	Buddhist	Anglican
Karen	AUS	19	14	Agnostic	Agnostic
Kathy	AUS	19	15	Nom. Protestant	Atheist
Ken	USA	22	15	Reformed Church	Jewish
Kevin	USA	20	16	Catholic	Catholic
Koehl	USA	18	17	Jehovah's Witness	Nom. Catholic
Laurel	AUS	20	—	Nom. Anglican	Nom. Anglican
Leanne	UK	18	—	No religion	No religion
Leslie	UK	23	16	Baptist	Not stated
Li (M)	UK	20	16	No religion	No religion
Logan (F)	USA	23	12/13	Presbyterian	Buddhist
Louise	UK	19	12/13	Nom. Anglican	Not stated
Lovette	USA	19	10–12	Agnostic	Atheist
Maggie	AUS	18	14/15	Presbyterian	Zoroastrian
Marcia	AUS	22	15	No religion	No religion
Marilyn	UK	22	17	Protestant	Catholic
Mary	AUS	21	16	Agnostic	Agnostic
Melissa	USA	22	14	Russian Orthodox	Not stated
Michael	UK	22	13	Pagan	Atheist
Mish	UK	21	13	Nom. Anglican	Nom. Anglican
Monica	AUS	17	—	Pagan	Pagan
Morgan	USA	19	12	Protestant	Nom. Protestant
Nika	USA	23	—	Protestant	Protestant
Olivia	USA	23	17/18	Agnostic	Atheist
Ollie	UK	18	—	Nom. Catholic	Nom. Catholic
Patricia	AUS	18	13	New Age	No religion
Percy	UK	22	—	Christian	Atheist
Pete	USA	22	13	Spiritual	Atheist
Rachel	USA	21	15	Jewish	Jewish
Ross	AUS	22	—	Nom. Catholic	Nom. Christian
Ruth	AUS	18	—	Pagan	No Religion

| NAME | COUNTRY | AGE | AGE BEGAN | PARENTS' RELIGION | |
				MOTHER	FATHER
Seamus	USA	22	13	Catholic	Catholic
Simon	AUS	20	12/13	No religion	No religion
Sophie	UK	20	15	Not stated	Agnostic
Sorrel	UK	19	—	Pagan	Pagan
Stella	AUS	18	12	No religion	No religion
Susan	AUS	23	16	Presbyterian	Presbyterian
Tanya	UK	22	15/16	Catholic	Nom. Protestant
Tim	UK	18	—	No religion	No religion
Tina	UK	18	14	Buddhist	Nom. Christian
Tom	USA	19	11	Catholic	Catholic
Vanessa	USA	19	13	Catholic	Catholic
Victoria	UK	19	13	No religion	No religion
Vivianne	AUS	21	—	No religion	No religion
Water (M)	UK	21	16	Not stated	Nom. Catholic
Wendy	UK	18	13/14	Atheist	Atheist
Yvette	AUS	17	15/16	No religion	No religion
Zack	USA	19	—	Witch	Nom. Jewish
Zoe	UK	19	15	Nom. Christian	No Religion

a Where a parent has changed religious affiliation, the last stated affiliation is listed. We have retained the country-specific name "Anglican" in the United Kingdom and Australia and "Episcopalian" in the United States, both of which refer to the Church of England. "Atheist" is used when the interviewee uses the term or indicates that a parent is antireligious. "Agnostic" is used to indicate parents who are open-minded about religion. "No religion" indicates that the parent is not religious but that no further information was provided about their attitude toward religion.

b "Nominal" is used when the interviewee indicates that the parent identifies with a religion but does not practice regularly. The absence of "nominal" indicates that the parent regularly practices the religion by attending church or participating in relevant rituals or ceremonies.

NOTES

Introduction

1. Although some people use the terms "Pagan" and "Witch" interchangeably, "Pagan" usually refers to a broader range of religious traditions, including Witches, Heathens, Druids, and others. Douglas is not a Witch but shares some of their Pagan practices. For more information see Ezzy 2004 and 2005.

Vignette: Beverly—A Ministers' Daughter (America)

1. Witchvox (www.Witchvox.com) is a well-respected and popular Pagan Internet site, founded in 1997 by Wren Walker and Fritz Jung (Hadden and Cowen 2000; Nightmare 2001). It is a U.S. site but has pages about and for Pagans in other parts of the world.

Vignette: Charles—From *Big Brother* to Witchcraft (England)

1. Drawing down the moon is normally done in a ritual, called an esbat, to celebrate the full moon. Traditionally the moon, which is conceived as a female divine, is drawn down into the Goddess, who manifests the moon's essence or energy.
2. A handfasting is a Wiccan marriage. If performed by a legally recognized minister, this is a legal marriage. But, it can also be done as a religious ceremony to signify either a lifelong commitment or a commitment for a shorter time period, most commonly a year and a day.
3. Path work is a form of guided visualization in which individuals meditate on sequential events, such as walking down a forest path or conversing with deceased ancestors.

Vignette: Ruth—Coming out of Depression (Australia)

1. Mabon is one of the eight festivals of the wheel of the year. Celebrated on the autumn equinox (21 March in Australia, and 21 September in the United States

249

and Britain), when day and night are of equal length, Mabon is a harvest festival, marking the turning of the year from light to dark.

Chapter 1: The World of Teenage Witchcraft

1. Sociological research indicates that most of those who join more stereotypical new religious movements are not seduced into them either but make a reasoned choice to join. Most leave within three years (see, for example, Stark and Bainbridge 1985; Richardson and Kilbourne 1986).
2. For a fuller discussion of sects of Paganism see Harvey 1997 and Berger 2005a.
3. Brigit Meyer (1999) argues that older notions of Witchcraft in the African community she studied were used by Evangelicals to introduce and reinforce Christian concepts of the devil.
4. For a fuller discussion of rituals see Berger 1999, Pike 2004, Magliocco 2004, and Bado-Fralick 2005.
5. There have been a number of excellent academic studies of this pre-1990 phase of Witchcraft; see, for example, Adler 1986, Berger 1999, Greenwood 2000a, Hume 1997, Hutton 1999, Pike 2001, Salomonsen 2002, York 1995.
6. Fourteen is the average age for those who told us when they first explored the religion. In the cases in Appendix B in which two ages—for example, 16/17—are given, we picked the older for purposes of this average. Where there is a three-year range, we picked the middle age listed.
7. This percentage is based on the number of teens between the ages of fifteen and nineteen in the 2000 U.S. census, which is the closest age category in the census to that used by Smith with Denton (2005).
8. A number of authors who write about Witchcraft have published several books, some of them with similar names. As it was common for the young Witches to have problems remembering exact titles, we have focused instead on the authors they found most interesting.
9. We did not consistently ask about magazines and were therefore dependent on those young people who chose to tell us about them.
10. Ronald Hutton (1999), Aiden Kelly (1991), and Issac Bonewits (1989) helped dispel the belief among many Witches that Witchcraft was an old religion that had been passed down from practitioner to practitioner.

Chapter 2: Coming Home to Witchcraft

1. The Cabot tradition was begun by Laurie Cabot, a Witch in Salem, Massachusetts, but is taught by others trained in this tradition. It is a very individualized tradition. Training occurs on a one-to-one basis with a mentor and student, not in a coven.
2. For an extended discussion of this issue see Ezzy n.d.
3. Being called a Witch by classmates is not necessarily viewed negatively. Often what is meant is the young person appears to be knowledgeable about the occult. At other times the label is an indication that the person is seen as different.
4. In his study, Lofland used the pseudonym Divine Precepts for the group.

Vignette: Karen—Magic, Ritual, and Self-Transformation
1. "Samhain" is pronounced *sōwain*.

Chapter 3: The Magical Self
1. Beltane, one of the eight yearly sabbats of the wheel of the year, is a celebration of spring and fertility. It occurs on 1 May in the Northern Hemisphere and 31 October in the Southern Hemisphere.
2. For a discussion of other new religions that incorporate similar self-help techniques, see Beckford 1984.
3. Binding spells are meant to stop someone from doing something but are not supposed to in any way harm that person.

Vignette: Victoria—Creating Pagan Community
1. The Goat of Mendes, a symbol of a goat inside a pentagram, is commonly associated with Satanism. It is believed by some to have been created by Elipas Levi, a nineteenth-century occultist, who linked the goat, which is commonly found in portrayals of Witches' sabbats, and the Egyptian god Ammon of Mendes, both associated with sexuality and fertility.

Chapter 4: Within the Circle: Community and Family
1. Gardnerians are Wiccans who have been trained in a coven that can trace its lineage back to Gerald Gardner, credited with founding the religion. This is one form of what is called traditional British Witchcraft.
2. Because of interviewing inconsistencies, we asked only thirty-four of the young Witches about the amount of time they spent on the Internet.
3. Like Witchvox.com, the Children of Artemis was one of the sites we used to advertise for respondents.
4. In her ethnographic study of a high school Satanist group in a southern U.S. community, Kathleen Lowney (1995) documents the use of fear by the group to gain power and reverse the status hierarchy in their high school. Satanism for these young people was a way both to critique the mainstream culture of their community and to help create a new sense of self.
5. We did not ask about the marital status of our informants' parents, although many volunteered the information.
6. McPhillips 2003 provides a detailed account of female Witches who arranged a first-menstruation ritual for their daughters.
7. See York 2003 for a comparative discussion of the world pagan faiths.
8. Stark and Bambridge 1985 refers to these types of organization as "client cults."

Vignette: Nika—The Goddess as Role Model, Healer, and Mother Earth
1. Like that of a number of the young Witches we spoke to, Nika's conception of Celtic prehistory may not be consistent with historical accounts. These more romantic and in some cases feminist accounts are one part of Neopagan literature,

certainly not accepted by all Neopagans but nonetheless popular with a significant segment of the population.

2. This is a pseudonym.

3. Starhawk (1994) wrote this novel, which incorporates her spiritual system, beliefs, and worldview.

Chapter 5: The Goddess Is Alive: Feminism and Environmentalism

1. Reserve Officers' Training Corps (ROTC) trains young men and women for U.S. military service. Scholarships are often offered as a lure for students for join.

Chapter 6: If It Harm None, Do As Thou Will

1. As the most common form of prayer among Christians is for health or healing, the Witches' emphasis on doing healing spells may be consistent with the norms and behavior of the larger society.

WORKS CITED

Adler, M. 1979. *Drawing Down the Moon.* Boston: Beacon Press.
———. 1986. *Drawing Down the Moon: Witches, Druids, Goddess-Worshippers, and Other Pagans in America Today.* Revised and expanded edition. Boston: Beacon Press.
Adriance, M. C. 1995. *Promised Land: Base Christian Communities and the Struggle for the Amazon.* Albany: State University of New York Press.
Alexander C., M. Rainforth, and P. Gelderloos. 1991. "Transcendental Meditation, Self-Actualisation, and Psychological Health: A Conceptual Overview and Statistical Meta-analysis." *Journal of Social Behavior and Personality* 6, 1:189–247.
Astin, J. A. 1997. "Stress Reduction through Mindfulness Meditation." *Psychotherapy and Psychosomatics* 66, 1:97–106.
Bado-Fralick, N. 2005. *Coming to the Edge of the Circle: A Wiccan Initiation Ritual.* Oxford: Oxford University Press.
Barbato, M. 2000. "Australians at the Brink of Death." In *Death and Dying,* ed. A. Kellehear, 208–22. Melbourne: Oxford University Press.
Barker, E. 1984. *The Making of a Moonie: Choice or Brainwashing?* Oxford: Blackwell.
Bauman, Z. 1993. *Postmodern Ethics.* Oxford, UK, and Cambridge, Mass.: Blackwell.
———. 1995. *Life in Fragments: Essays in Postmodern Morality.* Oxford, UK, and Cambridge, Mass.: Blackwell.
———. 2001. *The Individualized Society.* Cambridge: Polity Press.
Baumgardner, J., and A. Richard. 2000. *Manifesta: Young Women, Feminism, and the Future.* New York: Farrar, Straus and Giroux.
Beck, Ulrich. 1992. *Risk Society: Towards a New Modernity.* New Delhi: Sage.
Beckford, J. 1984. "Holistic Imagery and Ethics in New Religious and Healing Movements." *Social Compass* 31:259–72.
———. 1992a. *Religion and Advanced Industrial Society.* London: Routledge.

———. 1992b. "Religion and Modernity, Post-Modernity." In *Religion: Contemporary Issues*, ed. B. Wilson, 11–23. London: Bellew.

Bell, C. 1992. *Ritual Theory, Ritual Practice*. New York: Oxford University Press.

Berger, H. A. 1999. *A Community of Witches: Contemporary Neo-Paganism and Witchcraft in the United States*. Columbia: University of South Carolina Press.

Berger, H. A. 2005a. "Witchcraft and Neopaganism." In *Witchcraft and Magic: Contemporary North America*, ed. H. A. Berger, 28–54. Philadelphia: University of Pennsylvania Press.

———. 2005b. Introduction to *Witchcraft and Magic: Contemporary North America*, ed. H. A. Berger, 1–7. Philadelphia: University of Pennsylvania Press.

Berger, H. A., and D. Ezzy. 2004. "The Internet as Virtual Community: Teen Witches in the United States and Australia." In *Religion Online: Finding Faith on the Internet*, ed. L. L. Dawson and D. E. Cowan, 175–88. New York and London: Routledge.

Berger, H. A., E. A. Leach, and L. S. Shaffer. 2003. *Voices from the Pagan Census: Contemporary: A National Survey of Witches and Neo-Pagans in the United States*. Columbia: University of South Carolina Press.

Berger, P. L. 1967. *The Sacred Canopy: Elements of Sociological Theory of Religion*. Garden City, N.Y.: Doubleday.

———. 1969. *A Rumor of Angels: Modern Society and the Rediscovery of the Supernatural*. New York: Doubleday.

Berger, P., B. Berger, and H. Kellner. 1973. *The Homeless Mind*. New York: Random House.

Berry, T. 2000. "Christianity's Role in the Earth Project." In *Christianity and Ecology*, ed. D. Hessel and R. Ruether, 127–34. Cambridge: Harvard University Press.

Besecke, K. 2001. "Speaking of Meaning in Modernity: Reflexive Spirituality as a Cultural Resource." *Sociology of Religion* 62, 3:365–82.

Blain, J. 2002. *Nine Worlds of Seid-Magic: Ecstasy and Neo-shamanism in North European Paganism*. London: Routledge.

Blain, J., D. Ezzy, and G. Harvey, eds. 2004. *Researching Paganisms*. Walnut Creek, Calif.: AltaMira Press.

Bolen, J. S. 1984. *Goddesses in Every Woman: A New Psychology of Women*. San Francisco: Harper and Row.

———. 1989. *Gods in Every Man: A New Psychology of Men's Lives and Loves*. San Francisco: Harper and Row.

Bonewits, I. 1989. *Real Magic*. York Beach, Me.: Samuel Weisner.

Bouma, G. 1999. "Social Justice Issues in the Management of Religious Diversity." *Social Justice Research* 12, 2:283–96.

Bradley, M. Z. 1982. *The Mists of Avalon*. New York: Ballantine Books.

Bruce, S. 1996. *Religion in the Modern World*. Oxford: Oxford University Press.

Buber, M. 1958. *I and Thou*. Trans. R. Smith. New York: Collier Books.

Buckland, R. 1986. *Buckland's Complete Book of Witchcraft*. St. Paul, Minn.: Llewellyn.

Budapest, Z. 1986. *The Holy Book of Women's Mysteries*. Vol. 1. Revised edition. Oakland, Calif.: Susan B. Anthony Coven Number One.

Casanova, J. 1994. *Public Religions in the Modern World.* Chicago: University of Chicago Press.

Castells, M. 1996. *The Rise of the Network Society.* Oxford: Blackwell.

———. 1997. *The Power of Identity.* Oxford: Blackwell.

Christ, C. 1982. "Why Women Need the Goddess: Phenomenological, Psychological, and Political Reflections." In *The Politics of Women's Spirituality: Essays on the Rise of Spiritual Power within the Feminist Movement,* ed. C. Spretnak, 71–86. New York: Anchor Books. Reprinted from J. Plaskow and C. Christ, eds. 1979. *WomanSpirit Rising.* San Francisco: Harper and Row.

Clark, L. S. 2002. "U.S. Adolescent Religious Identity, the Media, and the 'Funky' Side of Religion." *Journal of Communication* 52:749–811.

———. 2003. *From Angels to Aliens: Teenagers, the Media, and the Supernatural.* Oxford: Oxford University Press.

Cobb, J. 1998. *Cybergrace: The Search for God in the Digital World.* New York: Crown.

Cohen, A. 1993. *The Symbolic Construction of Community.* London: Routledge.

Corcoran, K. 2005, 27 May. "Paganism Ruling Stirs Outcry." *Indianapolis Star.*

Cousineau, M. 1998. "Religion and Social Activism: The Grassroots Catholic Church in Brazil." In *Religion in a Changing World: Comparative Studies in Sociology,* ed. M Cousineau, 185–92. Westport, Conn.: Praeger.

Cowan, D. E. 2005. *Cyberhenge: Modern Pagans on the Internet.* New York: Routledge.

Crook, S., J. Pakulski, and M. Waters. 1992. *Postmodernization: Change in Advanced Society.* London: Sage.

Crowley, V. 1996. *Wicca: The Old Religion in the New Millennium.* London: Thorsons.

———. 1998. "Wicca as Nature Religion." In *Nature Religion Today,* ed. J. Pearson, R. Roberts, and G. Samuel. Edinburgh: Edinburgh University Press.

———. 2000. "Healing in Wicca." In *Daughters of the Goddess: Studies of Healing, Identity, and Empowerment,* ed. W. Griffin, 151–65. Walnut Creek, Calif.: AltaMira Press.

Csordas, T. 1994. *The Sacred Self: A Cultural Phenomenology of Charismatic Healing.* Berkeley: University of California Press.

Cunningham, S. 1988. *Wicca: A Guide for the Solitary Practitioner.* St. Paul, Minn.: Llewellyn.

———. 1994. *Living Wicca: A Further Guide for the Solitary Practitioner.* St. Paul, Minn.: Llewellyn.

Daschke, D., and W. M. Ashcraft, eds. 2005. *New Religious Movements: A Documentary Reader.* New York: New York University Press.

Davis, Erik. 1995. "May the Astral Plane Be Reborn in Cyberspace." *Wired* 3, 7:126–33, 174–81.

Davy, B. 2005. "Being at Home in Nature: A Levinasian Approach to Pagan Environmental Ethics." *The Pomegranate: The International Journal of Pagan Studies* 7, 2:157–72.

Dawson L. L. 1998. *Comprehending Cults: The Sociology of New Religious Movements.* Oxford: Oxford University Press.

———. 2001. "Cyberspace and Religious Life: Conceptualising Concerns and Consequences." Paper presented at the Center for Studies on New Religions (CES NUR) conference, London, 1 April 2001.

———. 2003. "Who Joins New Religious Movements and Why: Twenty Years of Research and What Have We Learned?" In *Cults and New Religious Movements: A Reader*, ed. Dawson, 116–30. Oxford: Blackwell.

———. 2004. "The Sociocutural Significance of Modern New Religious Movements." In *The Oxford Handbook of New Religious Movements*, ed. J. R. Lewis, 68–98. Oxford: Oxford University Press.

Denizet-Lewis, B. 2004, 6 June. "Friends, Friends with Benefits, and the Benefits of the Local Mall." *New York Times Magazine*, 30–35, 54–55.

d'Epinay, L. 1991. "Individualism and Solidarity Today: Twelve Theses." *Theory, Culture, and Society* 8:57–74.

de Tocqueville, A. 1969. *Democracy in America*. Trans. George Lawrence, ed. J. P. Mayer. New York: Doubleday Anchor. (Orig. pub. 1835.)

Eilberg-Schwatz, H. 1989. "Witches of the West: Neo-Paganism and Goddess Worship as Enlightenment Religions." *Journal of Feminist Studies of Religion* 5:77–95.

Elias, N. 1991. *The Society of Individuals*. Trans. E. Jephcott. Oxford: Blackwell.

Eller, C. 1993. *Living in the Lap of the Goddess: The Feminist Spirituality Movement in America*. New York: Crossroads.

———. 2000. *The Myth of Matriarchal Prehistory: Why an Invented Past Won't Give Women a Future*. Boston: Beacon Press.

Ellis, B. 2000. *Raising the Devil: Satanism, New Religions, and the Media*. Lexington: University Press of Kentucky.

———. 2003. *Lucifer Ascending: The Occult in Folklore and Popular Culture*. Lexington: University Press of Kentucky.

Ellwood, R. S., Jr. 1979. *Alternative Alters: Unconventional and Eastern Spirituality in America*. Chicago: University of Chicago Press.

Evans-Pritchard, E. E. 1937. *Witchcraft, Oracles, and Magic among the Azande*. Oxford: Clarendon Press.

Ezzy, D. 2001. "The Commodification of Witchcraft." *Australian Religious Studies Review* 14, 1:31–44.

———. 2003a. "New Age Witchcraft?" *Culture and Religion* 4, 1: 47–66.

———. 2003b. "What Is a Witch?" In *Practising the Witch's Craft*, ed. Ezzy, 1–22. Sydney: Allen and Unwin.

———. 2004. "Geographical Ontology: Levinas, Sacred Landscapes, and Cities." *The Pomegranate: The International Journal of Pagan Studies* 6, 1:19–33.

———. 2005. "I Am the Mountain Walking: Wombats in the Greenwood." In *Pagan Visions for a Sustainable Future*, ed. L. de Angeles, E. Orr, and T. van Dooren. 161–72. Woodbury, Minn.: Llewellyn.

———. 2006. "White Witches and Black Magic." *Journal of Contemporary Religion* 21:17–37.

———. Forthcoming. "Faith and Social Science: Victor and Edith Turner's Analyses of Spiritual Realities." In *Victor Turner and Contemporary Cultural Performance*, ed. G. St. John. New York: Berghahn.

Finley, N. 1991. "Political Activism and Feminist Spirituality." *Sociological Analysis* 52, 4:349–62.

Firestone, S. 1970. *The Dialectics of Sex: The Case for the Feminist Revolution.* New York: Morrow.

Foltz, T. G. 2005. "The Commodification of Witchcraft." In *Witchcraft and Magic: Contemporary North America,* ed. H. A. Berger, 137–68. Philadelphia: University of Pennsylvania Press.

Gallagher, A. M. 2000. "Woven Apart and Weaving Together: Conflict and Mutuality in Feminist and Pagan Communities in Britain." In *Daughters of the Goddess: Studies in Healing, Identity, and Empowerment,* ed W. Griffin, 42–58. Walnut Creek, Calif.: AltaMira Press.

Gardner, G. 1954. *Witchcraft Today.* London: Rider

Geertz, C. 1966. "Religion as a Cultural System" In *Anthropological Approaches to the Study of Religion,* ed. M. Banton, 1–46. London: Tavistock.

———. 1973. *The Interpretation of Cultures.* New York: Basic Books.

Gergen, K. J. 1991. *The Saturated Self: Dilemmas of Identity in Contemporary Life.* New York: Basic Books.

Giddens, A. 1979. *Central Problems in Social Theory: Action, Structure, and Contradiction in Social Analysis.* Berkeley: University of California Press.

———. 1987. *Social Theory and Modern Society.* Stanford: Stanford University Press.

———. 1991. *Modernity and Self-Identity: Self and Society in the Late Modern Age.* Stanford: Stanford University Press.

———. 1992. *The Transformation of Intimacy: Sexuality, Love, and Eroticism in Modern Societies.* Stanford: Stanford University Press.

Gilligan, C. 1982. *In a Different Voice: Psychological Theory and Women's Development.* Cambridge and London: Harvard University Press.

Goffman, E. 1963. *Stigma.* Englewood Cliffs, N.J.: Prentice Hall.

Goldenberg, N. R. 1993. *Resurrecting the Body: Feminism, Religion, and Psychotherapy.* New York: Crossroads.

Goode, Erich. 2000. *Paranormal Beliefs: A Sociological Introduction.* Prospect Heights, Ill.: Waveland Press.

Greenwood, S. 1998. "The Nature of the Goddess: Sexual Identities and Power in Contemporary Witchcraft." In *Nature Religion Today,* ed. J. Pearson, R. Roberts, and G. Samuel, 89–100. Edinburgh: Edinburgh University Press.

———. 2000a. "Feminist Witchcraft: A Transformatory Politics." In *Daughters of the Goddess: Studies in Healing, Identity, and Empowerment,* ed W. Griffin, 136–50. Walnut Creek, Calif.: AltaMira Press.

———. 2000b. *Magic, Witchcraft, and the Otherworld: An Anthropology.* Oxford: Berg.

Griffin, W. 2000. "Crafting the Boundaries: Goddess Narrative as Incantation." In *Daughters of the Goddess: Studies in Healing, Identity, and Empowerment,* ed W. Griffin, 73–88. Walnut Creek, Calif.: AltaMira Press.

———. 2002. "Goddess Spirituality and Wicca." In *Her Voice, Her Faith: Women Speak on World Religions,* ed. A. Sharma and K. Young. Boulder, Colo.: Westview Press.

———. 2005. "Web of Women: Feminist Spiritualities." In *Witchcraft and Magic: Contemporary North America*, ed. H. A. Berger, 55–80. Philadelphia: University of Pennsylvania Press.

Hadden, J. K., and D. E. Cowan, eds. 2000. Introduction to *Religion and the Internet: Research, Prospects, and Promises*, 3–24. New York: JAI Press.

Hanegraaff, W. 1999. "New Age Spiritualities as Secular Religion: A Historian's Perspective." *Social Compass* 46:145–60.

Harrington, M. 2004. "Psychology of Religion and the Study of Paganism." In *Researching Paganisms*, ed. J. Blain, D. Ezzy, and G. Harvey, 71–84. New York: Altamira Press.

Harrow, J. 1994. "Other People's Kids: Working with the Underaged Seeker." In *Modern Rites of Passage: Witchcraft Today.* Book 2, ed. C. S. Clifton, 93–104. St. Paul, Minn.: Llewellyn.

Harvey, G. 1997. *Contemporary Paganism: Listening People, Speaking Earth.* New York: New York University Press.

———. 1999. "Coming Home and Coming Out Pagan (but Not Converting)." In *Religious Conversion: Contemporary Practices and Controversies*, ed. C. Lamb and M. Bryant, 233–46. London: Cassell.

———. 2001. "Maori Diaspora Spirituality, Global Indigeneity, and the Construction of Academia." At http://www.cesnur.org/2001/london2001/harvey.htm.

———. 2005. *Animism: Respecting the Living World.* New York: Columbia University Press.

Heelas, P. 1996. *The New Age Movement.* Oxford: Blackwell.

Heelas, P., and L. Woodhead, B. Seel, B. Szerszynski, and K. Tusting. 2005. *The Spiritual Revolution: Why Religion Is Giving Way to Spirituality.* Oxford: Blackwell.

Helland, C. 2000. "Online-Religion/Religion-On-line and Virtual Communitas." In *Religion on the Internet: Research Prospects and Promises*, ed. J. K. Hadden and D. E. Cowan, 205–24. Amsterdam: JAI.

Helm, T. 2005. "Between Satan and Harry Potter: Legitimating Wicca in Finland." *Journal of Contemporary Religion* 21, 1:39–58.

Hodkinson, P. 2002. *Goth: Identity, Style, and Subculture.* Oxford: Berg.

Hoover, S. 1997. "Media and the Construction of the Religious Public Sphere." In *Rethinking Media, Religion, and Culture*, ed. S. Hoover and K. Lundby, 283–97. Thousand Oaks, Calif.: Sage.

Hopkins, S. 2002. *Girl Heroes: The New Force in Popular Culture.* Annandale, New South Wales: Pluto Press.

Howell, J. 1997. "ASC Induction Techniques, Spiritual Experiences, and Commitment to New Religious Movements." *Sociology of Religion* 58, 2:141–64.

Hume, L. 1997. *Witchcraft and Paganism in Australia.* Melbourne: Melbourne University Press.

Hutton, R. 1999. *The Triumph of the Moon: A History of Modern Pagan Witchcraft.* Oxford: Oxford University Press.

Ireland, R. 1999. "Religious Diversity in a New Australian Democracy." *Australian Religion Studies Review* 12, 2: 94–110.

Jacobs, J. L. 1989. "The Effects of Ritual Healing on Female Victims of Abuse." *Sociological Analysis* 50:265–79.

———. 1990. "Women-Centered Healing Rites: A Study of Alienation and Reintegration." In *In Gods We Trust: New Patterns of Religious Pluralism in America*. 2d. ed., ed. Thomas Robbins and Dick Anthony, 373–83. New Brunswick, N.J.: Transaction Publishers.

Jencson, L. 1998. "In Whose Image? Misogynist Trends in the Construction of Goddess and Woman." In *Spellbound: Women and Witchcraft in America*, ed. Elizabeth Ries, 247–68. Wilmington, Del.: Scholarly Resources.

Jennings, P. 2002. *Pagan Paths*. London: Rider.

Jorgensen, D. L., and S. E. Russell. 1999, September. "American Neo-Paganism: The Participants' Social Identities." *Journal for the Scientific Study of Religion* 38, 3:325–38.

Julian, R. 2004. "Living Locally, Dreaming Globally: Transnational Cultural Imaginings and Practices in the Hmong Diaspora." In *The Hmong of Australia*, ed. N. Tapp and G. Lee, 24–57. Canberra: Australian National University/Pandanus Books.

K, A. 1998. *Covencraft: Witchcraft for Three or More*. St. Paul, Minn.: Llewellyn.

Karp, D. 1996. *Speaking of Sadness: Depression, Disconnection, and the Meanings of Illness*. New York: Oxford University Press.

Kelly, A. A. 1991. *Crafting the Art of Magic: Book I*. St. Paul, Minn.: Llewellyn.

Kemp, C. 2000. *Catholics Can Come Home Again*. New York: Paulist Press.

Kohlberg, L. 1969. "Stage and Sequence: The Cognitive-Development Approach to Socialization." In *Handbook of Socialization Theory and Research*, ed. D. A. Goslin, 239–55. Chicago: Rand McNally.

Kostarelos, F. 1995. *Feeling the Spirit: Faith and Hope in an Evangelical Black Storefront Church*. Columbia: University of South Carolina Press.

Krueger, O. 2004. "The Internet as Distributor and Mirror of Religious and Ritual Knowledge." *Asian Journal of Social Science* 32, 2:183–97.

Lasch, C. 1979. *The Culture of Narcissism*. New York: Norton.

———. 1984. *The Minimal Self*. New York: Norton.

Lausanne Committee for World Evangelization. 2004. *Religious and Non-Religious Spirituality in the Western World ("New Age")*. Lausanne Occasional Paper No. 45, Forum for World Evangelization.

Letcher, A. 2000. "Virtual Paganism or Direct Action?" *Diskus* 6, http://www.unimarburg.de/religionswissenschaft/journal/diskus.

Levinas, E. 1969. *Totality and Infinity*. Trans. A. Lingis. Pittsburgh: Duquesne University Press.

Lewis, J. 2001. "Who Serves Satan? A Demographic and Ideological Profile." *Marburg Journal of Religion* 6, 2:1–10.

———. 2003. *Legitimating New Religions*. New Brunswick, N.J.: Rutgers University Press.

Lofland, J. 1966. *Doomsday Cult*. Englewood Cliffs, N.J.: Prentice Hall.

Lowney, K. S. 1995. "Teenage Satanism as Oppositional Youth Subculture." *Journal of Contemporary Ethnography* 23, 4:453–84.

Luhrmann, T. M. 1989. *Persuasions of the Witch's Craft.* Oxford: Blackwell.

————. 1993. "The Resurgence of Romanticism: Contemporary Neopaganism, Feminist Spirituality, and the Divinity of Nature." In *Environmentalism: The View from Anthropology,* ed. K. Milton, 217–32. London and New York: Routledge.

Lyon, D. 2000. *Jesus in Disneyland: Religion in Postmodern Times.* Cambridge: Polity.

————. 2002. "Cyberspace." In *Living with Cyberspace,* ed. J. Armitage and J. Roberts, 21–33. New York: Continuum.

Ma, V. 2000. "Woman Mysteries of the Ancient Future Sisterhood." In *Daughters of the Goddess: Studies of Healing, Identity, and Empowerment,* ed. W. Griffin, 201–16. Walnut Creek, Calif.: AltaMira Press.

Magliocco, S. 2004. *Witching Culture: Folklore and Neopaganism in America.* Philadelphia: University of Pennsylvania Press.

Manning, C. J. 1996. "Embracing Jesus and the Goddess: Towards a Reconceptualization of Conversion to Syncretistic Religion." In *Magical Religion and Modern Witchcraft,* ed. J. R. Lewis, 299–326. Albany: State University of New York Press.

Mantin, R. 2000. "'The Journey Is Home': Some Thealogical Reflections on Narrative Spirituality as Process." *Journal of Beliefs and Values* 21:157–67.

May, R. 1975. "Values, Myths, and Symbols." *American Journal of Psychiatry* 132, 7:703–6.

McGraw, B. 2004. "The Witch's Will: Magick as a Religious Social Ethic." Paper presented at the annual meetings of the Association for the Sociology of Religion, San Francisco, August.

McGuire, M. B. 2002. *Religion: The Social Context.* 5th ed. Belmont, Calif.: Wadsworth.

McNeil, M. 2005, 18 August. "Parent Can Share Wicca with Son." *Indianapolis Star.*

McPhillips, K. 2003. "Feminist Spirituality and the Power of Ritual." In *Practising the Witch's Craft,* ed D. Ezzy, 70–88. Sydney: Allen and Unwin.

Melton, J. G. 1978. *The Encyclopedia of American Religions.* Wilmington, N.C.: McGrath Publications.

Meyer, B. 1999. *Translating the Devil: Religion and Modernity among the Ewe in Ghana.* Trenton, N.J.: African World Press.

Michelet, J. 2003. *Sorceress: A Study in Middle Age Superstition.* Trans. A. R. Allinson. Kila, Mont.: Kessinger. (Orig. pub. 1862.)

Murray, M. A. 1971. *The Witch-Cult in Western Europe.* Oxford: Clarendon Press. (Orig. pub. 1921.)

Nightmare, M. M. 2001. *Witchcraft and the Web.* Toronto: ECW Press.

Nussbaum, M. 1986. *The Fragility of Goodness.* Cambridge: Cambridge University Press.

Oboler, R. S. 2004. "Nature Religion as a Cultural System?" *The Pomegranate: The International Journal of Pagan Studies* 6, 1:86–106.

O'Leary, S., and B. Basher. 1996. "The Unknown God of the Internet: Religious Communications from the Ancient Agora to the Virtual Forum." In *Philosophical Approaches to Computer-Mediated Communications,* ed. C. Ess, 233–69. Albany: State University of New York Press.

Orion, L. 1995. *Never Again the Burning Times: Paganism Revived.* Prospect Heights, Ill.: Waveland Press.

Pichardo, N. 1997. "New Social Movements." *Annual Review of Sociology* 23:411–30.

Pike, S. M. 2001. *Earthly Bodies, Magical Selves: Contemporary Pagans and the Search for Community.* Berkeley: University of California Press.

———. 2004. *New Age and Neopagan Religions in America.* New York: Columbia University Press.

Poletta, F., and J. Jasper. 2001. "Collective Identity and Social Movements." *Annual Review of Sociology* 27:283–305.

Raphael, M. 1996. "Truth in Flux: Goddess Feminism as a Late Modern Religion." *Religion* 25:199–213.

RavenWolf, S. 1993. *To Ride A Silver Broomstick: New Generation Witchcraft.* St. Paul, Minn.: Llewellyn.

———. 1999. *Teen Witch: Wicca for a New Generation.* St. Paul, Minn.: Llewellyn.

Reisman, B., and P. Schwartz. 2002. "After the Sexual Revolution." *Context* 1 (spring): 16–24.

Renfrow, D. 2004. "A Cartography of Passing in Everyday Life." *Symbolic Interaction* 23, 4:485–506.

Richardson, J. T. 1992. "Conversion Process in the New Religions." In *Handbook of Religious Conversion,* ed. H. N. Malony and S. Southard, 78–89. Birmingham, Ala.: Religious Education Press.

Richardson, J. T., J. Best, and D. Bromley, eds. 1991. *The Satanism Scare.* New York: Aldine de Gruyter.

Richardson, J. T., and B. Kilbourne. 1986. "Classical and Contemporary Brainwashing Models: A Comparison and Critique." In *Brain Washing/Deprogramming Controversy: A Sociological, Psychological, Legal, and Historical Perspective,* ed. D. Bromley and J. T. Richardson, 29–45. Lewiston, N.Y.: Edwin Mellen Press.

Rindfleish, J. 2005. "Consuming the Self: New Age Spirituality as 'Social Product' in Consumer Society." *Consumption, Markets, and Culture* 8, 4:343–60.

Roberts, K. A. 2004. *Religion in Sociological Perspective.* 4th edition. Australia: Wadsworth.

Rockford, E. B., Jr. 1985. *Hare Krishna in America.* New Brunswick, N.J.: Rutgers University Press.

Roof, W. 1999. *Spiritual Marketplace: Baby Boomers and the Remaking of American Religion.* Princeton, N.J.: Princeton University Press.

Rosenau, P. M. 1992. *Post-Modernism and the Social Sciences: Insights, Inroads, and Intrusions.* Princeton, N.J.: Princeton University Press.

Rubin, L. B. 1990. *Erotic Wars: What Happened to the Sexual Revolution.* New York: Farrar, Straus and Giroux.

Sacks, O. 1989. *Seeing Voices: A Journey into the World of the Deaf.* Berkeley: University of California Press.

Salomonsen, J. 2002. *Enchanted Feminism: The Reclaiming Witches of San Francisco.* London and New York: Routledge Press.

Shires, L. 2003. *Coming Home: A Woman's Story of Conversion to Judaism.* Boulder, Colo.: Westview Press.

Shutz, A. 1964. *Collected Papers.* Vol. 2. The Hague: Martinus Nijhoff.

Skinner, H., S. Biscope, and B. Poland. 2003. "Quality of Internet Access." *Social Science and Medicine* 57, 4: 875–80.

Smith, C., with M. L. Denton. 2005. *Soul Searching: The Religious and Spiritual Lives of American Teenagers.* Oxford: Oxford University Press.

Smith, C., and R. Faris. 2002. *Religion and American Adolescent Delinquency, Risk Behaviors, and Constructive Social Activities.* Chapel Hill, N.C.: National Study of Youth and Religion.

Snow, D. A., and C. L. Phillips. 1980. "The Lofland-Stark Conversion Model: A Critical Reassessment." *Social Problems* 27:430–47.

Starhawk. 1979. *The Spiral Dance.* San Francisco: Harper and Row.

———. 1994. *The Fifth Sacred Thing.* New York: Bantam.

Stark, R., and W. Bainbridge. 1985. *The Future of Religion.* Berkeley: University of California Press.

Starrett, B. 1982. "The Metaphors of Power." In *The Politics of Women's Spirituality: Essays on the Rise of Spiritual Power within the Feminist Movement,* ed. C. Spretnak, 185–93. New York: Anchor Books.

Stoller, P., and C. Olkes. 1987. *In Sorcery's Shadow.* Chicago: University of Chicago Press.

Sutcliffe, S. 2003. *Children of the New Age.* London: Routledge.

Swinton, J. 2001. *Spirituality and Mental Health Care.* London: Jessica Kingsley.

Taylor, C. 1989. *Sources of the Self.* Cambridge: Cambridge University Press.

———. 1992. *Ethics of Authenticity.* Cambridge, Mass.: Harvard University Press.

Taylor, M. L. 2005. *Religion, Politics, and the Christian Right: Post-9/11 Powers in the American Empire.* Minneapolis: Augsburg Fortress.

Telesco, P., and S. Knight. 2001. *The Wiccan Web: Surfing the Magic on the Internet.* New York: Citadel Press.

Tonnies, F. 1957. *Community and Society.* New York: Harper and Row.

Wald, D., A. Silverman, and S. Fridy. 2005. "Making Sense of Religion in Political Life." *Annual Review of Political Science* 8:121–43.

Wallis, J. 2005. *God's Politics: Why the Religious Right Gets It Wrong and the Left Doesn't Get It.* San Francisco: Harper and Row.

Weber, M. 1930. *The Protestant Ethic and the Spirit of Capitalism.* Trans. T. Parsons. London and Boston: Unwin Hyman.

Wilson, B. R., and K. Dobbelaere. 1994. *A Time to Chant: The S_ka Gakkai Buddhist in Britain.* Oxford: Clarendon Press.

Wright, S. 2005. "Satanic Cults, Ritual Abuse, and Moral Panic: Deconstructing a Modern Witch-Hunt." In *Witchcraft and Magic: Contemporary North America,* ed. H. A. Berger, 120–36. Philadelphia: University of Pennsylvania Press.

X, M., as told to A. Haley. 1965. *The Autobiography of Malcolm X.* New York: Grove Press.

York, M. 1995. *The Emerging Network: A Sociology of the New Age and Neo-Pagan Movements.* London: Rowman and Littlefield.

———. 2001. "New Age Commodification and Appropriation of Spirituality." *Journal of Contemporary Religion* 16, 3:361–72.

———. 2003. *Pagan Theology: Paganism as a World Religion.* New York: New York University Press.

————. 2004. "The Ethical Implications of Idolatry." Paper presented at the annual meetings of the Association for the Sociology of Religion, San Francisco, August.

————. 2005. "New Age and Magic." In *Witchcraft and Magic: Contemporary North America*, ed. H. A. Berger, 8–27. Philadelphia: University of Pennsylvania Press.

Zaleski, J. 1997. *The Soul of Cyberspace: How New Technology Is Changing Our Spiritual Lives*. San Francisco: Harper.

index

Page numbers in **bold** indicate vignettes.
Young Witches are indexed by first names to ensure their anonymity.

ABOUT THE AUTHORS

Helen A. Berger is professor of sociology at West Chester University of Pennsylvania. She is the author of *A Community of Witches: Contemporary Witches and Neo-Pagans in the United States* and *Voices from the Pagan Census: A National Survey of Witches and Pagans in the United States* (with Evan Leach and Leigh Shaffer) and editor of *Witchcraft and Magic: Contemporary North America*.

Douglas Ezzy is a senior lecturer in sociology at the University of Tasmania, Australia. He is the author of *Qualitative Analysis* and the editor of *Practising the Witch's Craft* and *Researching Paganism* (with Jenny Blain and Graham Harvey). He is fascinated with how people find meaning and dignity in the contemporary world.